A History of African Popu

Popular culture in Africa is the product of everyday life: the unofficial, the non-canonical. And it is the dynamism of this culture that makes Africa what it is. In this book, Karin Barber offers a journey through the history of music, theatre, fiction, song, dance, poetry, and film from the seventeenth century to the present day. From satires created by those living in West African coastal towns in the era of the slave trade to the poetry and fiction of townships and mine compounds in South Africa, and from today's East African streets, where Swahili hip-hop artists gather, to the juggernaut of the Nollywood film industry, this book weaves together a wealth of sites and scenes of cultural production. In doing so, it provides an ideal text for students and researchers seeking to learn more about the diversity, specificity, and vibrancy of popular cultural forms in African history.

Karin Barber is Fellow of the British Academy and Emeritus Professor of African Cultural Anthropology at the University of Birmingham. She was appointed CBE in 2012 for services to African studies. She is the author of a number of books and articles on African popular culture, including *The Generation of Plays: Yoruba Popular Life in Theatre* (2000) and *Print Culture and the First Yoruba Novel* (2012).

New Approaches to African History

Series Editor
Martin Klein, *University of Toronto*

Editorial Advisors
William Beinart, *University of Oxford*
Mamadou Diouf, *Columbia University*
William Freund, *University of KwaZulu-Natal*
Sandra E. Greene, *Cornell University*
Ray Kea, *University of California, Riverside*
David Newbury, *Smith College*

New Approaches to African History is designed to introduce students to current findings and new ideas in African history. Although each book treats a particular case and is able to stand alone, the format allows the studies to be used as modules in general courses on African history and world history. The cases represent a wide range of topics. Each volume summarizes the state of knowledge on a particular subject for a student who is new to the field. However, the aim is not simply to present views of the literature; it is also to introduce debates on historiographical or substantive issues and may argue for a particular point of view. The aim of the series is to stimulate debate and to challenge students and general readers. The series is not committed to any particular school of thought.

Other Books in the Series:

1. *Africa since* 1940 by Frederick Cooper
2. *Muslim Societies in African History* by David Robinson
3. *Reversing Sail: A History of the African Diaspora* by Michael Gomez
4. *The African City: A History* by William Freund
5. *Warfare in Independent Africa* by William Reno
6. *Warfare in African History* by Richard J. Reid
7. *Foreign Intervention in Africa* by Elizabeth Schmidt
8. *Slaving and Slavery in African History* by Sean Stilwell
9. *Democracy in Africa* by Nic Cheeseman
10. *Women in Twentieth-Century Africa* by Iris Berger
11. *A History of African Popular Culture* by Karin Barber
12. *Human Rights in Africa* by Bonny Ibawoh

A History of African Popular Culture

Karin Barber
University of Birmingham

CAMBRIDGE
UNIVERSITY PRESS

CAMBRIDGE
UNIVERSITY PRESS

University Printing House, Cambridge CB2 8BS, United Kingdom

One Liberty Plaza, 20th Floor, New York, NY 10006, USA

477 Williamstown Road, Port Melbourne, VIC 3207, Australia

314–321, 3rd Floor, Plot 3, Splendor Forum, Jasola District Centre,
New Delhi – 110025, India

79 Anson Road, #06-04/06, Singapore 079906

Cambridge University Press is part of the University of Cambridge.

It furthers the University's mission by disseminating knowledge in the pursuit of
education, learning, and research at the highest international levels of excellence.

www.cambridge.org
Information on this title: www.cambridge.org/9781107624474
DOI: 10.1017/9781139061766

First published 2018

Printed in the United States of America by Sheridan Books, Inc.

A catalogue record for this publication is available from the British Library.

Library of Congress Cataloging-in-Publication Data
Names: Barber, Karin, 1949– author.
Title: A history of African popular culture / Karin Barber.
Other titles: New approaches to African history.
Description: New York: Cambridge University Press, 2018. |
Series: New approaches to African history |
Includes bibliographical references and index.
Identifiers: LCCN 2017044206| ISBN 9781107016897 (hardback) |
ISBN 9781107624474 (pbk.)
Subjects: LCSH: Popular culture – Africa, Sub-Saharan – History. |
Africa, Sub-Saharan – Social life and customs.
Classification: LCC DT14.B355 2017 | DDC 306.0967–dc23
LC record available at https://lccn.loc.gov/2017044206

ISBN 978-1-107-01689-7 Hardback
ISBN 978-1-107-62447-4 Paperback

Contents

Acknowledgements

Writing this book turned out to be an engrossing and demanding project, and it took much longer than I expected. I am very grateful to my editor, Martin Klein, for his saintlike patience and encouragement over the years. I would like to thank colleagues and research associates at the University of Birmingham for their careful reading and constructive comments on various draft chapters: Maxim Bolt, Reginald Cline-Cole, Juliet Gilbert, Jessica Johnson, Rebecca Jones, David Kerr, Saima Nasar, Insa Nolte, Katrien Pype, Benedetta Rossi, Keith Shear and Kate Skinner. Paulo Farias read every chapter, some of them in several versions, and as always illuminated them with his insight and erudition.

I received valuable feedback from postgraduate students too, chief among them Surayya Adam, David Coughlin, Shuo Li, Pernille Nailor, Amy Redgrave, Carmen Thompson and Ceri Whatley. Their exuberant interpretations of African popular culture genres will remain with me for a long time to come.

Seminar participants at the University of Cape Town and the University of Cambridge gave me valuable help with formulating the approach to popular culture that I have taken in this book. I am particularly grateful to Heike Becker, Andrea Grant and John Iliffe for their comments. More recently, I was fortunate to be invited by Derek Peterson to present my work at a series of seminars at the University of Michigan in April 2017. I thank all the participants who generously gave their time to read and discuss the completed book manuscript, and I am especially grateful for valuable follow-up discussions with Kelly Askew, Gaurav Desai, Judith Irvine and Derek Peterson.

I would like to thank my friends and colleagues who generously provided photographs from their own collections: Kelly Askew, Lane Clark, Catherine Cole, David Coplan, David Kerr and Katrien Pype. The artist Victor Ndula kindly allowed me to reproduce one of his celebrated cartoons, and the South African rap star Zuluboy provided me with photos of himself in performance. I am grateful to Sapin Makengele for allowing me to use his brilliant narrative picture 'Examen d'un Polygame' for the cover of the book. I thank Chris Albertyn, Laura Fair, Dina Ligaga, Innocentia Mhlambi, Stephan Miescher, Duncan Omanga, Katrien Pype, Brett Pyper and Sipho Sithole for their advice on sourcing photos and help with contacts. I am grateful to 'Makali Mokitimi for permission to quote from her book *Lifela tsa Litsamaea-naha Poetry: A Literary Analysis* (1998) and her MA thesis, *A Literary Analysis of Lifela tsa Litsamaea-naha Poetry* (1982), and to Andy Chebanne and K. C. Maimane for helping me to contact her. The image of Barbot visiting the King of Sestro (Fig. 2) is reproduced, by permission of the Hakluyt Society, from *Barbot on Guinea: The Writings of Jean Barbot on West Africa, 1678–1712*, Vol. 1., edited by Adam Jones, Robin Law and P. E. H. Hair (London: Hakluyt Society, 1992).

Stephanie Newell has long been my ideal interlocutor on popular culture. I have enjoyed many conversations with her at different stages of the project – starting from her advice to take it on in the first place. I was given great encouragement by her generous initiative, with Onookome Okome, to convene a group of scholars in order to revisit, and take off from, my earlier efforts at conceptualising the field of African popular culture. Their contributions came out in two substantial volumes: a special issue of *Research in African Literatures* (2012) and an edited book, *Popular Culture in Africa: The Episteme of the Everyday* (2014). This shows clearly that whether or not *A History of African Popular Culture* achieves any of its aims, there is an abundance of energy and talent out there. A new generation of researchers is coming into its own, and is already revitalising the study of African popular culture.

CHAPTER 1

Introduction

History and Popular Culture in Africa

Popular culture in Africa is a product of everyday life. It is the unofficial, the non-canonical. It is usually taken to mean the culture of 'ordinary people': not the educated elites, politicians, military top brass and rich businessmen; not the people in power, the people who have legal or illegal bank accounts in Switzerland and send their children to boarding schools overseas; but rather petty traders, primary school teachers, taxi drivers, farmers, the unemployed, street children in the Congo and parents in Zimbabwe trying to feed their children when the inflation rate hit 79.6 billion per cent in 2008.

It is the dynamism of this culture that makes Africa what it is. But policymakers and media pundits looking at Africa from the outside give us very little impression of what everyday life is like. Apart from the occasional five-second sound bite from the man or woman in the street at a moment of crisis, we tend to be shown two alternative pictures: extreme images of famine and war, encouraged by NGOs that depend on them to raise funds, or a focus on 'tribal', 'traditional' cultures described as 'remote' and even 'exotic'. There are exceptions, of course, but in general, the Western media have not been particularly interested in the ordinariness of everyday life in Africa and people's resilience in solving ordinary problems – getting water every morning, paying school fees, mobilising hundreds of people in order to hold a suitable funeral for a respected relative. Nor do we hear much about their inventiveness and creativity, the hundreds of ways in which people go beyond bare survival to make something new, make a mark, attract attention, offer an interpretation of experience, articulate communal concerns or protest against what's going on. When Paul Zeleza visits family and friends, he says, he sees a different Africa from the one that prevails in Afropessimist discourses of 'deprivation, disease, despotism, and destruction': he sees the quotidian 'small joys of living, the gaiety and drunkenness in the bars and clubs, the intoxicating ecstasy and rowdiness at football and boxing matches, the uninvited and unpaid story-tellers in buses and taxis, ... carnivalesque crowds at political rallies or gathered on street corners watching and listening to some aspiring or accomplished comedian, preacher, and acrobat ... families assembled at home telling stories, watching television, or listening to the radio' (Zeleza 2003:viii). Nor are the perspectives of the policymakers, cultural officials, educational authorities and media pundits within Africa generally very different from those of outsiders.

The idea of *A History of African Popular Culture* is that popular forms of expression – music, theatre, fiction, songs, dances, pictures, poetry, jokes, sayings – emerge from everyday life on the ground, and that new genres are precipitated by new historical experiences. Africa has undergone massive, cataclysmic, transformative changes over the past 400 years, changes that have continually thrown up new situations and encounters. As people have grappled with these and attempted to get something out of them, they invented new creative forms to comment on them and put them into perspective. We see seventeenth-century commoners in Gold Coast city-states satirising their exploitative overlords, whose power had been fuelled by the Atlantic slave trade; nineteenth-century Yoruba villagers sharing poignant witticisms on the turbulence unleashed by long-lasting inter-kingdom wars; Sotho migrant labourers on the journey to the South African mines creating a new poetic genre to describe their experiences of travelling and arriving at the fearsome mine compounds; Congolese artists after independence painting 'reminders' of Belgian colonial rule and images of fortune-bearing mermaids for the sitting rooms of aspiring urbanites; Tanzanian rappers seeking to reach new continental and diasporic Internet audiences for their Swahili compositions in the era after structural adjustment; and, everywhere in Africa, people using mobile phones to document events on the ground, share music, promote activist agendas, make money transfers and imagine alternative worlds.

*could also say produce it
w so cial media*

New popular cultural forms not only emerge out of historical change, but also participate in it, embody it and comment upon it. They are part of history, in the sense that their production is a socio-historical fact every bit as empirical as agricultural production or patterns of trade. They are produced in specific historical circumstances and change with the times. They create new social and intellectual pathways and forge new kinds of social constituency, and these in turn shape historical developments. But they are also responses to history, interpretations of social reality from within and from below. For a historian, therefore, a new popular cultural form has a double life, as an object of historical inquiry and as one of its sources. And it is a unique source. The changing perspectives of ordinary people are rarely documented in official records. As Terence Ranger said in his pioneering study of the Beni dance, which swept Eastern Africa from the 1890s to the 1960s, popular culture gives unique access to the views of those people excluded from power and privilege:

> [S]tudies of popular culture are especially valuable for getting at the experience and attitudes of the "masses" and for giving expression to the reactions of the inarticulate … [T]he "masses" did not control formal means of articulating their desires – the universities, the pulpit, the press, the theatre, the political pronouncement – and … when spokesmen did emerge they were at instant risk. For this reason, we have to look at the informal, the festive, the apparently escapist, in order to see evidence of real experience and real response; to see how far "the people" have had to make use, even for this informal vocabulary, of the idioms of the masters; to see how far, on the other hand, creativity and spontaneity survive.
>
> (Ranger 1975:3)

If popular cultural forms are both objects of and sources for historical inquiry, they are also bearers of their own past. Present-day popular cultural forms often advertise their own novelty. Part of their appeal is that they follow and create fashion, pick up or coin new formulations, and outdo their competitors with newfangled gimmicks. But they also often draw on long-standing traditions of expression, and the same motif or formulation may be recycled for hundreds of years. They embody historical memory and a consciousness of continuity with the past, as well as an orientation to what is new and changing in social experience. Apparently new forms may recapitulate or repurpose remembered precursors. A presentist view of popular culture misses the inbuilt sense of where it came from and what it brings with it, which may constitute an important part of its meaning. Practitioners of relatively long-standing genres often have a keen consciousness of how these genres have changed over the decades. And when certain styles fall out of fashion, there may be pockets of the community who actively and nostalgically revive them. Themes and motifs may lie dormant and then crop up again. For all these reasons, a historical view is rewarding.

But there are two challenges for anyone rash enough to try to write a history of African popular culture. One has to do with 'popular culture': what we mean by the term, what baggage it brings with it, where its boundaries are, what it excludes and includes. The other has to do with 'history', with the temporality of cultural change in Africa, the immense variations in historical experience from one region to another and the mutability yet stubborn survival of cultural forms that, because they were unofficial, were rarely documented in detail until very recently.

Popular Culture as a Field

Popular culture has been audible and visible in Africanist research for many decades. Informal, unofficial performances, texts and artefacts have been ubiquitous and impossible to overlook. In the earliest African studies research, they were not conceptualised as a field of inquiry named 'popular culture'. But they kept cropping up, in the documentation of anti-colonial struggles or processes of urbanisation, migrant labour and industrial transformation. Anthropologists occupied themselves early on with everyday life and therefore with the expressive forms of ordinary people. Southern African ethnographies dating from the 1930s onwards, many of them associated with the Rhodes-Livingstone Institute, were particularly attentive to the cultural dimension of their subject matter (Becker 2012). There are Ellen Hellmann's vivid depiction of Rooiyard, a Johannesburg 'native slum yard', which she studied shortly before it was evacuated and demolished in 1934; A. L. Epstein and Hortense Powdermaker's Copperbelt studies, researched in the 1950s; and Philip and Iona Mayer's *Townsmen or Tribesmen*, documenting urban culture in East London. All these evoked the lives of urban migrant workers, including their recreations, tastes and ways of constructing a meaningful life.

Particularly noteworthy was J. C. Mitchell's *The Kalela Dance*, which, unlike the other Rhodes-Livingstone studies, took a specific popular performance genre as its central subject and described it in some detail, as a means of tracing ethnic and class relations in a Copperbelt town. In short, there is an abundance of material from early studies in African history and anthropology in which insights into everyday life and popular creativity are sedimented, but popular culture as a field had not yet come into its own.

One limitation of these early studies was that, though they drew on creative or expressive sources, they often did not attend closely to the forms themselves: they used creative arts as evidence of attitudes, beliefs and responses to experience, but without looking closely at *how* these arts express such things. They did not often seek to discover the nature of their constitution as creative forms – the conventions of the genre, the mode of composition, the internal structure, the intertextual allusiveness or the audience's ways of interpreting and understanding them. Yet it is only through their specific form, conventions and associated traditions of interpretation that creative expressions have meaning. What they say and do is inseparable from *how* they say and do it.

From the 1970s onwards, this inattention to 'the thing itself' began to change. There began to appear detailed, in-depth studies that made specific popular culture genres their central focus and attended closely to their properties as creative forms. In the 1970s and '80s, these studies included histories of Onitsha market literature, Ghanaian concert parties, Nigerian juju music and songs of protest and resistance in Mozambique, Zimbabwe, Kenya and South Africa. There have also been studies looking at the history of a whole range of interrelated genres in a specific social context, notably South African township culture in the pathbreaking work of David Coplan and, more recently, the shaping of music genres by national cultural policy and local taste in socialist and post-socialist Tanzania in Kelly Askew's brilliant studies. Forty years after Hortense Powdermaker's pioneering fieldwork, there has been an efflorescence of new research on leisure, a key study being Phyllis Martin's subtle and original account of the way social activity shaped time and space in colonial Brazzaville. From the mid-1990s onwards, we have seen a flood of new work on contemporary mediatised genres, coinciding with major shifts in the media landscape in Africa.

Two propositions in the landmark work of the 1970s have the potential to be taken further than they have been so far. One is the regional approach in Terence Ranger's 1975 history of the Beni dance. He sees the dance not only as an expression of ideas, but also as an organisational form, with a characteristic hierarchy of participants modelled on colonial military and civil officialdom. He is able to trace the spread of this organisational form over sixty years – coinciding almost exactly with the period of colonial rule – from Kenya into Tanganyika, Northern Rhodesia and Nyasaland, taking on different names and local characteristics in each place. (The Kalela dance was one such variant; it will be discussed in the next chapter.) This shows the advantages of a comparative approach based on material interconnections on the ground, rather than a parallelism based only on similarities perceived by the observer. Tracing the movement of cultural forms across wide areas presents formidable challenges to researchers, but it is crucial if we are to form an adequate picture of the mobility and dynamism of popular culture – or, to put it more accurately, the long-standing readiness of cultural practitioners and audiences to access and adapt new things from elsewhere.

The second is the proposition in Johannes Fabian's 1978 article 'Popular Culture in Africa: Findings and Conjectures', that ideas and creative energy may jump from one genre to another. He observes that the 'loud and colourful bursts of creativity in music, oral lore and the visual arts emerging from the masses' were ephemeral and volatile: genres would come suddenly into being, enjoy a period of efflorescence and as suddenly decline. But their animating themes were not necessarily thereby lost; rather, they might reappear in another form in a different context. His example is the topic of male – female relationships in Katanga, DRC (formerly the Belgian Congo, then Zaire): a focus of intense interest and anxiety in the context of migrant labour, urbanisation and increasing inequality. Fabian shows how this theme was elaborated first in popular songs, then in the Christian Jamaa movement and later in popular painting. This suggests that we need to look not only at how one genre mutates over time and spreads over space, but also at how different domains of social life may successively become the site where creative work on a dominant popular concern is concentrated.

Thus there is a lot of empirical and conceptual work still to be done to constitute popular culture as a comprehensive, comparative research domain across Africa. Nonetheless, it can now be said that African popular culture is a recognised subject – taught in university undergraduate and postgraduate courses and researched by an ever-growing and diverse cohort of scholars based within Africa as well as outside it.

If African popular culture has become a field, however, it's not really clear where that field's boundaries lie or by what criteria certain forms are included or excluded, and this is because of the ambiguities of the term 'popular'. It's a slippery, disputed term wherever it is used. In Africa, there is the added unease that a category shaped essentially by the class relations of the industrial West should be applied to the incommensurable historical experience of Africa. Some influential scholars therefore use the term more or less under protest, in quotation marks, for want of a better one.

At first, the term 'popular' was used in African studies to refer exclusively to new cultural forms created in response to colonisation and post-independence experiences. This category of genres, texts and performances does have a kind of intuitive coherence: observers have noted the upsurge during the twentieth century of new styles of music, painting, theatre and fiction, which all shared key aesthetic features, including a self-conscious differentiation from longer-established and more prestigious cultural repertoires. The new forms were identified as predominantly urban, syncretic, quickly changing, oriented towards modernity, often pursuing novelty and often commercial and produced by young, self-taught entrepreneurs working alone or in small groups. Fabian drew attention to this energetic creativity in the rapidly expanding African cities of colonial sub-Saharan Africa, and distinguished it from older oral traditional culture, on the one hand, and the European-inspired culture of the educated elites, on the other. In some of my own previous work (Barber 1987, 1997), I associated this type of popular culture with the fluid and emergent new urban intermediate classes who had left the culture of their fathers' farms and villages but had not been able to join the ranks of the new urban white-collar professional classes. While the longer-established 'traditional' cultural forms and the elite 'modern' forms associated with European models were recognised by cultural and educational institutions within and outside Africa (preserved in museums, put on university syllabi), the interstitial 'popular' forms were disregarded. The popular was a residual category, defined by what it was not. To give a theatrical example: a 'traditional' ancestral masquerade would be valued as cultural heritage, and a play in highly complex English by Wọle Ṣoyinka would be celebrated as the greatest of 'modern' written works, but a 'popular' improvised performance by a Yoruba travelling theatre company would be left out, despite the enormous and long-lasting impact of the travelling theatre genre in western Nigeria. But while this kind of colonial and post-independence popular culture was very striking, remarkably dynamic and well worth exploring as a category – all the more so because, as a category, it had previously been overlooked – it is a strange limitation to use a conception of popular culture that excludes everything that was produced before the onset of formal colonialism. It may suggest, though unintentionally, that African culture before colonisation was homogeneous, static and communal, as if everyone in a given society shared the same experience, perspective and means of expression. This, of course, was not the case, as the examples in Chapter 2 illustrate.

The very concepts of 'traditional' and 'modern, Europeanised' culture in Africa were a product of colonialism. And because the 'popular' was conceptualised by scholars as an interstitial category – neither traditional nor modern, but hybridising both and constantly inventing new things – it too became associated exclusively with the colonial and postcolonial periods. Perhaps we do need a label for the new, primarily urban, consciously novel but lower-class forms that began to emerge in the late nineteenth and early twentieth centuries. But to look exclusively at this category, whatever we decided to call it, would be to condemn us to a history that goes back barely more than a century.

This implied restriction on the temporal reach of the concept of the popular was accentuated with the new wave of work on African media genres, which has been so buoyant in the last twenty years and is much influenced by media studies approaches. It is now sometimes assumed that popular culture as a whole is synonymous with mass media, that the widespread use of media in Africa is new, and that therefore popular culture itself is a very recent phenomenon going back only thirty years or so. These assumptions – all of which are wrong – throw all the attention onto the immediate and excitingly rapid developments in the African digital revolution, and tend to overlook the previous history of media in Africa and their entanglement with the profuse production of still-vital non-mediatised popular culture.

All popular cultural forms have a past. What did the new colonial, postcolonial and post–digital revolution forms come out of? What were the precedents, models and resources their creators drew on? In precisely what ways did changing circumstances foster the generation of new forms? To what extent were these forms in continuity with what went before, to what extent a departure from it? These questions all solicit a longer historical view.

But pushing the idea of the popular back into precolonial times raises other conceptual problems. 'Popular' is usually taken to mean 'that which pertains to the people' – the 'common people', as distinct from the economic, political and social elites. We might ask whether common or non-elite people in precolonial Africa had distinctive cultural forms of their own. It is fair to say that in most African cultures, past and present, there has been a huge bedrock of shared forms, cultural expressions which people of all social levels would recognise and relate to. But there are also ways of treating these shared forms – realising them in performance or framing them in relation to other activities – which make social differences apparent. And in some well-documented cases, there were distinctive forms that belonged only to certain social strata. In some precolonial societies, there was such steep vertical stratification that royal, aristocratic and noble strata evolved cultural traditions inaccessible to commoners, and commoners evolved a repertoire unknown to, or avoided by, their social superiors. But inequality is a matter of degree. All societies, even the most egalitarian, make differences of status between categories of people, and these differences are marked and enacted through cultural means. It doesn't really make sense to say that some precolonial societies 'had' popular culture while others did not. To complicate things further, when twentieth-century popular cultural forms incorporated and recreated older oral forms, they often drew on genres previously associated with the privileged strata. Modern Malian popular music raids the griots' oral repertoire of aristocratic epic and praise chants to speak to a new and much broader national and international audience. Thus a history of popular culture needs simultaneously to recognise the many instances of cultural expressions of protest, satire and self-assertion by disadvantaged and oppressed strata throughout history, and to keep in view the porousness of cultural boundaries, the substratum of shared forms and the repurposing of genres over time.

A sociological definition of popular as 'pertaining to the common people' also has its problems for more recent periods, right up to the present day. It remains an open question to what extent elites are culturally distinct from non-elites in any given social setting, and in what ways. Cultural differentiation changes over time, for example when the cultural markers of an elite's privilege become more widely available and lose their leverage. In Nigeria, early in the twentieth century,

a school education was a powerful mechanism for social advancement; in the second half of the twentieth century, the expansion of the
primary school system meant that one had to go to grammar school
to gain any social advantage; and today, there is a jobless underclass
in Lagos made up of university graduates. Cultural differentiation
also varies over space, because of different histories of class formation. Industrialisation in South Africa, for example, makes it possible
to talk about a distinctive 'working-class culture' in a way that would
seem inapplicable in many other parts of sub-Saharan Africa.

Everywhere in Africa, social mobility, aspirational self-positioning
and the uncertainty and fragility of economic and occupational status all mean that neither the elite nor the non-elite are ever bounda-
ried, empirically enumerable categories. Members of an elite group
almost always have poor relatives; the most disadvantaged often have
pathways to the better-off though clientship or communal solidarity. Subjectively as well as objectively, the boundaries of social strata
are fluctuating and indeterminate. Neither elites nor non-elites are a
monolithic group; rather, they are often unstable congeries of social
groupings, between which there are many fault lines as well as shared
interests.

The culture participated in by privileged sections of society, no
less than popular culture, has been volatile and shot through with
cross-currents; not a mere clone of metropolitan models, but 'groping toward alternative forms of cultural and political expression'
(Erlmann 1996:60), a process which has often involved incorporating popular materials rather than holding them at arm's length. And
conversely, forms initiated by elites were often taken up by non-elites
and popularised. The concert party in the Gold Coast began as an
expensive entertainment in English, accessible only to the educated
coastal elites; by the 1950s, it used Akan and a smattering of other
Ghanaian languages, incorporated highlife bands rather than Western-
style dance music, expanded comic sketches into full-blown dramas
and travelled the country playing to rural as well as urban audiences.
The *taarab* music of East Africa, similarly, was an Arab-inspired genre
performed by male orchestras for the elite of Zanzibar; it was taken up
on the mainland, popularised and indigenised initially by a woman of
slave origin, Siti binti Saad, who became a highly influential star in the
1920s and '30s (Topp Fargion 1993). In an influential early critique of
the concept of 'the popular', Stuart Hall argued that in British social
history there is no fixed category of cultural form or content that can

be permanently identified with the common people. Rather, there is constant movement and interchange between 'preferred' and 'marginalised' cultural forms, the result of shifting power relations and mutual assimilation, so that what is seen as 'popular' is itself a site of struggle (Hall 1981). The temptation to identify certain genres, themes or styles as inherently and permanently 'popular' is one which Africanist scholarship, also, needs to be wary of.

And, in addition to the two-way flows between elites and non-elites, it must be recognised that there have always been cultural forms that belong to the whole population or attract audiences drawn from all social backgrounds. Roger Chartier, in his studies of early modern European popular culture, suggested that specific cultural forms cannot be mapped neatly onto class structures; rather, audiences with particular tastes convene around particular genres or styles. In other words, rather than audiences being pre-constituted by class or social status, they may be convened by shared taste, which cuts across social distinctions. In Nigeria, juju music flatters the big men who patronise it and whom it praises, but appeals to a wide cross-section of the population because of its evocation of a deeper shared aesthetic and ethos (Waterman 1990). Yoruba popular theatre companies were sometimes invited to perform for affluent social clubs, where the ambience was very different from their usual venues, crowded with rowdy impoverished youths, but where the sources of satisfaction that drew these spectators – the linguistic versatility, the moral affirmation – were the same (Barber 2000). And some genres, such as rap, may attract a specific subsection of the population along lines of youth or generation rather than class or educational status. While cutting across some social divisions, taste constituencies may at the same time give expression to new ones, establishing new forms of belonging and exclusion.

'Popular' is a term laden with contradictory values, attracting both championship ('the voice of the people') and disdain ('low-class trash'). Most scholars of African popular culture, myself included, have adopted a positive, sympathetic view, focusing on the dynamism, creativity and inventiveness of popular forms. But this does not mean that the opinions and values expressed in popular texts are themselves always positive or sympathetic. Popular culture gives form to the whole spectrum of ideological and emotional impulses, including violent and reactionary ones (see Kaarsholm 2006). As we will see in later chapters, there are popular texts that sycophantically extol brutal dictators, pillory independent women and denounce Lebanese and

Indian traders as vermin. Popular forms like the *chimurenga* songs of the Zimbabwean guerrillas could be used coercively to ensure peasant compliance even while articulating a liberatory message.

Nonetheless, in the texts and performances we are going to look at, what we hear most often is collective affirmation. We keep hearing voices that evoke the presence of 'us, the poor' in contrast to 'them, the rich and powerful'. We keep hearing expressions of sarcasm, outrage and challenge. We also keep hearing the eloquent, plaintive assertion that though inequality is a condition of life, the poor have dignity and moral worth and may one day escape their condition; that the powerful and advantaged have an obligation to assist the weak and disadvantaged; that individual self-realisation can only take place through relatedness to other people; and yet that everyone needs to shift for him- or herself and be resourceful and self-reliant within the bounds of social propriety.

Popular Culture in History

If the category 'popular' is a conundrum, the idea of writing a history (a *short* history) of the popular culture of the whole continent seems a downright impossibility. In the first place, there is the huge diversity of social forms and historical experience across Africa. The great empires and kingdoms of West Africa, the ancient cosmopolitan cultures of the Swahili coast, the Coptic Christian core of Ethiopia and the medieval spread of Islam across the Sahara were juxtaposed with small-scale societies whose interaction with other communities was relatively restricted until the nineteenth and twentieth centuries. The ravages of the Atlantic slave trade unleashed more intense forces along the coast of western and central Africa than farther inland. The impact of settler colonialism in Kenya, Zimbabwe and South Africa was different from that of the essentially mercantile colonialism of West Africa, though both had extremely brutal phases and both were exploitative. Thus the legacy of the past, which shaped more recent popular culture, is a patchwork of strongly contrasting experiences.

In the second place, though social change has been extremely rapid all over Africa, it did not happen in step across different regions. Battered by wave after wave of compressed, high-speed, sometimes brutal social, economic, political and technological change, African people have been constantly adapting and innovating while also trying to preserve what is daily being erased and obliterated. But in this short span, there have been striking differences in the timing and tempo of change from one African region to another. Up to the Second World War, for example, in French Equatorial Africa, the availability of schooling and general literacy – an important influence on popular culture everywhere – lagged twenty-five years behind the rest of West Africa (Martin 1995:51). Industrial mining, which restructured labour relations and stimulated new cultural forms across much of southern Africa, took off in Johannesburg in the 1890s, but in the Zambian Copperbelt only in the late 1920s. Independence and majority rule, ushering in new official cultural policies and unofficial responses, was attained by Ghana in 1957, by many African countries in the early 1960s, by Portuguese Africa in 1975, by Zimbabwe in 1980 and by South Africa only in 1994. Not only this, but new social, economic and political forms often turn out to be layered on top of existing arrangements rather than superseding them. There is a simultaneous co-presence of old and new temporalities, an interlocking of presents, pasts and futures that Achille Mbembe evokes thus: 'the postcolony encloses multiple durées made up of discontinuities, reversals, iner-tias and swings that overlay one another, interpenetrate one another, and envelop one another: an entanglement' (Mbembe 2001:14). So a historical narrative that tried to move chronologically through the decades would turn into a series of bewildering zigzags.

In the third place, what kind of narrative can be written about expressive forms that are constantly emergent, ephemeral, embedded in daily life, given to extraordinary bursts of activity and rapid trans-mutation? Often oral or partly oral, often improvised, almost always disregarded by the official agencies that have the means to record them, popular genres by their very nature lack documentation until the very recent period, in which they became the object of scholarly (and sometimes government) interest.

And finally, it is in the nature of a creative work, whether formed of words, images, sound or movement, partially to escape time. Creative works are put 'out there' by their creators in order to attract the attention and response of others. This gives them the potential to be detached from the here and now and be recreated, repeated or recontextualised in another time and place. It is not just that people copy forms that are already in existence and thus perpetuate them; it is also that, in the very act of presenting a work to an audience, the maker puts it into a kind of suspension. It no longer belongs wholly to him or her, nor can it be wholly appropriated by listeners, viewers or readers. It exists in a state of potential. Each reinterpretation or recontextualisation 'completes' the work in a different way. Audiences for African popular creative works are noted for the active role they assign themselves in the constitution of a work's meaning. They often take responsibility for finding the significance of a work for themselves, including by bringing extraneous knowledge to bear on it or attaching a meaning that resonates with their own experience. As circumstances and experiences change, so do the ways in which audience members 'complete' the work.

Thus creative works have a transtemporal or multitemporal character. In oral genres, this character is evident in the text itself, which has passed through successive mouths, each of which has slightly or significantly changed it. The orally transmitted text does not belong entirely to the moment in which it was first enunciated, nor entirely to the latest occasion of its recreation; rather, it belongs to all the stages of transmission layered upon one another.

Popular creative works are thus not only often volatile and patchily recorded; even when they are recorded in detail, they cannot be pinned down to a particular historical point.

From the Ground Up

The starting point for me is on the ground, in the creativity of everyday life – the quotidian, often unremarked creativity of people going about their business, improvising, shifting for themselves and producing commentaries of all kinds on the situations in which they find themselves. Adaptability, resourcefulness and invention are the stock-in-trade of everyday life.

Everyday speech, for example, is a fundamental site of often brilliant innovation. People play with language, make up new expressions to name new experiences, comment humorously and sarcastically on everyday life. This had already been noted in some of the early Rhodes-Livingstone ethnography. In a Copperbelt town in the 1950s, migrants from many backgrounds adapted Bemba as a lingua franca, infusing it with loan words and christening it CiCopperbelti. It was used in ingeniously humorous acts of naming and describing. The residents of the early style of round house in the locations were nicknamed 'Aba mu mabottle' ('bottle dwellers'); those who lived in one-room houses could be saluted by a visitor with the question 'You might be in the dance hall – where are the drums so we can dance?' '*Simyamfule*' ('switch off the light while I undress') categorises your petticoat as a cheap one you'd be ashamed to let your lover see. With witty and imaginative epithets like these, the Copperbelt migrants generated, for new objects in their experience, not only a vocabulary, but also a means of ordering and evaluating them. CiCopperbelti thus 'served Africans as a means of placing their own distinctive stamp on this otherwise alien and oppressive milieu' (Epstein 1992:xvi).

Such everyday linguistic creativity has been noted all over the continent. Sixty years after Epstein's observations on the Copperbelt, Mbugua Wa Mungai describes the linguistic prowess of the *matatu* (private minibus) drivers of Nairobi, with their verbal punches and fireworks. The *matatu* environment is a space in which images, sounds and verbal formulations circulate and are carried around in and on the vehicles themselves as well as from one participant in the scene to the next. Pictures of famous rap artists, celebrities and Spider-Man are juxtaposed with painted quotations from the Bible, proverbs and boasts; stereos blasting out rap mingle with *matatu* drivers' oaths and curses, jests and threats, and passengers' narratives, for 'on *matatu*' – one customer told Wa Mungai – 'they exchange stories about their hard lives; corruption, potholed roads, the rain, joblessness'. From informal situations like this, elements emerge which may be taken up and absorbed into existing genres – the transgressive style of *matatu* influences other cultural forms, such as the Mugiithi dance style and urban rap – or may become the seeds of a new genre: the *matatu* passengers' narratives of personal experience, Wa Mungai suggests, 'merit serious study in their own right'.

From innovative, improvised performances, new genres emerge as conventions become established and past performances are copied, improved upon or deliberately diverged from. The testimony of born-again women at revivalist Christian 'night vigils' in western Nigeria in the 1980s, though billed as spontaneous outpourings prompted by the movements of the Holy Spirit, quickly became elaborate performances with narrative conventions, performative styles and even costumes and props (Oyegoke 1994). Speech is always a fertile field for innovation. But everyday creativity extends much beyond this, into styles of dress, gesture and behaviour of all kinds.

Tracing the life of everyday experiments and innovations on the ground offers the possibility of a generative approach to creative

FIGURE 1 Work in progress: Sapin Makengele in his Kinshasa studio.
Courtesy Katrien Pype.

works, not starting from a finished text, object or performance and
then contextualising it, but starting from a given context and tracing
the emergence of a form, its circulation, consolidation, expansion and
recycling. It is an approach that understands cultural forms as work
in progress (Figure 1). People everywhere seek to take materials and
practices circulating in everyday life and shape them into more elaborated forms that attract attention and interpretation. They do so in
order to get a handle on changing experience.

Interpreting Popular Works

My central aim is to bring full attention to the thing itself: the popular
cultural forms that are the subject of this book. I hope to put readers in a position where they have the background and the tools actually to engage with the pamphlets, play texts, songs and all the other
forms that emerged from the conjunctures of African history. Each
chapter, therefore, is built around two or more detailed examples
(different genres, different parts of the continent); my hope is that

the complexity, subtlety and impact of these forms will become more available for appreciation and understanding.

As with all creative works, 'reading' them is not a simple procedure. It involves attending to ambiguities, exaggerations, ironies, allusions and silences. No creative work can be paraphrased: it says and does through its own form. No creative work is an island entire of itself: it belongs in a network of other works; it emerges, as I have already emphasised, from a field of resources – formulations, themes, motifs, models – circulating in the social environment; it establishes and at the same time is established by the constantly emerging conventions of a genre; and its meaning to audiences depends on what they themselves bring to it. As I will conclude in the final chapter of this book, a two-ended model of a 'producer' passing messages or meanings to a 'consumer' does not begin to capture the constant simultaneous productivity and receptivity of cultural activity. Production is a form of consumption of other texts, other works (a poem is a 'cannibal consumer of earlier poems', as the deconstructive theorist J. Hillis Miller rather startlingly put it); consumption, conversely, is a form of production of meaning, as audiences apply specific registers of cultural knowledge to the work, and also apply the conclusions they draw from it to their own lives. To look at one popular pamphlet, one *chimurenga* song or one television drama in isolation leads to a practice of cherry-picking meanings to support a preconceived thesis.

Given the incredible demands that interpretation places on the researcher, it can only ever be a utopian ideal, an ever-receding horizon. But it is worth reaching as far towards it as the available data allow. Unlike the apparently more 'readable' forms of the questionnaire and interview, popular culture genres are framed in the local producers' and participants' own terms. They develop perspectives on topics that people themselves feel are interesting, attractive or important. They do so in a manner felt to be appropriate and adequate to the topic. A joke at a bus stop or a proverb quoted over a beer may encapsulate a vast hinterland of shared experience; how much more so an elaborated form like an ever-extending Sotho oral autobiographical poem or a three-hour Ghanaian improvised concert party play, which draw on the resources of the joke, the proverb and a multitude of other circulating materials and create a larger construct, iridescent with sparks of wit, pathos, prejudice, common sense and social criticism. If this were not the case, would people invest the time, effort and resources in creating and recreating them? Many creative works are highly valued forms – worked upon, made memorable, often quoted and constituted in order to give pleasure.

Furthermore, creative works are not mere reflections of pre-existing attitudes and emotions which could be expressed through other means. They are the sites where popular consensus is created, and where unformulated feelings and ideas are given a shape and a name and are spread and shared. This is one reason why they are so often quoted.

The focus of this book is therefore mainly on identifiable, elaborated creative genres which are locally valued. The book seeks to explore the circumstances in which they emerged, the cultural resources they drew on and the new experiences they were created to speak to. Underlying these salient forms are the habits and choices of everyday existence, which may be part of unremarked routines but which feed into creative works. Behind the history of cultural innovation and change, there lie inconspicuous, sedimented practices and understandings which may quietly endure over centuries. There is a substratum of popular attitudes and assumptions discernible across the continent which the evidence suggests has long been in place, and which may have manifested in different guises but continued to provide a kind of moral compass over the generations.

Only history permits a narrative of human action turning multiple potentialities into particular actualities. Only ethnography, insofar as it is the study of the incremental, quotidian, often unremarked and unrecorded experience 'on the ground', can trace the actual emergence of cultural and social forms (institutions, practices, relationships) as it occurs. In these ways, ethnography is profoundly historical, and history is profoundly ethnographic. I therefore draw on both disciplines.

Instead of trying to write a watertight synthetic overview of popular culture in the whole of sub-Saharan Africa, I will look at key examples drawn from different places but link each of them to parallel cases elsewhere on the continent. Instead of trying to move steadily forward through chronological time, I will focus on transformational moments, arranged roughly in historical sequence, but each radiating backward and forward in time. Instead of looking at an array of finished products ('popular art'), I will explore the ways in which particular scenes of experience – in domestic life, sociality, labour and political action – stimulated the generation of new forms of cultural expression. Such generative sites or moments from which new cultural forms emerged from the seventeenth to the twenty-first centuries include social dislocations and transformations in the era of the slave trade; missionary interventions, schools and the spread of popular literacy; mining and migrant labour; rapid urbanisation and the expansion of road and rail networks; flashpoints in the history of anti-colonial mobilisation and its successor forms of post-independence critique; and the effects of recent media privatisation and deregulation in the context of accelerating globalisation. Needless to say, these were not the only transformations that stimulated new popular cultural forms in Africa. I have chosen to focus on particular moments and sites where the historical ethnography is particularly rich and the emergent popular genres particularly interesting and well documented. But this is for illustrative purposes only; I hope readers will be encouraged to explore other generative sites and other popular cultural forms. Much more could be said, for example, about visual art, dance and music than I have room for in this short book; much more attention could be paid to changes in household structures and family relationships, transformations in the rural economy, the rise of conservation and the tourist trade and a host of other key themes in African studies.

So this study is not intended to be comprehensive or authoritative. My approach has the merit, at least, of being in sympathy with its subject matter. If popular culture itself is uneven, moving in fits and starts, episodic, elusive, repetitive yet focused on novelty, then this history of popular culture echoes those qualities in being open-ended, non-definitive, partial and intended to stimulate further work rather than have the last word.

CHAPTER 2

Early Popular Culture: Sources and Silences

A central aim of any history of popular culture is to retrieve the voices of the underdogs – to recover the genres and cultural forms in which the unprivileged strata of society expressed their view of life. In Africa, before the twentieth century, there were many different forms of hierarchy and inequality – as well as some of the most notably egalitarian societies in the world. In the most steeply unequal societies, commoners, slaves, and the poor did forge cultural genres that articulated their own perspectives on the world, to some extent distinct from those of royalty, the aristocracy and the wealthy, and often critical of or satirical about them. The strata into which these hierarchical societies were divided rarely conformed to a neat binary model of elite versus common people. As we will see in the case of Mande and other Sahelian societies, stratification could involve multiple nested social layers each vehemently maintaining its difference from all the others. In many societies, mutual dependence and obligation between patrons and clients counteracted solidarity among the disadvantaged. In slave-holding societies, slaves could become powerful and rich while still suffering various kinds of social stigma and disadvantage. Nonetheless, traces of expressive forms from as early as the seventeenth century show that there were struggles between rich and poor, advantaged and disadvantaged: and that the poor and disadvantaged created genres to satirise their superiors or affirm the value of their own experience. These voices are worth retrieving.

The problem, however, is the nature of the evidence about these early non-elite forms. Almost all popular culture before the late nineteenth century, when popular literacy began to spread, was oral – and oral transmission is always an unpredictable mixture of stability and volatility, so that one can never be sure how far present-day versions are in continuity with the forms and genres of 100 or 200 years ago. There are some written historical sources that shed light on oral non-elite culture, and these are fixed and, in that sense, more reliable. But much of the earliest written information, from the seventeenth century or before, comes from the observations of foreign travellers and traders who, even if they paid long visits to Africa, probably did not have a full understanding of what they heard and saw. They certainly did not spend much time in the company of the poor and servile classes. In some societies where there were local literate elites, we find in their writings occasional hints of the popular genres they were at pains to distance themselves from. Only in the mid to late nineteenth century were there new kinds of educated African elites who began to take an interest in popular traditions, now recast as collective ethnic heritage in the face of colonial encroachments.

As is the case elsewhere in the world, popular cultural forms are less well documented than those produced by elites. 'Aristocratic', 'royal' and 'noble' strata would demonstrate and consolidate their status not only through lavish displays of material wealth, but also by their command of creative resources: the praise songs of bards, the carefully transmitted genealogies, histories and epic poems, elaborate musical performances and dance. They could afford to invest in techniques of textual elaboration, employ specialists to compose and transmit verbal arts and, in some cases, acquire literacy with which to preserve them. Visitors to their realms, impressed by elaborate court performances, would describe them in accounts of their travels. One of the earliest examples is the fourteenth-century Moroccan traveller Ibn Battuta, who was greatly struck by the elaborate feast-day performances at the royal court of Mali, and described them in lavish detail: the armour-bearers carrying 'splendid weapons, quivers of gold and silver, swords ornamented in gold', the massed singers, the thirty slave drummer boys in their red and white uniforms, the royal bards standing before the king to recite poetry of praise and exhortation. He was clearly impressed and enthralled, even if, with an outsider's arrogance, he found one aspect of the festival – the bards' bird costumes – 'comical' and 'laughable' (Ibn Battuta 1994:961–2). But if the common people, away from the court, had their own poetry, music, dances and narratives, these were not witnessed or recorded by Ibn Battuta.

These are the limitations of the early evidence. But the very lacunae and silences in the record reveal something about popular culture. What they show is its relational character. Even the most antagonistic forms of popular expression – bawdy satirical lampoons targeting the aristocracy, for example – established rather than denied a relationship between the social strata. Aristocratic cultural refinement was likewise constructed in relation to what was assumed to be the ordinary people's lack of refinement, and would have had no meaning apart from this contrast. In many cases, the aristocracy's attitude of disdain towards commoner culture was mixed with a desire to incorporate and shape it. This revealed both a fear of the lower orders and a desire to keep them on side. Power essentially depended on having a following, and the relationship between patron and followers, the lord and his retinue, could be negotiated and expressed through the sensitive mutations of popular performance arts.

This chapter, then, is about the nature of the evidence for early (pre-1900) African popular culture and what this evidence can tell us about the experience of non-privileged people in relation to their social superiors. The lacunae and silences in the record, as much as the glimpses of popular expression, tell us something about the nature of social hierarchy in these societies – and about the crucial role of art forms in its construction and perpetuation.

Early Written Evidence

Up to around the 1820s or 1830s, the written records come mainly from areas where there was contact with Islam and Christianity or with the Atlantic and Indian Ocean trades, making it possible for literate observers to leave some kind of record. They contain occasional glimpses of popular performances and festivities, but no detailed information, let alone transcriptions of texts. There are also some written sources by foreign literates who settled permanently in Africa in the seventeenth century. These include the Portuguese Jesuit missionaries in Luanda, Angola, who produced extensive texts on local history and culture, and the Dutch settlers in mid-seventeenth-century Cape Town.

When travellers did comment on popular forms, they could be disparaging about them. But they could also give a vivid impression of the raucous vitality of some popular genres. There's an example of this in the travel narratives of two European merchants who traded in the Gold Coast in the late seventeenth century: Jean Barbot (see Figure 2), who was an agent of the French Royal African Company, and Willem Bosman, who entered the service of the Dutch West India Company at the age of sixteen and spent most of his career on the West African coast engaged in the Atlantic slave trade. As the Atlantic trade intensified, a belt of ports and city-states along the coast went through a period of rapid expansion and accumulation. This mercantile dynamism made possible increased occupational specialisation and steepening hierarchy. A small urban elite of royals and nobles monopolised economic, political and administrative power. Their privileges, forbidden to other strata, included the right to own slaves, trade where they wished, keep drummers and horn blowers and hold festivals. Their households were large, swollen with slaves, clients, bonded commoners and other dependants. Beneath them in the hierarchy were urban commoners who had their own households; they ranged from comparatively prosperous traders and artisans to poor porters and hawkers and indigent day labourers who went from place to place looking for work. The urban population's food supply came from the town's dependent villages, where slaves or free peasants worked land controlled by the urban elite and paid taxes or tribute to them. Urban commoners who were not dependent on a noble had to buy their food in the town market, making more acute the differentiation between the well-off and the poor. Steep differences in status went hand-in-hand with a fluidity which allowed people to move up the hierarchy or forced them to move down it, according to their economic success. A prosperous trader could buy noble status through a formal procedure, and thus gain the right to privileges reserved for this class, while a trader, craftsman or cultivator who fell on hard times might have to take up waged labour or even scavenge for food (Kea 1982: 40).

This fluidity meant that differences in status had to be continually asserted and reinforced. They were enacted and publicly displayed through material goods, clothing, manners and retinues, and upheld by strict sumptuary laws. The nobles accumulated trade goods and money. They built two-storey houses and filled them with costly furnishings. They invested heavily in valuable cloth, displayed gold ornaments and moved around with slave attendants. Jean Barbot described them as 'wonderful proud and haughty': 'for if a man by his subtilty or industry has raised himself so as to become rich, or be in considerable

FIGURE 2 Barbot visits the King of Sestro, 1681. Courtesy Hakluyt Society.

office, he never goes about the streets without a slave, who carries his
wooden stool, to rest him wheresoever he makes a stop. He seldom
moves his head to look at any other person, unless it be one above
himself in wealth or place; or if he happens to speak to his inferiors, it
is done in a lofty, disdainful way' (Barbot, quoted in Kea 1982:293).
These inferiors – urban commoners of limited means – wore coarse
linen, and the rural people wore barkcloth or homespun cotton. Slaves
had to go bareheaded by law.

Popular discontent could be signalled by tax riots, banditry and
theft. But there were also established cultural performances through
which the lower orders could vent their outrage. Willem Bosman
noted that at Axim and 'above one hundred Towns at the same time',
there was an annual festival eight days long,

> accompanied with all manner of Singing, Skiping, Dancing, Mirth
> and Jollity: In which time a perfect lampooning Liberty is allowed, and
> Scandal so highly exalted, that they may freely sing of all the Faults,
> Villanies and Frauds of their Superiours as well as Inferiours without
> Punishment, or so much as the least Interruption; and the only way to

stop their Mouths is to ply them lustily with Drink, which alters their
tone immediately, and turns their Satyrical Ballads into Commendatory
Songs on the good Qualities of him who hath so nobly treated them.

(Bosman, quoted in Kea 1982:291–2)

If only we had a transcription of these 'Satyrical Ballads' and
'Commendatory Songs', which Bosman of course failed to provide!
All the same, we can learn a lot from Bosman's description. First is
simply the confirmation that in this highly unequal society, commoners or non-elites did indeed have distinctive poetic and other performance genres at their disposal through which to voice their own point of
view on the lords who ruled them. Second, there is the licence allowed
to the commoners, for a defined period, to abuse and lampoon the
nobles: a kind of 'ritual of rebellion' that has been documented all
over the world and is seen by Bakhtin, in his study of carnival, as the
quintessence of popular culture. And third, Bosman's account of the
festival at Axim draws attention to the singer who taunts and insults
a wealthy target until the latter pays up, when he switches to fulsome
praise. This kind of praise singer is a well-known figure, which has
been documented for later periods and in other culture areas of West
Africa. It underlines the fact that these popular performances were
constituted to express a relationship between common people and
elites. They were not self-contained: they asserted people's right to
speak, shout, dance and sing in the face of elite disdain – and also to
extract rewards from those targets by shoring up their prestige.

In other early sources, it is apparent that even when a cultural
performance was staged by the elite, non-elites would introduce
popular elements. In Cape Town, after its establishment as a supply
base for merchant shipping in 1652, the Dutch governor and almost
all estate owners established their own orchestras made up of slave
musicians brought in from many places of origin – the local Khoikhoi
area, as well as Java, Malaya, the Malabar coast, Madagascar, West
Africa and Mozambique. This mixed underclass brought their own
musical instruments, techniques, melodies and styles to form a new
syncretic music, which later spread beyond the Cape and contributed greatly to the evolution of South African popular music up to
today (Coplan 2008:15). Another example, remarkable for its vivid
detail, is a description by a Catholic missionary resident in Luanda,
Angola, of the festivities that were held in 1620 to celebrate the beati-
fication of the famous Jesuit Father Francisco Xavier. This massive

civic event, which involved gun salutes, streets decorated with artificial flowers, flags and lanterns, music, dances, praise-poetry competitions and a carnival-like procession featuring enormous, fantastical figures mounted on floats, was organised by the city's white and creole Christian elites. The figures on the carnival floats included three white giants, which were said to have been brought from Portugal, though people did wonder how such huge creatures could have fit on the ships. They also included a diminutive black figure, supposed to be the white giants' father, who hurled incessant abuse at his 'sons'. This figure, and his licence to insult the white characters – again reminiscent of rituals of rebellion and the inversion of hierarchy – may have come from a popular custom among the black and slave population of the city. Almost certainly the praise-poetry performances, in which bards competed to extol the saint, drew on indigenous African repertoires. And the whole institution of carnival itself, though appropriated by successive ruling regimes to consolidate their own position, became a resilient and enduring popular form. In an overview that starts from reflections on the Luanda festivities of 1620, David Birmingham writes:

> The dynamic continuity of popular culture has been little ruffled by the coming and going of contrasted regimes. Spanish Hapsburgs in the 1580s, Protestant Netherlanders in the 1640s, Brazilian planters in the 1660s, Portuguese mercantilists in the 1730s, black creoles in the 1850s, army monarchists in the 1880s, white republicans in the 1910s, "fascist" authoritarians in the 1930s, industrialising capitalists in the 1960s, nationalist revolutionaries in the 1980s. The carnival and similar feast days always represented a flexible response to the traumas of change, a tight hold on the values of the past, and an ironic portrayal of how to exorcise contemporary devils.
>
> (Birmingham 1988:93)

The implication of this is that no matter where the specific ingredients of the Luanda carnival originated, it early on became a popular local institution which successive political regimes tried to appropriate but affected only superficially.

The popular-elite relationship could work both ways. It was not only that the popular genres were constructed over against the elite: elites also created genres in counterpoint to popular ones. The deliberate act of differentiating themselves culturally from the popular strata implicitly linked them. Elite and popular genres were interdependent and mutually defining. In the north of what is now Nigeria, a long tradition of Islamic knowledge had embedded high levels of Arabic literacy in a small concentration of learned Muslims, who had coexisted for centuries with a pagan or only partially Islamised majority. This literate elite mastered complex forms of Arabic versification and adapted them in order also to compose verse and historical chronicles in Hausa, which they wrote in a modified Arabic script known as *ajamī*. In the late eighteenth century, a reformist movement arose among the Muslim elite of the neighbouring Fulani people, leading to the jihad launched by Usuman dan Fodio in 1804. This movement aimed at reforming the Muslim population that had only partially converted or had accommodated local pagan customs. The intellectual leaders of the movement, Shehu Usuman dan Fodio, his brother ᶜAbdullāhi b. Muḥammad, his son Muḥammad Bello and his daughter Nana Asma'u, among others, composed vast quantities of Islamic homiletic and theological verse in Arabic, Hausa and Fulfulde in order to push forward the reformist agenda. Among these writings were poems in praise of the Prophet, envisioning the afterlife and warning against the corruption of the world; poems describing the course of the jihad; poems outlining the duties of rulers and ruled; and poems lamenting the deaths of pure and pious Muslim leaders. The poets often wrote cooperatively and with tremendous urgency: after the fall of Alkalawa in 1808, for example, they 'wrote prodigiously ... to provide historical records to guide future generations' (Boyd 1989:27). The poetic style was complex and highly refined; the authors set a high value on scholarly achievement. But as instruments of proselytization, the poems had to be widely disseminated. Fulfulde and Arabic texts had to be translated into Hausa, and then carried from place to place to be performed orally for the general populace (Hiskett 1975:19).

Thus elaborate and erudite poetic texts were brought into alignment with popular styles in order to achieve their purpose. They had to be accessible. But at the same time, they had to oppose and denounce popular profane genres; indeed, one reason for their creation was to provide a counterblast to two well-established types of local oral tradition. The flourishing tradition of Hausa court poetry, which was non-Islamic or only partly Islamicised, aroused the reformers' ire because of its excess and its glorification of figures other than the Prophet; but how much worse was the demotic tradition of songs of praise and satire which were performed at public festivities such as marriages and age-grade ceremonies, and in private meeting places such as prostitutes' parlours. We know about these genres because the reforming elite launched fiery denunciations of profane culture. Later in the nineteenth century, the non-Islamic but aristocratic praise poetry was extensively documented. The praises of chiefs and office holders from the fourteenth century onwards are well represented in the Kano Chronicle, compiled in the late nineteenth century from existing written chronologies, oral court traditions and, possibly, written family records (Hunwick 1993). But the popular recreational and satirical songs of everyday life were not written down. Their form and content can only be guessed at from twentieth-century manifestations of these traditions, on the assumption that 'popular song at that time was much as it is now ... part of a tradition that has not changed in its essentials' (Hiskett 1975:6) – a view reminiscent of David Birmingham's description of the long-term continuity of the Luanda carnival as a popular form. We'll return to this point later. The key point for now is that both commoner and elite genres seem to be constituted not as self-contained traditions, but relationally – each with one eye on the other.

Oral Sources

Apart from the clues provided by such written sources as these, the main resource has been speculative reconstruction based on non-elite oral traditions recorded in recent times but assumed to be of ancient provenance. This raises problems of temporality, for oral genres recorded in the twentieth century have often passed through many generations of transmission and cannot be said to 'belong' definitively to any one era: they are multitemporal, or transtemporal. Nonetheless, they give an impression of what popular genres might have been like in the past, perhaps over long periods.

In the highly compartmentalised hierarchical societies of the West African Sahel, we can see a much more complicated stratification of cultural forms than could be covered by the binary division into 'elite' and 'commoner'. Each social layer seems to have had its own genres and styles of performance, which other strata were ostensibly excluded from. A striking example is Mamadou Diawara's reconstruction, from oral sources, of the hierarchy of performance genres in the Soninke kingdom of Jaara in Mali. Each layer of the highly stratified precolonial social order had its own distinct performance genres. *Hooro* (free people) were distinguished from *komo* (people of servile status). *Hooro* were further divided into patrons (*tunkanlenmu*) and clients (*nyaxamalo*); patrons were further subdivided into princes and commoners, while the client category was made up of separate endogamous groups of blacksmiths, cobblers and wordsmiths or griots. The people of servile status, *komo*, were divided into servants of royalty and aristocracy, on the one hand, and the slaves of private individuals, on the other. The slaves of private individuals were further divided into slaves of ancient stock and recently acquired slaves. All these layered categories, apart from the recently acquired slaves, had their own distinctive traditions of verbal art. The texts of the royal servants, for example, were a formally learned genre, *tanbasire*, and were dignified and gravely performed, while the songs of the slaves of ancient stock – the lowest social category to transmit oral historical traditions – were a ludic genre called *worson suugu* that was informally learned and was 'accompanied with underarm drums, hand-clapping, indecent dances and mimes' (Diawara 1989:114). And the lower strata jealously guarded their exclusive right to their genres:

> The lively style of the music of the *komo* may prompt a free man to sing it; but should one of the slaves of ancient stock catch him at it, even if he is only humming, his house will be invaded by everyone in the village entitled to perform this music. The musicians improvise songs insulting the unlucky victim; men and women perform indecent dances. The person they aim at is obliged to offer his apologies to this frightening troupe and give them presents.
>
> (Diawara 1989:120)

Thus, in the sharp stratification and compartmentalisation characteristic of West African Sahelian societies, each of the many social subdivisions fiercely defended its own traditions and repudiated those of other layers. But in doing so, they upheld the structure as a whole, in which each compartment took responsibility for maintaining its place vis-à-vis the others. And there were threads linking the strata too. The historical traditions of the *hooro* were transmitted and performed by a *nyaxamalo* group, the bards or griots. Though *hooro* families were the 'owners' of their historical and praise traditions, they were not necessarily able to recall or perform these traditions themselves. They depended on the griots for that, just as the griots depended on their *hooro* patrons for sustenance. Here again, we see divisions that indicate relationships.

A recurrent theme in the examples we have looked at is the idea that the popular genres were informal and improvised, in contrast to the dignified and formal genres associated with the elites. I've suggested that one reason for the absence of detailed information about popular genres from early periods might be that, on the one hand, the literate elites and visitors did not think them worth describing in detail, and, on the other hand, the popular performers preferred the freedom of improvisation to the rigours of careful transmission. But the example of the ancient kingdom of Rwanda shows that there is another side to this argument. Despite the extraordinary elaboration of the aristocratic genres and the extreme rigour with which they were transmitted, a case can be made for the greater resilience of the popular improvised genres.

The cultural and political life of the kingdom of Rwanda revolved around the king (the Mwami) and his court. The Tutsi pastoral aristocracy maintained a cultural distinctiveness which differentiated them strongly from the agricultural Hutu majority: they consumed milk rather than grain, cultivated refined manners and perfected the martial and poetic arts. Extraordinary attention was paid to the composition, preservation and faithful transmission of a number of genres most closely associated with royal power. The semi-mystical figure of the Mwami was maintained by rituals, the practice of which was encoded in *ubwiru*, oral poems that were secret, rigorously memorised by hereditary specialists and protected from loss by being divided into sections, which were distributed among different families who were tasked with transmitting them word-for-word down the generations. A second court genre was *igisigo*, dynastic poems composed and transmitted only for the Mwami and his descendants, by specialist bards who had no other duties and who answered directly to the king. Remarkably, not only were the bards of the early twentieth century able to perform a separate poem for each of nineteen successive Mwami, but they were also able to attribute the authorship of each of these poems to a named royal bard from the reign of Cyilima II Rujingura (1675–1708) onwards. Unlike *ubwiru*, these dynastic poems were not secret and the bards could teach them to anyone who wanted to learn, but they were couched in a characteristically 'veiled' or riddle-like style, which required very complicated processes of interpretation before any determinate meaning could be discovered. They were thus a prestigious aristocratic genre only understood by courtiers who had the leisure to master the techniques of exegesis.

Some court genres, however, were more loosely transmitted and more open to appropriation and recasting by the non-aristocratic majority. *Ibiteekerezo* were historical narratives transmitted by official court historians, but they could be performed at court in the evenings for entertainment and could be varied and recreated by the teller. This style of narrative could be picked up by lowly court functionaries and carried to commoner households, where they could be retold for pleasure, fame and recompense. There was a popular narrator called Gahaniisha, for example, who had picked up the stories when his father was a tanner at the Mwami's court. But not all historical narratives lent themselves equally to capture; those that passed into popular repertoires tended to be the most colourful and fantastical. The popular narrators would modify them in the retelling, often increasing the prominence of female characters and introducing topical anachronisms. These versions would be added to a popular repertoire of marvellous legends and tall tales not found in the elite sphere – tales of hunter heroes and miraculous births (Smith 1975).

Among commoners, creative storytelling was a widespread talent; tales of the marvellous, most often told by women and children, were creatively varied and blended, giving the impression, Smith tells us, of 'unlimited abundance'. There was a lot of scope for individual invention, and storytellers added all kinds of symbolic, fantastic, moving or horrifying details, feeding in a wealth of material drawn from everyday life: comic anecdotes, witticisms and strings of proverbs or riddles, sometimes to the point where the narrative thread became a mere vehicle for a display of verbal fireworks. This freewheeling creativity was not known at court.

So the aristocracy invested in preservation, exact transmission and hermetically impenetrable texts, while the commoners invested in imaginative variation, invention and appropriation from all available sources. But there's a contradiction here. Precisely because of their restriction to a narrow aristocratic base and the complete control that the Mwami and his court sought to exert over them, the aristocratic traditions were vulnerable to manipulation for political ends. The eminent historian Jan Vansina suggested that the very idea of a tradition of dynastic poems unchanged and unchallenged for 300 years is an artefact of the expansionist nineteenth-century Rwandan state. The tightly controlled royal traditions, he suggests, were redesigned to suit changing vested interests: the popular traditions, widely and freely disseminated, were more variable, but also less vulnerable to deliberate manipulation (Vansina 2004). For our purposes, the question is not about the historical truth or otherwise of the aristocratic and popular traditions. The question is about the nature, qualities and social constitution of the genres themselves – what they were like, what views they expressed, when and where they were performed and by whom – and to what extent we can assume that they, or something like them, existed in the past. Popular genres which seem informal and fluid may in fact retain their forms and themes over long periods, while carefully controlled and elaborated aristocratic genres, associated with political competition and the exercise of power, may be subject to systematic revision.

African oral popular genres over the *longue durée* thus present us with a peculiar paradox. On the one hand, historians have remarked on the slow-moving tenacity and deep continuity of popular culture, such that forms observed in the seventeenth or eighteenth century are still resilient in the twentieth. On the other hand, there is abundant evidence of the capacity of popular creators to invent new forms and invest in novelty, and for innovations to catch on, spread like wildfire and then die down – to the extent that these characteristics have been identified by some scholars as the hallmarks of what is 'popular'. The combination of endurance and innovation is, indeed, what makes popular culture both a challenge and a fascinating magnet for social historians.

Later Written Evidence – the Scribal Elite and Two Popular Poets

It is from the first half of the nineteenth century that we begin to get more detailed evidence about the popular songs, anecdotes and commentaries that people produced in response to their own experience. This is not because people did not produce such commentaries in earlier periods, but because it was only in the late nineteenth century that local literates, capable of retrieving and understanding forms circulating fifty years earlier, found them significant enough to write down.

In some cases, this was because local African historians began to look for sources for the precolonial era. Historical memory is very often lodged in key textual formulations, such as praise epithets, songs and proverbs, and the authors of local histories drew heavily on them. Samuel Johnson's great work *The History of the Yorubas* (published in 1921, but completed in the 1890s) constantly quotes popular sayings and 'ditties' coined in response to specific events in the wars that, from circa 1830 to 1893, engulfed most of what is now south-western Nigeria. The common people are continually present in his text, commenting sometimes patriotically and sometimes cynically on the progress of the wars. Their laconic and witty extemporised songs (which Johnson often links to popular dances) seem to have run across the region and across enemy lines like bush fires. They caught 'the spirit of the times' (Johnson 1921:331), and sometimes that spirit seems to be one of bewilderment and sorrow in the midst of all the military triumphalism. An Ijaye song complains of the convergence of rapacious enemies around the town:

> Ibadan kidnaps, Fiditi kidnaps
> Daily the men of Agọ kidnap in our farms
> Daily the men of Agọ capture for service behind our walls [i.e. capture people just outside the town in order to enserf them]
> This matter to me is like a dream!
>
> (Johnson 1921:345)

Johnson quotes these songs and sayings as keys to the meaning of the whole long-drawn-out and extremely complex sequence of inter-kingdom wars and alliances. These events, in Johnson's telling, were meaningful partly because of their impact on the population at large – an impact that was encapsulated in people's immediate, creative and memorable commentaries.

There were other members of the African literate elite whose interest in oral texts was not historical so much as literary, philosophical or religious. They collected proverbs and divination poetry as repositories of the collective 'wisdom of our fathers'. But more surprisingly, at least two such scholars, on opposite sides of the continent, also took a keen interest in the topical works of popular poets from fifty years earlier, remembered by their communities not as anonymous bearers of tradition or testimony to popular shared experience, but as distinctive, named, original individuals. In Kenya, the Swahili poems of the oral poet Muyaka bin Haji (1776–1840) were collected by an Islamic scholar, Mwalimu Sikujua, who wrote them down in Arabic script in the late 1880s. He then helped an English clergyman, the Reverend W. E. Taylor, to transliterate these texts into Latin script and translate them into English. In Nigeria at around the same time, the Reverend E. M. Lijadu, a Yoruba clergyman, collected and transcribed the songs of an oral poet, Aribiloṣo (who died soon after Muyaka, in 1848), and published them in the form of a delightful memoir in Yoruba that combines an account of Aribilọṣọ's life with the songs he composed in response to his experiences.

Both poets lived through turbulent times: the late phase of the slave trade and the stepping-up of interference by foreign powers. Aribilọṣọ's Ẹgba region of western Nigeria was in the eye of the political and military storm that followed the collapse of Ọyọ, the most powerful of the Yoruba kingdoms. This precipitated the mass movement of refugees and soldiers southward, the breakup and relocation of whole towns and the creation of new settlements on novel political patterns – among them Abẹokuta, the principal city in Aribilọṣọ's area. Spreading warfare involved almost all the Yoruba city-states, and threats came from the Fulani in the north and the Dahomeyans in the west. Warfare increased the supply of slaves and led to a surge in the export of Yoruba slaves, just as the British nominally abolished the slave trade and the British naval squadron started patrolling the coast of West Africa from 1807 onwards. Aribilọṣọ himself was enslaved in his youth, but managed to redeem himself before he could be sold overseas. British missionaries were beginning in a small way to arrive in Abẹokuta just at the end of Aribilọṣọ's life.

Mombasa, the home of Aribilọṣọ's contemporary Muyaka, had an even longer history of external embroilment. The Swahili coast was active in long-distance Indian Ocean trade from a very early period, and Swahili merchants and middlemen exported ivory and spices as far as India, Persia and Mesopotamia. They developed a unique literate Islamic civilisation from around the ninth century, characterised by stone houses, elegant dress, poetry and Islamic learning. Interaction resulting from long-distance trade fostered linguistic and cultural mixing, not least in the Swahili language, with its African Bantu base and extensive importation of Arabic vocabulary. The Portuguese had arrived 1498 and consolidated their presence by building Fort Jesus in 1593. They were succeeded by Omani Arabs, who ruled Mombasa through a garrison of Arab soldiers – Mazruis – until the latter, with the support of the Swahili patricians of Mombasa, stopped paying tribute. Complicated power struggles ensued that involved other islands along the coast such as Pate, Lamu, Pemba and Mafia. When a coup in 1806 brought Seyyid Said to power in Oman, he decided to make Zanzibar his headquarters and, with the support of the British government, assert overlordship of the whole East African coast. Mombasa struggled against him and the islands that recognised him, and Muyaka was one of Mombasa's spokespeople. Many of his poems were about this political and military struggle.

Thus, the two poets, Muyaka and Aribiloso, were shaped by the uncertainties unleashed by foreign incursions and long-drawn-out, multifaceted local warfare. Both of them composed oral topical poems commenting on events as they unfolded. Both were loved and remembered by their local community. Both used popular verse forms. Muyaka composed mainly in the *shairi* form, which consisted of four-line stanzas with a fixed metre and rhyme scheme, suitable for short poems of topical interest aiming at wide appeal (Abdulaziz 1979:102), unlike other, more elaborate Swahili verse forms. Aribiloso composed in the style of the Oro cult singers characteristic of the Egba region.

Lijadu's memoir gives a vivid sense of the low status of itinerant singers in Aribiloso's time. He says that when Aribiloso was a child, he liked to follow the Oro singers around, copying them and gradually learning to compose and perform songs for himself. His parents were terribly upset. His father warned him that the Oro singers were all good-for-nothings and were never respected in their lives. But Aribiloso

> was unable to heed these warnings. After a while, it took such a hold of him that he sometimes spent three days without coming home; and he neglected the work that his father gave him to do. His father couldn't stand this, so he drove him out of the house. But this did not bother Aribiloso, because he had places to stay everywhere that he went to sing, and he was given food as well.

Even when his father's friends and relatives, believing Aribiloso was deranged, tied him up and dosed him with medicines, they could not break him of the habit. His mother 'burst into tears, because she was terribly upset; she called Aribiloso and begged him to listen to her; that he shouldn't let these bad words [the Oro songs] become a habit, because those who had done it before him had died paupers'. Aribiloso replied with an extempore verse:

> See how the entire world speaks ill of Oro-singers
> Wishing them a bad end
> But before I, Aribiloso
> Meet a bad end
> The civet cat will turn into a dog, the antelope will become a horse
> Horses will turn into people.

In the end, his parents despaired of changing his behaviour and let him pursue his chosen calling in peace (Lijadu 1886, my translation).

Thus, though Oro singers were considered poor and disreputable, their art could also bring them the community's affection and esteem.

Muyaka's status was somewhat different. He was from an old family in Mombasa and was a client of two of the Mazrui governors, whom he used to visit in the old Portuguese area of town. They admired his poetry and exchanged verses with him. But he was not of patrician status, and does not appear to have been at all well off. In one verse he laments

> I wish I could cut a smart dash
> So that wherever I pass I might appear prosperous;
> I no longer care to cast away this poverty, having been so much
>   slandered and insinuated against
> That my clothes are full of lice and that I scratch my body too much!
>   (Abdulaziz 1979:109)

Both Aribiloṣo and Muyaka commented satirically, humorously, philosophically and sometimes passionately on contemporary people, politics and events. Their compositions were spread, treasured and passed on by members of their communities. The poems passed into everyday discourse: fragments of them became quotable as proverbs or catchphrases. Lijadu says of Aribiloṣo: 'It's amazing to see how his sayings, songs and proverbs have spread among the Egba – just look, he himself has died and his life-story too has died with him, but the words of his songs and proverbs remain alive on our lips up till today.' Many of Muyaka's metaphorical formulations were also picked out and used as proverbs by his hearers (Abdulaziz 1979). In other words, these two poets were popular not only in the sense that they were of fairly humble status and drew on and articulated an experience shared with ordinary people, but also in the sense that their formulations were loved and appreciated to the point that they passed into everyday language. In both cases, also, their texts relied on extensive local knowledge to decipher their allusions. Both the Swahili *mashairi* and the Yoruba Oro song genre were deliberately created to be enigmatic and opaque, challenging the listener to complete the allusion or figure out the reference. To people not immersed in the local situation, the poems would convey little; the listener is drawn in as an accomplice to participate in the constitution of the text's meaning. They were thus popular in the further sense of being deeply embedded in local discourse.

The fact that the popular poetry of Muyaka and Aribiloṣo – relatively recent, attributable to named authors, topical and allusive – was prized by local African intellectuals in the late nineteenth century shows that these particular members of a literate elite, whether Christian or Muslim, were still very much in touch with – or part of – a wider collective experience and expression. Unlike the Fulani reformers in the 1804 jihad, they set out not to bury popular genres, but to praise them. Nonetheless, what they did was essentially to transpose or translate these texts into a different sphere, that of print literacy, accessible only to a minority. And that brings us to the wider effects of Christian missions, literacy and the press.

Christian Missions and Print Literacy

Samuel Johnson, who recorded so many popular songs in his *History of the Yorubas,* and E. M. Lijadu, who collected and wrote down Aribiloṣo's popular songs, were both Anglican clergymen. After Muyaka's verses had been collected and transcribed by a Muslim scholar, a Christian clergyman helped him put them into print. The key role played by churchmen in the research and recording of oral traditions was no accident.

Christian missionaries, from the early nineteenth century onwards, were catalysts for far-reaching changes in popular experience and outlook. Writing in various scripts existed in Africa before the arrival of missionaries. The Arabic alphabet was used by Qur'anic scholars across the West African Sahel and along the East African coast, and it was adapted for writing African languages including Fulfulde, Mande languages, Nupe and, most extensively, Swahili. The Tuareg had an ancient Lybico-Berber script, *tifinagh,* which they used mainly for writing about private and amorous affairs. The Coptic Ge'ez script of Ethiopia supported the creation of a large written literature dating from the fourth century AD. But the nineteenth-century Christian missions brought new regimes of reading and writing. Their key innovations were the printing press, the ideal of mass literacy and the link they made between literacy and social progress as well as personal self-betterment. This involved new disciplines of time, space and sociality, overlaid on older social forms.

To implant their evangelical message, Christian missionaries had to get at everyday life. They introduced social regimes built around literacy and faith, in many cases abstracting people from kin and residential networks and constituting new communities around the mission station. They introduced new disciplines of time and space. R. W. J. Shepherd of the Lovedale Institution in South Africa described the traditional Nguni round house as 'the root cause of the low standard of Bantu life' and advocated square buildings, internally partitioned for the sake of personal privacy but with large windows for the sake of illumination. Rather than clustering in a semicircle around the big house of the village chief, the new square houses were to be built in orderly rows, emphasising an ethic of individual merit and hard work rather than patronage and customary hierarchy. Schools and churches seated their classes and congregations in uniform rows in square, straight-walled rooms. Even when desks and chairs were not available, the strict regime of regular columns and rows was maintained in schools across British Africa. Disciplines of time were equally emphasised: clock time was associated with self-regulation. Anna Hinderer, who, with her husband, David Hinderer, ran the CMS mission for seventeen years in Abẹokuta and then in Ibadan, in what later became Nigeria, describes the start of lessons in their Ibadan school: 'We see the people hastening towards us as nine o'clock approaches, for the one hour for school is too precious to be wasted by being five minutes too late' (Hone 1877:296–7). These new ideas of spatial and temporal regulation were taken up and partly adopted, partly satirised, in popular cultural forms throughout the colonial period. Numerous comic scenes in twentieth-century Ghanaian concert party and Yoruba popular theatre show characters excessively preoccupied with telling the time by clocks or enormous watches strapped to their arms, or people obsessed with making lists and reading memos, or people determined to make others line up in orderly queues – or in military formation, a parallel and related development. Visual art began to depict the interiors of modern, square houses, with square pictures on the walls and chairs arranged in formation. Fiction referred to dates and precise times of day. All this was on a knife edge between emulation and mockery, where it was never certain which prevailed.

Print literacy was central to the missionaries' project. They believed that Christian books could reach places the individual missionary could not go, could stay within families and communities exerting a quiet influence and could become an instrument of individual reflection and self-examination. And to maximize the speed and breadth of its impact, the printed word had to be in local African languages. From the moment they set foot on African soil, European missionaries got to work translating sacred texts, devising orthographies, producing tracts and newsletters and creating word lists and grammars. Important linguistic work was done, new vocabulary was imported or invented, local linguistic structures were sometimes distorted in the effort to make the African language convey the Christian message. Missionaries established versions of African languages – often based on an amalgamation of several local dialects – which in due course were adopted as the standard for print, media and educational purposes, overriding the numerous variants that were actually spoken. And as missionary texts travelled, they were recast in local terms. Bunyan's *The Pilgrim's Progress* was translated into more than eighty African languages, and its illustrations recreated in local styles. Its images, plot structure and literary style were all gradually absorbed into local popular culture and given new life in secular African-language fiction and drama as well as Christian discourse. The 'impact' of mission-instilled literacy was not restricted to a dyadic centre-periphery relationship; still less was it a one-way transaction: the African mission field shaped the way Bunyan was seen in England, and the texts, images and ideas associated with the book spread through multiple capillaries in a network of generative points across Africa, and continued to work in unpredictable ways (Hofmeyr 2004).

The Christian literates formed a new elite whose privilege was defined by its proximity to colonial power. They became civil servants, teachers, catechists and government and mercantile clerks. They asserted their privilege by styles of life, registers of speech and distinctive forms of dress; they saw themselves as urban, enlightened and 'civilised', in contrast to the bushmen, illiterates and pagans of the rural hinterlands. But this class was not clearly demarcated. Literacy, the single most powerful engine of social mobility in the colonial period in Africa, though in practice restricted to a minority, was in principle obtainable by all. People aspired to better themselves through schooling, and where formal church or government school places were not sufficient, entrepreneurs set up private schools, and autodidacts sought to increase their knowledge through private reading and participation in literary and debating societies.

Writers and editors among the educated elites in coastal West Africa and South Africa quickly detached themselves from the control of missionary presses and set up publishing enterprises of their own, producing newspapers and pamphlets on civic, political and cultural issues. They depicted the African print sphere that they were creating as thoroughly modern, a platform from which to launch advancement towards a better future, and definitively superior to the oral sphere of most of the population. But from the beginning, there were popular voices in these texts. Popular poets were captured in print. The first Yoruba novel was about low-life Lagos and was bursting with popular anecdotes, allusions and sayings. Many newspapers published street ballads, folklore and jokes gathered from everyday speech. Print literacy (and the idea of print literacy) from the very beginning was entwined with a whole range of live performance–oriented genres. Throughout the twentieth century, popular fiction and poetry written in African languages continued to recreate oral-like effects. And in turn, new twentieth-century live performance genres were often oriented towards literacy without actually depending on it. The managers and actors in West African popular travelling theatres spoke of 'writing' plays which were entirely unscripted and improvised; oral poets in South Africa might write a poem, but then perform it without referring to the written text; or they might hold a piece of paper in front of them as they performed, but without reading it. Writing in some circumstances thus became a kind of reference point for what was a predominantly oral mode of creativity.

The social consequences of the inception and spread of popular literacy have been profound. Throughout the twentieth century, the majority of primary school pupils did not succeed in continuing into secondary – let alone tertiary – education. Dubbed 'primary school leavers' in West Africa, they formed the backbone of a new urban workforce of artisans, traders, clerks and skilled workers. Producers and consumers of twentieth-century popular cultural forms are often described in scholarly studies by means of lists: shoeshine boys, bread sellers, taxi touts, tailors, seamstresses, hawkers. Many of these people had a few years of primary school education and were able to read (more easily in their mother tongue than in English), write letters and decipher the billboards that sprang up advertising theatre, dance and film shows.

Schooling fed into popular culture not only through literacy, but also through instruction in visual art, dance and drama. In these arts, there was almost always a tension in colonial educational policy between inculcating European forms and values and fostering and preserving a distinctive 'African' creativity.

This large and ever-expanding constituency of primary school leavers, partially conversant with European art forms, literate but not sufficiently to obtain high-status white-collar jobs, was one of the major seedbeds of twentieth-century African popular culture.

Tradition and the Vitality of Oral Culture

Literacy had an increasing, profound and undeniable influence on popular culture in Africa throughout the twentieth century. But it did not supersede or displace oral culture. Up till today, popular culture producers have drawn on and continued to revitalise inherited oral traditions at a number of levels and in a number of different ways. Some have taken up a genre formerly associated with monarchy or nobility and converted it to a popular cause. Sunjata, the magnificent epic of the medieval empire of Mali, was created to uphold the status and legitimacy of the rulers and their noblemen. These social categories no longer exist, but Sunjata is ubiquitously performed by popular musicians to exalt national and regional identities. The story is taught in children's school texts, and the musical tradition, accompanied by the traditional *kora* lute, has become the basis for one of the most widely appreciated popular music styles worldwide. In South Africa, A. T. Qabula took the style of Zulu praise poetry, the most extensive forms of which are associated with chiefs, and turned it into praises of the Council of South African Trade Unions, which he performed at mass political rallies (Gunner 1989). Other popular performers incorporated token fragments of well-known oral genres into newer performance genres: Yoruba popular theatre, projecting itself as modern and distinct from older masquerade theatre, nonetheless took every opportunity to insert traditional drumming, the recitations of diviners, incantations and hunters' chants into its plays (Barber 2000). Newly established institutions like the popular theatre troupe Mufwankolo of the Congo used television drama to ponder and explicate an old, orally transmitted proverb (Fabian 1990). And amongst the exceptionally rich and vigorous traditions of verbal art in Somalia, a new oral genre, *heelloy*, was created in the twentieth century. It was open to new categories of performer, notably women, and was able to speak of new experiences – parliamentary debates, industrial strikes (Johnson 1995). Oral genres have therefore flourished through continual initiatives to adapt, transform and recreate them in response to new historical experience. Even the most recent mediatised genres, products of late twentieth- and early twenty-first-century economic, political and technological change, still continue to recycle older oral repertoires.

One aim of this chapter has been to dispel the idea, unintentionally suggested by the 'traditional-popular-elite' triad that was used in early studies of popular culture in Africa, that the 'traditional' was a homogenous, shared, consensual, communal and unchanging culture, and that cultural divisions and oppositions between social strata only came into force in the colonial era. After colonisation, the past came to be seen as 'tradition', 'cultural heritage', now belonging to all, to the whole nation or ethnic group. The triadic definition pointed to a truth, not about the past, but about the present: in the colonial and postcolonial worlds, precolonial genres had indeed come to be seen as 'tradition', more or less undifferentiated and collective, but available for editing, writing down, revising, restaging and presenting as a badge of identity.

The concept of tradition did, of course, exist outside the colonial sphere, but it was not conceptualised as one field of relations and processes over against another alternative set. Elders would appeal to the concept in adjuring their younger relatives to do things the right way: 'Let us do what we have previously been doing, so that things can stay as they have previously been.' Maintaining the forms established by previous generations was not a matter of passively accepting what had been passed down, but rather an alert and creative effort to keep things on the rails, reinstall institutions that were always at risk of fading, shore up arrangements and make them stick. Wọle Ṣoyinka captures this hauntingly in his play *Death and the King's Horseman*, when the Praise Singer exhorts the King's Horseman, with mesmerising intensity, to commit the required act of ritual suicide. In the time of their forebears, he says, 'the world was never tilted from its grooves', and 'it shall not be in yours' (Ṣoyinka 1984:148). The danger of tilting from the groove, of dislocation and disintegration, was an ever-present, long-standing threat that had to be met with determined constructive action. Willem Bosman witnessed, in the late seventeenth-century Slave Coast, a particularly striking ritual of rebellion: on the death of a king, the community would deliberately plunge into lawlessness, with robbery on all sides, until the new king was announced and forbade it, whereupon it would cease immediately (Bosman 1967 [1705]:366a). Here, it seems, was a dramatization or enactment of the need for sovereignty: chaos was allowed to break out to underline and reaffirm the need for a socially created order vested in the person of the king. In another part of the West African coast, again according to Bosman, the role of 'Cabocero's, or Chief Men' was to 'take care of the Welfare of the City or Village, and to appease any Tumult' (ibid.:132). Tumult seems to have been an ever-present possibility, and the instituted authorities were put in place to damp it down. The possibility of breakdown, of the world running out of its groove, always had to be confronted.

Tradition, then, was an active process of creation and maintenance of social form. But it was not a cultural/aesthetic category that competed for space with another order of cultural production. This only happened with the emergence of a class of colonial 'new men', whose position issued from their proximity to the colonial power and their mastery of colonial repertoires. Tradition now became a category with boundaries, offering one set of options that contrasted with another, 'modern' set. The two main categories through which African culture used to be habitually represented in museums, art galleries and university courses owed everything to this bifurcation of the field. 'Tradition' became not an active, vigilant preservation and recreation of the sociocultural forms a community had agreed to constitute, projected forward into the future, but instead a legacy or even remnant from the past, needing documentation before it disappeared, a source of pride and nostalgia. The 'modern', on the other hand, was all about the future: African intellectuals who were vested in European repertoires spoke in terms of lack, of the need for more literacy, more conversion, more enlightenment in order to achieve a better future. Different combinations of a sanitised tradition and an anticipated modernity were envisaged in local intellectual traditions.

These attitudes to tradition were fostered through the spread of popular literacy and were, to some extent, adopted by non-elite cultural producers. The boss of a Yoruba popular theatre company in the 1980s once told me that they charged more for plays based on traditional myths, because they were 'heavier' and required 'research', unlike plays based on anecdote and everyday experience. The early manifestations of popular culture that we have tried to trace in this chapter are elusive as an object of historical inquiry. But those genres, performances and creative resources of the past, which we have only been able to glimpse in the archive or very tentatively reconstruct from oral sources, are nonetheless in some sense still alive and present to popular culture producers today. They appear in myriad forms and transformations, in ongoing 'traditions of invention' (Guyer 1996).

CHAPTER 3

Mines, Migrant Labour and Township Culture

As an engine of transformation, mining was one of the most rapid, far-reaching and devastating innovations in Africa's recent social and economic history. In the relations between the mining companies and the workers, the struggle between capital and labour was revealed in its starkest form. This was especially apparent in gold mining, for fixed international gold prices meant that the only way to increase profits and absorb increased production costs was to tighten the screws on labour. The history of mining is one of continual battle: ruthless subjection of the workers to inhumane conditions and unremitting resistance, individual and collective, formal and informal, by the workers. The rapacity and brutality of the mining companies and their larger international finance companies are startling. And this was not even the most consequential feature of mining in Africa. All mines – of gold, copper, tin, coal and diamonds – needed immense concentrations of labour, which they had difficulty recruiting. In societies that were grounded in subsistence agriculture, there was no need for men to sell their labour for low wages in dangerous and unpleasant conditions underground. Mining companies therefore sought, with the connivance of the colonial state, to separate or partially separate agricultural producers from their land. By means of taxation and recruiting methods that in some cases amounted to forced labour, they drove thousands of young men underground. African populations sought to extract some advantage from the situation: in the earliest days of the mining industry, some chiefdoms, such as the Sotho and Pedi in South

Africa, organised their youth to work in the mines in order to acquire guns for the defence of the kingdom, and later, individual young men were attracted to the mines by the promise of new sources of personal independence. But their gains were slight in comparison with the massive profits extracted by the mining companies.

Mining was not a colonial invention. Gold mining already existed in West Africa before the Portuguese arrived in the fifteenth century; the states of the Gold Coast had built up their power on the back of the gold trade for centuries before British conquest paved the way for the Ashanti Goldfields Corporation to begin its operations (Crisp 1982). In Katanga, waves of African conquerors recruited the local farmers to work in copper, iron and gold mines from the late seventeenth century onwards (Higginson 1989:6). In Southern Rhodesia, gold mining dated back to the fourteenth century and perhaps earlier, and the gold trade with the east coast of Africa was the basis of the rise of the state of Great Zimbabwe until its abandonment in the sixteenth century (Van Onselen 1976:11). Shallow gold mines had been worked, and exhausted, by local populations before the big gold find in South Africa unleashed the industrial revolution there. The difference was one of scale, intensity and technology.

Industrial-scale mining threw up new towns. Gold in large quantities was discovered on a Transvaal farm in South Africa in 1886; within a decade, an arc of mining towns had sprung up along the gold reef, and at the apex of the arc was Johannesburg, with a population of 100,000 people who had flooded in from all over the world (Callinicos 1981:8). Enugu, Eastern Nigeria's 'coal city', was a brand-new settlement in 1915, laid out by the governor general, Lord Lugard, and reflecting colonial hierarchies of class and race in its spatial segregation. The towns of the Zambian Copperbelt took off with terrific speed after the inception of large-scale copper mining in the late 1920s.

Mining hurled people together from different ethnic, linguistic and regional backgrounds. Investors, speculators, prospectors and engineers were attracted from all over the world. The workforce was heterogeneous from the beginning, especially in the South African gold mines, where labour was recruited from all over southern Africa, and workers from Botswana, Lesotho, Malawi and, above all, Mozambique outnumbered those recruited within South Africa right up to the 1970s. Congolese and Zambian copper mines and Zimbabwean gold mines competed for labour from each other and neighbouring countries.

But especially in the settler colonies, where a white population feared the growth of a black urban proletariat, it was not intended that the mineworkers should live permanently at the mining centres or settle their families there. Instead, patterns of migrant labour were instituted. They varied from one region to another, but the essential idea was that miners worked for specified periods in the mine, often living in a mining compound as single men, while their wives and children remained in the rural areas maintaining the household. At the end of their contracts, the miners were expected to return to their villages. In this way, the mining companies avoided paying the miners a full living wage; their wives and children were supported by agricultural work in the village. In practice, in South Africa, where this system reached its most complete manifestation, the miners' wages were not enough to live on, but the 'reserves' where their households were based became increasingly overcrowded and depleted until the miners' families could not eke out a living from the soil either. An oscillating mutual dependency and mutual need became the norm. In the Copperbelt of Northern Rhodesia and the Congo, mining companies had moved by mid-century towards a system where housing, social services and leisure facilities such as cinema halls, libraries and sports fields were provided. This resulted in a more settled population, with migrants returning to their home areas, if at all, only after long residence in the mining centres. In West Africa, which was almost free of European settlers, miners (coal and tin miners in Nigeria, diamond miners in Sierra Leone, gold miners in the Gold Coast) tended to be recruited from nearer the mines and to have frequent or even uninterrupted contact with their villages. Since farmers were not expropriated and herded into reserves, it was possible for subsistence agriculture to continue. Migrant labour associated with mining thus had less far-reaching social and cultural impact in West Africa than in central and southern Africa.

Even South Africa, where the state was most bent on preventing the emergence of an urban proletariat, there was counter-pressure in the opposite direction. The mining companies needed a stable workforce; social order in the towns was better served by settled family units than by a concentration of lone male workers; many black employees, such as domestic workers, factory workers and providers of services, were needed on a permanent basis; and some urban dwellers, who had come in search of a better life, were reluctant to return to the farm. Hybrid compromise arrangements developed. On the Rand, mineworkers were corralled in guarded male-only compounds. The more senior mine employees were allowed 'married quarters' outside the compound walls. And beyond the mining compounds, informal black or mixed urban townships grew up, allowing a family life of sorts, as well as a legal and illegal informal economy in which prostitution and liquor distilling were key means of survival. During and after the Second World War, manufacturing in South Africa expanded dramatically, and this increased the demand for a stable urban workforce; at the same time, the state began to take more determined measures to get rid of the informal, mixed, inner-city townships such as Sophiatown and replace them with more distant purpose-built locations such as Soweto and Orlando. This pattern of divided residential space, where the aim was to control African residents, confine them to certain areas and avoid the cost of providing basic social amenities, was associated not only with mine towns, but with any urban centre in South Africa where there was a large African labour force recruited to work in white enterprises.

Thus the ground was prepared for the emergence of several new cultural impulses. In the mine compounds, workers of different national, linguistic and ethnic origins found a way to live together by a dual orientation: on the one hand, they emphasised their ethnic solidarity with fellow 'homeboys'; on the other hand, they developed a common linguistic and cultural idiom with which to interact with other groups. At the same time, as circular migrants, they also created cultural means to bridge and articulate the dislocation between the city and their rural homes. In the townships, the shifting, precarious urban population, thrown together by chance and necessity, created a heterogeneous culture in which people of different origins, occupations and opportunities came together in a common struggle for survival. This chapter will look at the cultural forms that emerged from these three sites: the mine compounds, the migrants' journeys and the townships. The central focus is on South Africa, and on the formative years of the mining industry in the first half of the twentieth century. But many of the structures and situations described here existed in variant forms in other mining areas and persisted, with modifications, right up to the end of the century.

Down the Mine

Working in a mine of whatever type was gruelling. But perhaps the hardest were the gold mines of the Rand. The gold ore was abundant, but was deep and had a low yield. This demanded heavy capital investment, which in turn meant that massive-scale, frenetic, nonstop production was required in order to realise a profit and produce dividends for shareholders. From the earliest days of the industry, the South African gold mines operated at high speed and on a huge scale. Lewis Nesbitt, a British-Italian mining engineer, spent three years (1912–15) working on the Rand. The scene he evokes in his memoir, *Gold Fever* (Nesbitt 1936), is astonishing. In each mine, multiple shafts were sunk more than a mile deep, each carrying pipes for air, water and electricity cables as well as huge metal lifts carrying eighty men at a time in their iron cages, which hurtled to the different levels, bouncing on their cables as they came to rest. From the shaft, horizontal galleries were opened at regular intervals of depth, and from the galleries, slanting stopes or channels were cut to allow the miners access to the thin gold-bearing strata in the rock face. In the stopes, teams of miners drilled dozens of deep holes, packed them with great charges of dynamite a hundredweight at a time and blasted the rock, which fell in avalanches. Other teams of 'lashers' shovelled the broken ore-bearing rock into wagons that ran along a rail in the galleries to the mine shaft, where they were tipped into skips and carried up to the surface in the lifts, ten tons at a time. Here they were again transferred to rail trucks and were pushed to the battery house, to be pounded to dust by giant mechanical pestles that worked 'day and night … moving with a ceaseless rhythm' and with a sound that could be heard for miles (Nesbitt 1936:85). Nesbitt constantly evokes the ear-splitting noise: 'Now there was nothing but a deafening crackling of rapid blows, interspersed with the more metallic clangs of the boys' iron maces beating on those stabbing chisels, as thick as the arm of a man. A chisel became stuck, the machine could not turn it; a hissing and shuddering, a crunching and whistling, most uneasy and terrifying, was heard' (ibid.:62). He emphasises the breakneck pace and the brutality with which this pace was enforced: 'At the end of the long train comes the threatening boss boy, laying about him with a large stiff piece of rubber tubing, a formidable weapon' (ibid.:63). Above all, he dwells on the devastation to the miners' lungs caused by breathing the mine dust, full of 'minute particles with points far finer than that of any needle and edges

FIGURE 3 Miners going underground at the Robinson Deep Gold Mine, Witwatersrand, South Africa, around 1900.

infinitely sharper than that of any knife' (ibid.:30–1). Miners were esti-mated to have an average of eight years of active work before they were killed by silicosis, caused by this dust. The white miners, with whom Nesbitt was most familiar, often decided to risk early death from dis-ease or disaster because of the 'lordly wages'. The African workers were paid far less. After the introduction of contracts tying them to specific mines and legal controls preventing them from seeking other work at the end of the contract, they were also paid less than they could have earned in more congenial occupations above ground. In this way, the devouring mines made a profit.

Labour in the mines was not seen by the workers as productive. Rather, the mine consumed workers, exhausting them, wrecking their bodies, tossing them aside and sucking in replacements. As Rosalind Morris put it in a profound reflection on the theme, 'the miner – unlike the capitalist to whom surplus value accrues – does not experience his work as a process of accumulation, with productivity enabling consumption. Rather, the miner himself is consumed in time' (Morris 2008:99). In the Tswana language, migrant workers distinguished between *mmereko*, waged labour they did for the whites, and *tiro*, fulfilling labour which contributed to the building of a household through the increase of a herd of cattle, the growth of crops, the rearing of children and so on (Moodie 1994:29–30). The mine became a beast, and human beings became parts of its machinery. In the title of David Coplan's book on the poetry of Sotho migrant mineworkers, the migrants experience their lives as taking place 'in the time of cannibals'. The mine devours its own attendants. At the same time, however, the gruelling labour could be experienced as a form of initiation into manhood. The interpersonal violence that pervaded the industrial process was experienced as productive in the sense that it established both black and white workers as men.

Diversity and Uniformity in the Mining Compound

The South African mining compound was a large rectangular barracks-like building, the sides of which consisted of rows of dormitories, each accommodating between fifteen and fifty men on concrete bunks. In the centre was a large open space where inmates could do their washing, socialise, play sports and so on. The compound also contained a refectory, providing a monotonous but free supply of unpalatable meals, and a compound shop, where imported food and other luxuries were sold at inflated prices. The compound was accessed via a single gate. This derived from the early worker housing at the diamond mines, where a prime concern was to prevent workers making off with stolen diamonds. In the gold mines, there was no fear of the workers stealing large lumps of broken ore, and they were free to leave the compound after working hours to visit friends in other compounds or to spend time in the nearby township. However, the enclosed structure was retained as a means of population control: unrest could be quelled, numbers monitored and abscondment limited. The compound was run on highly hierarchical and authoritarian lines, with a white compound manager and his white assistants at the top, and tiers of African supervisors, interpreter-clerks, 'police boys' and dormitory bosses below. Outside the compound were single small houses and sets of married quarters for the higher-paid and more permanent employees, and beyond that were the quarters of the European staff. These arrangements made apparent the tension between the mining industry's need to retain workers and its fear of an emergent urban proletariat. One reason for the recruitment of workers from far afield, in addition to the perennial shortage of labour, was that foreign migrants were less likely to be able to abscond to alternative employment during their contracts but were easier to get rid of at the end; in theory, at any rate, they had nowhere to go but home.

The mine authorities in South Africa found it expedient to consolidate ethnic blocs within the heterogeneous workforce. Men from the same area were put together in the dormitories, with their own spokesmen. There were patterns of recruitment to particular parts of the production process that fostered ethnic pride. And the authorities encouraged rivalry between ethnic groups by means of ethnically defined teams for sports and dance contests. Workers, too, found it congenial to congregate with other homeboys. Moodie describes groups of northern Sotho sitting together, talking about home, recalling shared experiences and telling stories from their rural background; their longing for home could only be assuaged by the construction of ethnic capsules within the heterogeneous compound. Delius shows how chieftaincy politics was a vital focus of debate among Pedi migrants, and how political strategies they worked out in the mine compounds were carried back to the homeland (Delius 1996). In this way, ethnicity-as-culture became more defined; people became conscious of 'having', and asserting, a specific culture, distinct from – and parallel to – those of other groups. But at the same time, they went beyond ethnic loyalties. They developed a lingua franca, learned about each other's customs and, in the very act of asserting their 'own' cultural forms, represented them as in some way commensurable or parallel to those of others. Moreover, many of the organisational structures they developed to perform 'traditional' culture were actually new inventions, modelled on bureaucratic or military forms and potentially therefore supra-ethnic.

The best-documented illustration of this double impulse – to both affirm 'home' culture and transcend it – is the 'tribal' dancing which flourished in all of the southern African mining sites, and indeed in other places where people of different ethnic origins were thrown together: 'Each African township, location or compound has its pitches where dancing teams from different tribes perform every Sunday afternoon and on public holidays' (Mitchell 1956:1–2). Charles Van Onselen describes Saturday and Sunday afternoons in the Southern Rhodesian gold mine compounds, when the Ndebele would perform the *nxuzu* dance with 'rhythmic clapping of hands on legs'; Karanga Shona would do the *Zangoma*, associated with spirits responsible for illness; Shangaans of eastern Mozambique would dance the *shimbo* and *mutzongoya*, 'celebrating the role of women in society'; the Ngoni of Northern Rhodesia would dance the *ngoma*, 'with home-made musical instruments made from gourds'; Mashukulumbwe people from north of the Zambezi did a 'stick-throwing dance'; while the Yao did *mbeni* and the Tonga did *mganda*. The mine compound became a kind of showcase for ethnic diversity, each ethnic group producing its 'own' 'typical' dance. Visitors could even be invited to the mine to witness the amusements of the happy black workers (Van Onselen 1976).

Mine-site dance is brilliantly illustrated by J. C. Mitchell's pioneering ethnography of the Kalela dance in Northern Rhodesia. Mitchell explains that Kalela was the most popular of the many styles of team dancing that flourished on the Copperbelt, mainly because the songs were topical, witty and in the Bemba lingua franca that, according to Epstein (see Chapter 1), was locally known as CiCopperbelti, because it was so heavily adapted to multi-ethnic urban work conditions and full of slang and loan words from other African languages and English.

The Kalela dance was performed by teams of men, dressed in a uniform and moving in a circle in single file to the music of drums and songs composed by members of the group. As with the Beni dance (Ranger 1975), to which Kalela was related, the Kalela dancers' style was associated with urban modernity. The uniform of the particular team that Mitchell describes in detail consisted of 'grey slacks, neatly pressed singlets, hair with partings, and polished shoes'; they had a 'Doctor' character wearing a white operating gown with a red cross on the front, and a 'Nursing sister' (the only woman performer) dressed in white, who went round with a mirror and handkerchief sprucing up the dancers. The head of the team was a 'King', elected by members, who functioned as organiser and treasurer and collected subscriptions when members were going to other Copperbelt towns to participate in dance competitions or were planning to hold a feast. The King dressed in a suit, tie and hat, and didn't perform but walked among dancers, greeting them. It was his second-in-command, the Dance Leader, who invented steps and composed the words of the songs, fresh ones being continually composed while dated ones were discarded.

Eighteen of the nineteen members of this team came from the same subgroup of the Bisa people, and one of their aims was to compose songs in praise of their own local chief. To this extent, they affirmed continued ties with their rural background. But their songs also extolled the team itself for its fine appearance and desirability, criticised mercenary good-time girls and denounced greedy parents demanding too many cattle in bride wealth for their daughters, all themes which expressed shared preoccupations of the mineworkers regardless of 'tribe'. Some songs lampooned other ethnic groups (for example, the Lamba for their alleged preoccupation with adultery cases), reflecting a consciousness of the multi-ethnic mine culture. And while some songs lamented the singers' inability to speak other languages of the mine location, others boasted about the team's proficiency, explicitly showcasing their ability to transcend or navigate between ethnic affiliations:

> I sing in Henga, I sing in Luba
> I sing in Zulu and Sotho
> I take Nyamwanga and Soli and put them together
> I stopped the Lwena language for it is very common,
> The Nyakyusa and Kasai and Mbwela languages
> Are the remaining languages. (Mitchell 1956:8)

Thus, though the team was to some extent actuated by 'home' politics and loyalties, it was also the product of a multi-ethnic environment. Though observers of the time referred to Kalela as a 'tribal' dance, it did not belong to any one ethnic group. It was danced all over the Copperbelt by people from different parts of the Northern Province. It was thus like a kind of template or envelope into which any group of people from a given home area could insert their own performance style and assert their own identity. Like the Beni dance, Kalela went one step further than the 'tribal' dances belonging to specific ethnic or local groups, in the direction of constructing forms that expressed the cultural parallelism or equivalence between groups.

Also like the Beni dancers, the Kalela dancers appeared to mimic colonial forms: police, army, officialdom. Ranger read the Beni dancers' attitude as one poised between satire and emulation. Ambiguity and free play between alternatives characterised the whole culture of the mining settlements. Just as the 'tribal' dimension of Kalela linked the team members back to their home communities, so the

'European' dimension linked into other forms available at the mining sites: in the Luanshya location, mineworkers could engage in ballroom dancing just as readily as in 'tribal' team dances. In the larger Southern Rhodesian mine compounds, alternatives to 'tribal dancing' were 'tea meetings', 'big dinners' and European-style dancing. James Ferguson subsequently interpreted these ambiguities and this scope for the play of alternatives as offering miners a choice of modes of self-making: between being 'local' (oriented towards the rural home and tradition) and being 'cosmopolitan' (oriented towards the urban and the European) (Ferguson 1999). It is interesting that in Kalela and related forms, the two alternatives appear to be folded together, and that the poise between mimicry and mockery represented a space of freedom and even power, because it was where opposing alternatives were held in suspension, and thus where potentiality was concentrated.

Finally, a crucial point about the dance societies: if the performative attitude was ambiguous, the organisational structure was efficacious. The model of elected leadership, responsible officials, account-keeping by the treasurer, bureaucratic membership procedures, formal communication with other dance teams and so on was, on one level, part of the show, consonant with the ambiguous representation of colonial authority (the doctor with the big red cross and the officious nurse with her mirror and handkerchief surely provoked laughter as well as admiration). But on another level, these organisational structures were real, not only a 'preparation for power' with an eye on future decolonisation, but also – at particular flashpoints of political confrontation – the actual means of mobilisation, as we will discuss further in Chapter 5. Expressive forms (the performance of dance, music and songs) and organisational forms (the hierarchical structure of the dance societies' membership, their procedures and processes) were not two separate faces of popular experience, but a single phenomenon which must be taken as a whole. This is what Ranger demonstrated, and what Mitchell's pioneering study of the Kalela dance also richly illustrates.

Joining the Sundered Fabric: *Lifela* of the Sotho Migrants

The oscillating existence that mineworkers were generally forced to sustain in settler colonies between mining camps and their usually impoverished and overcrowded home areas led some early anthropologists to conceptualise them as 'men of two worlds', switching between a rural, traditional identity and an urban, industrial, modern one. The question that was asked was how they managed the cultural and cognitive divide. How, and to what extent, were they 'proletarianised'? What was the nature of the gulf between 'townsmen' and 'tribesmen'? How did migrants adapt rural institutions and networks in order to survive in town? Later ethnography rejected the bifurcated model and proposed that migrants' experience was one whole. The question was how they managed the multiple cultural and organisational repertoires available to 'make sense' of their experience, hold the different panels of their existence together and build a meaningful life. One of the ways they did this was through the creation and performance of new expressive genres.

A moving and fascinating example of such genres is the Sotho migrant workers' poetic genre *lifela*, a 'complexly evocative word-music' (Coplan 1994:8). A *sefela* (the singular form of the word) is a long, continually evolving poetic composition recounting the personal experiences of its composer, expanding as he adds more material over time. It is recited in a rapid rhythmic chant, is open-ended in form, loosely structured and partly precomposed, partly improvised in performance. Its full name can be translated as 'songs of the inveterate travellers' or 'songs of the adventurers', and it is associated specifically with the journeys made from Lesotho to the mines of South Africa by migrant labourers. In these continually emerging texts, Sotho men commented on 'the woes of their journey, what they have left behind at home, and the problems with which they are going to contend in a new world' (Maake 2012:69).

Sotho labour migration has a long history. The kingdom of Lesotho had its origins in the early nineteenth-century movement of peoples unleashed by the rise of the Zulu military leader Shaka. A minor Sotho chief, Moshoeshoe, led his followers to a place of safety in the Drakensberg-Maloti mountain range and established a fortress kingdom with its headquarters on the virtually impenetrable plateau of Thaba Bosiu, and reigned over this kingdom from its establishment in 1823 till his death in 1870. A series of wars with the Boers of the neighbouring Orange Free State in the 1850s and 1860s, which resulted in the loss of much of the kingdom's fertile lowland territory, made military strength the dominant concern of the Sotho. Guns and cash were needed. Wage labour had begun to emerge as early as the 1820s, but

when the Kimberley diamond mines opened in 1867, the powerful ruling lineage, the Bakoena, was able to organise mass labour migration,
sending young men in large groups to work in the mines during the
agricultural off-season. The mines' acute labour shortage and, at this
point, the existence of alternative sources of income for the kingdom
(till the end of the nineteenth century, it was the grain basket of the
region) meant that the Sotho could command high wages and insist
on being paid in guns as well as cash (Kimble 1982). Labour migration was therefore state policy, organised by the chiefs for the benefit
of the kingdom's defences rather than individuals' material well-being.

Throughout the twentieth century, labour migration grew in
importance and became essential to the survival of the kingdom's
population. By the time of Lesotho's independence in 1966, the fertile
land had become so depleted as a result of drought, disease, overcultivation and overgrazing, that 30 per cent of the adult male population
had to work as migrants at any one time.

David Coplan, the principal ethnographer of *lifela*, argues that it
was the involvement of the chiefs in the exploitation of the young
men's labour that led to the creation of a new poetic genre. Other
groups that also were massively involved in migrant labour in the
region adapted older, existing genres of praise poetry to speak of the
new experiences of the mines. Xhosa, for instance, composed *izib-
ongo* about the mines. This was possible, Coplan suggests, because
the Xhosa chieftaincy was already discredited and defeated, and the
genre was no longer synonymous with its power. Men were compelled
into migrant labour as individuals in response to taxation and labour
recruitment drives by the Chamber of Mines, rather than sent out
by their chiefs. The Sotho, by contrast, were compelled by their own
powerful chiefs to go to the mines; *lithoko*, the praise genre of chiefs
and royals, could not be taken over by the migrants to speak from the
other side of the experiential coin. There is some evidence that it was
in the early years at Kimberley that the new genre was created. After
the gold industry got under way from 1886 onwards, Sotho migrants
shifted to the Rand, but up till today, *lifela* can refer to all mines as
K'hemele or Gemele (Kimberley), or as Libere (De Beers), as if that
were the foundational experience in the creation of the genre (Coplan
1994:68–9; Wells 1994:285). Maake has added the suggestion that
only the Sotho created a new genre to speak of the migrant miners'
experience, because only they journeyed from an enclave state through
hostile countryside, where the Boer farmers of the Orange Free State

needed their labour and resented their trek to the mines, intercepting and harassing them along the way (Maake 2012). Until the railway reached Basutoland in 1906, migrants travelled to Kimberley and later to the Rand on foot or in produce wagons. Both of these means of travel were dangerous; the migrants travelled in large groups for protection, and the performances apparently arose along the way, or retrospectively to commemorate the courageous undertaking.

A detailed and truly historical account of the emergence of the genre is frustrated by the fact that actual texts only began to be recorded in the 1970s, a problem we have already encountered for other genres in Chapter 2. Nineteenth-century observers commented on Sotho traditions of courtly rhetoric, storytelling and chiefly praise poetry, and written texts of the latter were produced as early as the 1920s. The term *lifela* was apparently first used in the Beersheba mission station in the 1840s to refer to Christian hymns, only afterwards extended by the migrant labourers to what may have seemed a parallel innovation, their own improvised compositions (Wells 1994:266). However, the archives apparently do not provide any record of the migrants' genre. The popular, informal, lower-class genre was either not known to the missionaries and officials who were in contact with the Sotho, or not considered worthy of documentation. Thus, though we may accept that the genre has existed since the nineteenth century, we have no concrete evidence about its content or form until around 100 years after its inception. And as a fluid, semi-improvisatory genre, it is constitutionally subject to change.

It was a new genre, but it did not spring from nowhere. Coplan carefully traces its relationship to the older praise genre *lithoko*, and more particularly initiation poetry, in which individual young men in the initiation school improvised self-praise. Initiates' *lithoko*, like migrant miners' *lifela*, were couched in the first-person singular and focussed on self-description. But whereas *lithoko* were formulaic, often drew on an older if not archaic vocabulary and were restricted to a certain range of themes, *lifela* were wide-ranging and freewheeling, allowing their creators to comment on all aspects of their novel experiences.

After the railway was built, the nature of the journey changed, but it remained fraught with risk and strange experiences. The theme was still prominent in texts recorded in the 1970s and '80s. Here is a *sefela* performed by Molefi Letlatsa and recorded by 'Makali Mokitimi in 1982:

FIGURE 4 *Sefela* performer, Lesotho. Courtesy David B. Coplan.

I want to praise the train.
Train, you are praised yet you do not know it ...
Smoke it takes out through nostrils, the fawny
The cunning with red eyes
You walk quickly, where are you going train?
"I go to Mohlehli's in the Lowlands" ...
A tall smoke, smoke of train
It can go up looking at the mountains
Train bores holes on the mountains
You know it bored Mount Majoba a hole ...
The day I knew the train
I arrived at Maseru station
I found a child of a European, a guard.
He was hairy on the chest

FIGURE 5 Mphafu Mofolo performing *sefela*. Courtesy David B. Coplan.

Some was grown so long on the arms.
I asked this very European
Where the train of ours, deserters, is.
I saw him looking at himself, keeping quiet,
He then looked at his arm.
When he did like that he was looking at his watch.
He said "Baag bitjie Nguni Mosotho"
The man was talking what made no sense.
"It is here at the corner coming."
He was wearing a green shirt.
Immediately it arrived,
It arrived, stopped at once.
A newcomer, I was amazed,
I was standing high on the platform,

I was looking this way and that way.
On the ears it had blinkers.
Water pipe on its head,
Water tank on its shoulders,
On its back it was carrying coal.
It left, it coughed,
As if it was going to throw us away.
It sneezed as if it was sick,
As if it had a cold, the train
The train left habitual walkers on the valley
It will have to come back
To come for us.
Ramakabaula a man of the people
I have long been travelling places,
These places I know them all.
Debts I have caused while travelling,
I even pay for sleep. (Mokitimi 1982:376–8)

In this extraordinarily vivid and poignant text, the poet transmits the shock of seeing the steam train for the first time. Everything about it is strange, including the hairy white guard with his incomprehensible dialect, the engine's appearance, the noises it makes, the route it takes, boring holes through mountains. By describing the train as an animate being – with a head, ears, shoulders and a propensity to catch cold – the poet paradoxically heightens the machine's inhuman speed and power. Yet this train belongs to the migrants: it is 'the train of ours, deserters' (deserters because they are abandoning their homesteads) and 'will have to come back' to collect the people it left behind. We seem to see it in the very moment when an alarming new experience is accommodated into the known world of everyday life.

While the migrants depict themselves as heroic adventurers facing dangerous odds, they also frequently sound a note of pathos. Hardship drove them to the mines. Molahlehi Makakane explains that it was his sister's dire need that made him give up school and become a migrant worker – which only led to more poverty:

Look and see how destitute I have become,
These days I have been impoverished by lack of schooling,
I find myself on my knees under rocks.
I attended school at Thabana-Morena
At Mount Tabor Secondary School.
When I came to my home

> I found my sister in tears
> Saying: "Mother, buy me a blanket I am in rags,
> I haven't even got a small piece on my shoulders."
> ....
> I felt humiliated and made a resolution
> Gentlemen, I went to see Tsolo, son of Lenonyane.
> "Please Tsolo fill contract forms for me to cross the border,
> I join the white man's work place." (Mokitimi 1998:180–1)

Another *sefela* describes the experience of arriving at the mine compound and being forced to strip for a medical examination. Moroba Moroba resisted ('I said: "I never go to the doctor when I am not sick, poor vagabond"'), but he was forced to go. They had to stand in a line: 'We were men, we were one hundred and fifty'. The incomprehensible command was barked out: 'Undress.' 'Now, "Undress" I did not know it. / Old chap, I am caught by trembling, I am shivering' (Mokitimi 1998:179). Other *lifela* describe the mine shaft itself, and the frequent deaths underground:

> When it first thundered, the thunder
> It thundered terribly while we were in the mine shaft.
> Oh, how those rascals ate up Raboletsi's son,
> They ate up Sello, the gentleman.
> I even became hesitant to write to his parents. (Mokitimi 1998:158)

In the mining compounds, groups of Sotho miners would stage competitions, all contributing a sum of money to a pool, which would be collected by the performer judged by common consent to be the best. The act of performance itself, as well as the content of the *lifela*, was an assertion and demonstration of manhood. *Lifela* contain heart-rending, vivid and hilarious passages describing privations and humiliations of induction into the workforce and the terror of the labour underground. But as Coplan eloquently argues, *lifela* did not just reflect new experiences, they stretched a textual bridge between home and mine. Anxiety about the families they had left behind, memories of their former existence as herd boys whose adventures were on the bare or snowy mountains of Lesotho, stories about their courtship and marriage, all served to keep home alive in the mining compound and their endurance in the mines alive in the minds of their auditors at home.

And – again, unlike the older tradition of *lithoko* praise poetry – the male adventurers' genre had a counterpart in *seoeleoelele*, the chanted poetry of women adventurers. Single women, women deserted by their migrant husbands, women who made a living in shebeens, sang songs of affliction and defiance accompanied by provocative *famo* dancing. Their poems boast of a personal autonomy equivalent to that of the male migrants:

> Chabane, I am going away.
> I am a person living in difficulties:
> I live by cheating [migrant] workers.
> I'm not working; I'm a wandering divorcer [philanderer],
> I, a little girl of Lesotho.
> Give me a ticket, gentlemen, a ticket and my stick.
> When I leave, I wander about;
> I am going home, home to Lesotho. (Coplan 1994:182)

And the shebeens bring us to the township.

The Township

In all African countries with a large settler population, cities were racially divided. The white residential and business areas were separated from the African quarters. In many towns, this resulted in the emergence of townships, overcrowded informal settlements with shanty housing and inadequate water and sanitation. As we have seen, townships grew up around all the mining centres, but they also existed in other big industrial and administrative centres, wherever migrant populations came to look for work. The state intervened to varying degrees.

In Johannesburg, there was already a permanent black urban population by the beginning of the twentieth century, along with semi-permanent migrants who came and went. Their numbers grew as the industrial, manufacturing and service sectors grew alongside the mining industry, sucking in more labour, and as pressure on black rural dwellers sharply increased after the 1913 Land Act, which forced numerous whole families off their land. In the early years, most of these urban settlers found accommodation in the inner-city townships. The 1923 Urban Areas Act required the Johannesburg Municipality to move them out of town, but this could not be implemented as long as no alternative accommodation was available. As more people flooded in, the pressure on the inner-city spaces became intense. Landlords made fortunes by buying up building plots, erecting rows of flimsy one-room shacks and renting them out at extortionate rates. These were the 'slumyards': unsanitary and overcrowded, but in the 1930s the sites where a new urban culture was forged from the heterogeneous population that inhabited them. Central to this culture was illicit liquor, which women brewed and sold, often as the centrepiece of a weekend all-night *marabi* party involving music, singing and dancing. Because the liquor had to be brewed at top speed to reduce the risk of detection, it was made as strong as possible and often fortified with a bizarre mixture of chemicals. Shebeen queens could make good profits from a batch of *skokiaan*, but they could also lose everything when a police raid caught them, fined or imprisoned them, and threw the brew away.

We can get vivid glimpses of life in the slumyards from two novels written by people who lived in them in the 1930s: Peter Abrahams's *Mine Boy* (1946) and Modikwe Dikobe's *The Marabi Dance* (published in 1973, but written in the 1950s and '60s). Both are set in the real slumyards where their authors had lived as young men – Abrahams in Malay Camp near Vrededorp, Dikobe in Molefe Yard in Doornfontein. Both novels are, above all, an evocation of the collective life of the township.

Peter Abrahams's protagonist is Xuma, a migrant from the north who has just arrived in Johannesburg knowing no one. Late in the evening, he turns up in the small Malay Camp slumyard and is taken in by Leah, the tough but kindly shebeen queen of the neighbourhood. Here he meets the diverse inhabitants, African and Coloured, in varying states of hope and decrepitude. The following Monday, one of the yard's inhabitants, Johannes, who alternates between drunken bravado and sober good sense, takes him to the mine and fixes him up with a job. Because of his immense strength and courage, Xuma is immediately taken on by one of the white miners as a 'boss boy' in charge of 500 underground workers. His first impression of work in the mine is that it is arid and unproductive: the back-breaking work pushing sand trucks does not seem to make the mine dump any bigger or the heap to be moved any smaller, and they have to keep repeating it every day (42). Nonetheless, it is 'a man's work' (5); labour is manly, and working alongside white men (106) creates a kind of equality and freedom not experienced outside the mine.

> The only place where he was completely free was underground in the mines. There he was a master and knew his way. There he did not even

fear the white man, for his white man depended on him. He was the
boss boy. He gave the orders to the other mine boys. They would do for
him what they would not do for his white man or any other white man.
He knew that, he had found it out. And underground his white man
respected him and asked him for his opinion before they did anything.
It was so and he was at home and at ease underground. (63)

Comradeship in labour does not mean friendship ('They work
together. That's all' [63]), until the climax at the end of the novel,
when Xuma leads a protest and his white boss, a radical, comes over
to the side of the miners.

His position as boss boy allows him to stay in the township rather
than move into the mine compound. He sees the compound miners
marching into the mine in the early morning and returning, guarded
by *indunas* and mine police, after their shift. While their conditions are
harsh but orderly, life in the slumyard is chaotic but vibrant. The heterogeneous inhabitants, who at first puzzle Xuma ('A strange group
of people, these ... Nothing tied them down. They seem to believe in
nothing. But well, they had given him a bed ...' [6]), begin to reveal
their pasts, and their capacity for loyalty and kindness as well as despair and violence. And it is the slumyard and the wider urban environment that is the imaginative centre of the novel. Freedom, alienation
and belonging are evoked in the traversal of urban space (Jones
2012): strolling during leisure time, running from the police, walking
to vantage points outside the city and viewing it, 'a mass of shadowy
buildings and twinkling lights', and behind it the mine dumps, 'huge
towering shadowy shapes that reared their heads to the sky' (25).

Vivid moments of creativity occur in the street. When Leah gets a
pair of new shoes, she and 'Daddy', an elderly denizen of the slumyard, enact the promenade of a fine gentleman and lady, to the delight
of all in the street. On another occasion, two 'swankies', dressed iden-
tically ('in violent purple suits with wide-bottomed trousers and long
jackets that reached down to their knees, straw hats, red shirts and
black ties ... a red handkerchief in the left hand and a light cane in the
right'), come out to show off their finery: 'they strutted and danced
from the one side of the road to the other', followed by a cheering and
laughing crowd. The intermittent solidarity and brilliance of township life is condensed in a description of a night-time dance. Men
and women form a circle on the corner of the street, clap and stamp
a rhythm and hum or sing a melody. Couples take turns going to the
centre of the ring and miming courtship:

A couple stepped into the ring. With commanding movements the man called the woman to him and told her to go on her knees in front of him. Disdainfully the woman danced away. Again the man commanded. The woman ignored him. He made to grab her. She danced away and evaded him.

The women in the ring applauded her, the men encouraged the man.

The man pulled himself up to his full height, and, trembling with anger, commanded the woman to go on her knees to him. Her eyes showed fear before his wrath, she cowered away and edged backward. The man stepped forward. The woman stepped back. Again he commanded and the trembling of his body was violent. But cowering fearfully, the woman refused to go on her knees to him ....

Suddenly the man in the ring turns and dances up to the woman. He now pleads. He does not command any more. And pleading, he goes down on his knees. The woman dances a victory dance, full of triumph.

The women in the ring joined with her in her victory. The men share his humiliation with him.

Her victory dance stops suddenly. And lovingly she dances up to him, also pleading. She too goes down on her knees. They embrace each other....

The couple stepped back. Another couple stepped into the centre of the ring. And so it went on. (55–6)

Such moments of improvised performance, viewed with wonder by the newcomer Xuma and described in loving detail by Abrahams, encapsulate the vitality of the slumyard culture, its capacity to innovate and forge a common expressive idiom for people of highly diverse backgrounds. It works as a touchstone both for Xuma's own courtship and for his gradual discarding of prejudices against Coloureds, Africans of other ethnic groups and even white people. Paddy, his white boss, at the same time becomes increasingly conscious of Xuma's independence and integrity, and at the end of the novel they unite in a vision of a world where being human would transcend racial identity. The township dance is surely a central emblem of the process of forging commonality and fellow-feeling, even while partisanship remains (the men support the male character in the performance, the women the female one).

For Abrahams, whose father was an immigrant from Ethiopia and whose mother was a Coloured, who left Vrededorp, the place of his birth, at the age of twenty to live in Britain and Jamaica for most of his adult life and became a left-wing pan-Africanist journalist, these themes of overcoming difference were central. His novel reached a Western and international audience first, and it was only gradually that some of his writings filtered back to a township audience via serialisation in *Drum* magazine (Peterson 2018). By contrast, Modikwe Dikobe, who arrived in Johannesburg at the age of ten from the northern Transvaal, lived in different parts of the city most of his life until he retired to Bophuthatswana in 1977, and while in Johannesburg worked in jobs not far removed from those of his slumyard characters: as a newspaper vendor, clerk, bookkeeper and night watchman. He was also a union organiser, which led to a banning order and the loss of his job during the State of Emergency in the early 1960s.

His characters in *The Marabi Dance* take the squalor, vitality, heterogeneity and intermittent solidarity of the township for granted. The very first paragraph puts the slumyard before us with stark matter-of-factness:

> The Molefe Yard, where Martha lived, was also home to more than twenty other people. It served a row of five rooms, each about fourteen by twelve feet in size. When it rained, the yard was as muddy as a cattle kraal, and the smell of beer, thrown out by the police on their raids, combining with the stench of the lavatories, was nauseating. (1)

The central character, Martha, has grown up there. Her parents have taken her out of school after Standard V because she has begun to hang around with boys, and they feel that continuing their painful investment in her education would be a waste. She is attached to George, a glamorous but irresponsible *marabi* musician (allegedly based on a real *marabi* star, Solomon 'Zuluboy' Cele), who plays the piano at the shebeen queens' all-night weekend parties and draws Martha in to sing for them. Eventually she becomes pregnant, upon which George decamps. Martha becomes a single mother and grows out of her youthful enchantment with the *marabi* culture.

As the title of the novel suggests, the theme is not the experiences of a protagonist for their own sake so much as a patchwork evocation of the culture of the slumyard and township, and the interrelated fortunes of the network of people caught in its ambience. The slumyard residents are, like those in Abrahams's novel, rootless. Martha's father, Mabongo, wants to marry her to a rural paternal cousin, to make amends for his own broken promise to marry into this family twenty years before, but he and his wife do not know the traditional procedures; Martha herself has not been taught the customary ways of behaving; unlike the more home-rooted cousins, the Mabongo family do not know traditional medicines. Nor do they have a stable existence in the city: Mabongo loses his job on the whim of his employer after twenty years of faultless service and is thrown into a desperate, hurried search for another job – without which he will lose his pass and his right to stay in the city where he has lived most of his adult life. Later, he enlists in the army and goes overseas; Martha's mother dies impoverished, leaving nothing, as she ironically states, except a bequest to the whites who have exploited her: her own daughter, for domestic service.

The heterogeneity of the township is unobtrusively stitched into the tapestry by Dikobe's repeated recourse to fragments of Sotho, Zulu and Afrikaans, often translated but not always, and never marked as foreign: they just make up the linguistic mix in which the township people exist. Speaking of a mixed-race gang leader 'who could not finish a sentence in a single language', Dikobe goes on to observe: 'The residents of Vrededorp were mixed as the league of nations: Malay, Coloured, Indians, Africans, Afrikaners and English, separated by no-mans open ground. There were even a few Damaras. The children all played together and understood each other' (75).

Martha's maturation at first involves a decision not to accept the marriage to her more rural kinsman when her heart is in the *marabi* culture of the town. But *marabi* is treated ambivalently in the novel. It is lower class. Respectable people 'knew Marabi as a dance party for persons of a "low type" and for "malala-pipe", pipe-sleepers, homeless ruffian children' (2). Martha's involvement in *marabi* culture, marked by the rivalry of violent youth gangs, not only cuts short her schooling but also scuppers her singing teacher's attempts to launch her into a respectable career as a performer at elite events, and leads to her flight with George, her seduction and pregnancy. Later, after she and her child have been relocated to a two-bedroom house in the new estate at Orlando, paid for by the well-meaning wife of Mabongo's now-repentant boss, she repudiates the low-life *marabi* world entirely. Now she wants something more respectable. George returns, and he too gives up his former way of life and marries her. The solitary *marabi* musician who tries to attend their wedding is excluded.

Dikobe described himself as a 'petty bourgeois running with the working class' (Sole and Koch 1990:217), whereas Martha's trajectory appears to be in the opposite direction. But Dikobe's 'petty bourgeois' status was itself the product of assiduous self-betterment: he attended night school, registered for correspondence courses and typing lessons, read voraciously to improve his English. While in Peter Abrahams's *Mine Boy* the desire for 'the things of white people' is regarded as a disease, in *The Marabi Dance* it's regarded as a step towards self-realisation as a respected member of society. The tension in *Mine Boy* is between white and black (as well as between rural and urban); the tension in *The Marabi Dance* is between a sympathetic evocation of the down-at-the-heels glamour of the world of *marabi* and the aspiration to get out. But there are points of contact between the two novels: not only the evocation of the life of the township, but also an optimistic vision of human potential. Xuma and Paddy overcome barriers to unite in support of the workers' struggle. Martha is depicted as a talented, independent-minded young woman who makes a life for herself as a single mother and is not condemned for this in the novel; and though muted, political radicalisation ends this narrative too. George's return to Johannesburg after seven years' absence is precipitated by a labour struggle in Durban, where he has been working for a bus company. The workers form a trade union; the employer is alarmed and tries to force some of the workers inform on their leaders. George says he 'would rather walk the streets without work than sell his own people' (114), so he leaves his job and returns to Martha.

From the mid-1930s onwards, the government began to dismantle the relatively central slumyards and relocate their populations to purpose-built peri-urban 'locations', such as Orlando, where Martha moves. Ellen Hellmann studied the Rooiyard slumyard in 1934, just before it was demolished, and evokes the inhabitants' anxiety and fear, their reluctance to go so far out of town that the cost of transport to work would be high and shebeens would not thrive for lack of customers (Hellmann 1948). 'Marabi dwindled and vanished at the end of the 1930s, as the conditions which supported its existence disappeared' (Sole and Koch 1990:211). *Marabi* music was replaced by large jazz bands for organised dances in township community halls.

Several things emerge from these two novels: the distinctive life of the township slumyards, linked to the mines, on the one hand, and to rural home places, on the other, but distinct from both; the emergence of a vibrant but unstable township culture revolving around music, dance and illicit liquor; the insistent running thread of resistance to and resentment of white exploitation, repression and arrogance (a repeated source of resentment in *The Marabi Dance* is white people calling adult African men 'boys'); and the everyday creativity which

FIGURE 6 South African township jitterbuggers, 1950s. Courtesy David
B. Coplan, *In Township Tonight!* (1985).

could burst out in all-night dancing, in spontaneous street theatre and
in the haunting songs of the *marabi* musicians. Neither *Mine Boy* nor
The Marabi Dance articulates a hard-line opposition to the oppressive
racial capitalism and incipient apartheid of mid-twentieth-century
South Africa. Both, rather, suggest a yearning to transcend or escape
from it. In both, the ultimate goal of political struggle is respect and
harmony between races and classes. At the conclusion of *The Marabi
Dance*, Martha reflects, 'We are made out of the same river mud as the
white people. The world was made for all to live in and like each other'
(115). But both also show the resources the anti-apartheid struggle
would draw on to achieve its eventual victory: the energy, resilience,

defiance and refusal to be crushed that comes out so vividly from their depictions of township life.

A version of township culture survived and came to fuller efflorescence in the few black residential areas which were freehold and thereby enjoyed a stay of execution until the late 1950s and early 1960s; these included Alexandra, Newclare and, most famously, Sophiatown. Sophiatown survived as a mixed suburb of Johannesburg through the 1940s and '50s, until the implementation of the Group Areas Act led to its final destruction in 1960. It was a raucous, vital, heterogeneous community in which ethnic groups and races lived side-by-side, street gangs forged a new hybrid slang and an exceptional concentration of musicians and writers articulated the frustrations and injustices of incipient apartheid. Affirming an urban, non-ethnic identity amounted to a declaration of independence.

> Through the invention of the "homelands", millions of Africans were reconceived as foreigners and told they came from places that, prior to their forced removal there, they had never been ... Faced with the life-threatening consequences of such ethno-cultural strait-jacketing, many black South Africans affirmed their right to more complex, mobile, and expansive identities. They drew on precedents and resources of neighbouring and distant cultures with an eclecticism that defied all ethnic cultural moulds.
>
> (Nixon 1994:4)

Drum magazine used to feature articles on 'tribal customs', but an incoming editor in the early 1950s changed all that, responding to the desire of the township for a more cosmopolitan outlook. As one contributor to the magazine wrote, 'Ag, why do you dish out that stuff, man? ... Tribal music! Tribal history! Chiefs! We don't care about chiefs! Give us jazz and film stars, man! We want Duke Ellington, Satchmo, and hot dames! Yes brother, anything American.' This statement has been quoted by numerous scholars to illustrate the township's outward-looking cultural perspective. *Drum* became a forum for a whole generation of young writers and musicians who flourished in the cultural mix of Sophiatown. The appeal of American culture was multiple: it was *not* the place of origin of British and Boer colonisers; its jazz, blues, soul and other musical styles were super-modern and fashionable, but also recognisable and congenial because of their African roots; and the large racially oppressed black industrial working class in South Africa had affinities with its counterparts in America.

The culture of the Harlem renaissance articulated a defiance of racial oppression with which urban South Africans could identify (Nixon 1994; Bank 2011:57). Several of the stars who began their careers in South Africa – among them Miriam Makeba and Hugh Masekela – migrated under high apartheid to the United States, where they continued to voice South African experience.

This core topic – the cultural forms generated in the context of mines, migrant labour and townships – radiates out chronologically, thematically and geographically. I have only touched on a few selected aspects of it.

Chronologically, the study of changes in the culture of mine towns and settlements extends to the present day. Mining is still an engine of social transformation, and new themes have emerged: the international trade in illicit or unethical diamond mining in Botswana, Angola and elsewhere; the increase in artisanal open-cast or shallow-pit mining by private local entrepreneurs; the new collective complicities and antagonisms at work in the 2012 massacre at the Marikana platinum mine in South Africa; and the films, poetry and media interventions that followed. Further research could reveal the cultural genres to which all of these transformations, for better or worse, have given rise.

Thematically, the subject of South African township culture extends far beyond the urban settlements that grew up around mines. Whereas mining was the generative experience in the townships and compounds of the Rand, in Durban, the single-sex male hostels for factory workers were where the beautiful choreographed a cappella male choir song genre *isicathamiya* was created. This genre has been studied in insightful detail by Veit Erlmann in his masterpiece, *Nightsong*.

Geographically, there are rewarding comparisons to be made between South African township culture and the cultural activities of workers in the compounds, squatter camps and *cité indigène* of Katanga. Some of the most influential work in the whole field of African popular culture was set in the mining towns of Zaire/DRC. Johannes Fabian, Ilona Szombati-Fabian and Bogumil Jewsiewicki have documented and profoundly interpreted the new forms of popular expression, notably the paintings produced by entrepreneurial urban artists in these towns. Though it had antecedents in the rapidly urbanising mining settlements of the 1920s and further impetus in the 1950s, this style came to its fullest efflorescence in the 1960s after independence, at a time of relative economic prosperity and urban stability. The paintings – which fell into well-established genres and were produced and sold in large numbers, as many as 500 a day – were mainly purchased by wage-earners seeking to decorate their living rooms in an urban, respectable style. They thus represented the aspiration to upward mobility in mining town life, but in the view of these scholars, they also revealed the formation of a historical consciousness not shared with the elites and foreign visitors who bought the pictures less frequently and did not favour the subgenres that dealt with the recent political past. Comparisons can also be made with the social and cultural activities of the mining towns in Nigeria, Sierra Leone, the Gold Coast, Southern Rhodesia and Angola, and especially in the Northern Rhodesian Copperbelt, where Hortense Powdermaker documented mineworkers' leisure activities in the 1950s with unusual inclusiveness and freedom from constraining stereotypes. 'Life on the ground' in the township – the everyday life that is so vividly evoked as the central subject of *Mine Boy* and *The Marabi Dance*, where parties, gossip, music, dancing, singing, street burlesque and film shows are all an inextricable part of the unremitting effort to carry on from day to day – has been the direct or indirect subject of a sustained tradition of ethnography from the 1940s to the present day, in South Africa and beyond.

CHAPTER 4

The City and the Road

Roads, Railways and Ports

West Africa, unlike East and southern Africa, did not attract many colonial settlers. The land was not taken over by white farmers. The colonial economy was mainly about the extraction of produce using the labour of African small farmers more or less in their existing configurations. Taxation was used not so much to force the population into migrant labour as to force households to grow cash crops and sell them at prices determined by cartels of big European commercial firms. There was migrant labour, and in many areas it was the norm for young men, especially, to go and work in mines, on privately owned farms and plantations or on public works in order to raise enough money to get independence from their fathers, marry and set up their own households. But the large-scale dispossession of African subsistence farmers from their land and the resulting permanent circulatory migration patterns characteristic of southern Africa did not happen in West Africa. The colonial economy was geared up to take over existing mercantile networks and make them work in Europe's favour. The great cities of West Africa were neither new mining settlements like Johannesburg nor towns of white settlers with segregated black locations for the African population who worked for them. Many West African cities were ancient trading entrepots. A few were created as colonial administrative centres but became centres of trade as well. Long-distance trade based on complex networks that crossed regions and ethnic groups long preexisted colonial conquest. Trading caravans had been crossing the Sahara since the early Middle Ages, and from the sixteenth century, the Atlantic coast was locked into European trade, which extracted upwards of twelve million human beings in the slave trade, as well as gold and ivory, in exchange for guns, cloth and other manufactured goods.

This deep and long-established mercantile culture produced cultural forms oriented to innovation and display. When the great Alaafin of Ọyọ, in the mid-eighteenth century, held a festival to which all the subordinate kings of the region were invited, he was rivalled in his magnificence by his friend the king of Popo, whose location on the coast enabled him to profit from the Atlantic trade. Every time the Alaafin changed into a yet more sumptuous robe, the king of Popo – who had probably supplied the cloth to him in the first place – was able to match him. Eventually, the Alaafin's weavers and tailors hit on a ruse: they covered a piece of ordinary cloth all over with floss of the silk-cotton tree. From a distance, this looked spectacular. 'When the sun shone upon it, it reflected a silken hue to the admiration of all; when the breeze blew, detached flosses of silk floated all around his majesty.' The assembled kings and princes were convinced that this was a rare and costly imported fabric, 'something so superior, that none but the great ALAFIN of ỌYỌ alone possessed! The crowd went into an ecstatic frenzy about it, and shouted an applause' (Johnson 1921:179). Novelty and acquisition of goods others did not possess was a key mark of status.

Until the late nineteenth century, European traders tended to stay on the Atlantic coast of West Africa and rely on middlemen to deliver goods from the interior. But when the scramble for Africa got under way, European governments perceived a need to 'penetrate', and merchant firms abetted and benefitted from their efforts.

The first incursions were by river, and the aim was to lay claim to any territory that could be reached by ship. In Senegal, for example, the French government drew up a plan in 1879 to build a great inland arc of transportation: from St Louis to Kayes by river, from Kayes to the middle Niger by rail, and onwards down the Niger. Thus they would be able to claim control of a vast territory across the West African Sahel. When the railway segment turned out to take a long time to build, they went ahead and launched a river vessel on the middle Niger anyway, carrying its component parts overland and assembling them at Bamako. It made its first voyage in August 1884, two months before the start of the Berlin Conference, at which West Africa was divided up between the European powers. On great waterways that opened into the sea, ocean-going steamers began to be taken upriver, and riverine stern-wheel vessels, not suitable for ocean conditions, were taken to the river mouths and stationed there permanently. The river Gambia, the lower Volta and the Oil Rivers and Niger Delta all began to be plied with the vessels of French and British merchant companies, which hastened to invest heavily in the necessary ships, fuel dumps, repair yards, warehouses and buying stations with wharves.

Once their claims to African territory had been formalised, European governments began building railways. This huge investment involved importing vast quantities of materials and machines and mobilising enormous amounts of labour, often by compelling local chiefs to conscript men in a system akin to forced labour. The rail lines progressed rapidly: between 1896 and 1909, twelve major railway construction projects began in Sierra Leone, Nigeria, the Gold Coast, Dahomey, French Guinea, Ivory Coast, Togo, Senegal and Cameroon. All ran from a coastal port straight into the interior, and railway stations were built in areas calculated to be rich in produce. Even before this, submarine telegraph cables had been laid to connect Europe to selected West African ports; these now became the favoured starting points for the rail lines, since they gave colonial administrators and engineers quick communication with their home governments. Commercial firms followed quickly, establishing buying stations at the points where they believed the best sources of produce to be.

Rail led inevitably to the development of 'feeder' roads, which were needed to facilitate the carriage of bulky produce to the railway stations. Initially these were built out from the rail stations at right angles and came to an end in the target produce-collecting areas. Road building, like rail construction, needed huge capital investment even when the roads were not tarred (as most of them were not): bush had to be cleared, bridges or ferries built. Lorries, up to the First World War, were inefficient, and private cars were few and far between. Nonetheless, it was demands from road users that changed the nature of the import-export economy. They wanted the dead-end 'feeder' roads to be joined up so that there was a road network. As this was done, it became possible for the small traders (many of them Lebanese and African) who had run the lorry business transporting produce to the rail stations, where the big European firms bought it, to gain independence from the big firms and increase their marginal gains by travelling across the country to find the best prices from producers and buyers. Rail remained important until the 1950s, but from the 1920s onwards, roads increased by leaps and bounds both in mileage and in economic centrality.

Some of the reasons for the tremendous drive by colonial governments to build railways and then roads will be apparent already. Rail and road 'opened up' the continent. The primary motive was economic: transport infrastructure made possible the efficient 'evacuation' of produce from, and the importation of European manufactured goods into, every part of the country, including the depths of the rural interior. A second motive was control. In the early days of colonial conquest, a handful of white colonial officers attempted to hold down vast territories, the southern parts in dense forest criss-crossed with footpaths, without maps or communications. Sir Rex Niven, one such colonial officer, describes in his memoir his main task while serving in the Kabba region in the early 1920s: erecting telegraph poles. He buzzed along forest paths on a motorbike marking out the spots, and on one occasion buzzed right into a crevasse. Telegraph preceded rail and road, loping through the bush with long loops of cable, making it possible for lonely outposts to communicate with their HQ in Lagos. And as colonial rule became established, control over local populations, and specifically over labour, was facilitated by the widening network of communications. A third motive was 'enlightenment', or 'civilisation'. Opening up the continent via road and rail meant exposing the benighted tribesman to modern influences (always, however, to be carefully selected and censored). And finally, as Brian Larkin has argued in a dazzling discussion of technological infrastructures in northern Nigeria, the colonial powers were wide awake to the capacity of great steam locomotives, giant iron bridges, the vision of straight, smooth, shining roads, to impress and overawe the natives.

A schematic map of the early colonial rail and road penetration into West Africa would look curiously similar to a schematic diagram of the deep-level gold mines in South Africa discussed in Chapter 3. The huge vertical mineshaft that went straight down thousands of feet into the ground was like the railway shooting straight up into the interior; the vast, electrically powered cages that rushed up and down were like the locomotives speeding up and down the railway. At right angles from the mineshaft were the tunnels, spaced at regular intervals, leading to different layers of the reef, and off from them slanted the stopes, giving access to the thin strata of gold-bearing ore, which the miners drilled and blasted; at right angles to the rail line were the feeder roads, leading off from strategically placed stations, to give access to the rural areas; and into the feeder roads ran footpaths from the villages where the cash crops were produced. The commercial firms in West Africa, in conjunction with the colonial government, were mining the agricultural produce of the land. The curious term 'evacuation', used of accessing, transporting and exporting crops, seems to apply with equal force to the extraction of minerals from the bowels of the earth.

As the roads snaked out across the land, a culture of the road developed. At first very limited, commercial vehicle ownership gradually increased, and so did the aspiration to own a private car – at first only realised by the town chiefs, whose community would join together to buy one for him to confirm his status, and by super-rich businessmen. Lesser folk rode bicycles, but that too was a great status symbol, indicating clerkly, white-collar occupation. So you have to think of these roads as buzzing with life. Traffic was not the smooth anonymous flow people may be used to in some other parts of the world. It was noisy, competitive, sociable (overcrowded mammy wagons), cantankerous (breakdowns, drivers cursing each other, speeding) and always unpredictable.

Cities

The building of transport networks was inseparable from the growth of cities. West African ports and major inland cities doubled or trebled in population between the 1920s and 1950s. They are, of course, still growing – it has been predicted that more than 50 per cent of Africa's population will be urbanised by 2030, with half a dozen cities of more than ten million people. But the 1920s to the 1950s was a period when there was a major take-off, and when the expansion of the cities was seen as remarkable, unprecedented and requiring a response. The new power of the city, as a concentration of both the good and the evil associated with modernity, found its most vivid expression in the innovative popular cultural forms that were created by urban dwellers.

Cities were where changes imposed or induced by colonial rule were most concentrated and experienced most immediately. The seemingly bizarre attempts of colonial municipal authorities to regulate housing, markets, waste disposal, work and leisure activities and the very use of urban space and time (they were always expelling 'vagrants', bulldozing 'slums', ringing bells or firing cannons to mark the hour) were inseparable from the opportunities that rapid social change threw up. In West Africa, the principal cities were commercial and administrative centres rather than industrial hubs, as in South Africa, discussed in Chapter 3. They offered huge, dynamic markets. Peter Gutkind evokes the scene: 'literally thousands of African traders ... crowd the sidewalks, the alleys, the public squares, the bus parks, the industrial areas – indeed, it seems that in West African towns every available space bristles with traders from the very young to the very old' (Gutkind 1974). In addition to trading of all scales and types, the city offered opportunities for cooking food for sale, artisanal trades such as tailoring, shoe mending, watch and radio repairing, vehicle maintenance, services such as shoeshining, laundry and porterage: all occupations of the informal sector, where access was unregulated and initial outlay was small. Intense overcrowding and competition for the small income such work offered created an entrepreneurial dynamism and a need to hustle, improvise and combine several lines of work to make ends meet.

The city was also where amenities such as schools and hospitals were concentrated, and where people with some schooling could seek white-collar jobs in government or commercial offices. Young people (especially young men) with a primary-school education did not want to hang around in rural villages working on their fathers' farms – they wanted to get a foot on the ladder of waged or salaried employment, which could, with luck, lead to a prestigious position in society and form the basis of a future involvement in the more lucrative end of the trading spectrum.

Literacy, as we saw in Chapter 2, became a major engine of personal and social transformation, and when places in mission or government schools failed to meet demand, many people made assiduous efforts to increase their educational qualifications through night school, self-teaching or private commercial colleges of dubious standing. Across Africa throughout the twentieth century, writing was increasingly put to work in ordinary contexts of everyday life. People seized on the possibility of making lists, creating registers, keeping accounts, writing letters, inscribing birthdates, noting remedies, spells and prayers, recording religious experiences and compiling personal memoirs and communal histories. Through selective and imaginative uses of writing, people developed new modes of self-management and of social and political projection (Peterson 2004; Barber 2006; Mbodj-Pouye 2013).

It was the aspirational intermediate classes, with some schooling but not enough to be considered part of the 'highly educated elites', who were the main creators of the new popular cultural forms associated with West African cities. The moral uplift that the missionary endeavour had associated with reading and writing was translated into a more secular idea that literature provides 'lessons' of all kinds – practical guidance, hints, tips and useful facts, as well as strong moral models of how to behave and how not to behave. These 'lessons' were vividly articulated in a whole range of popular genres.

After the Second World War, temporary economic buoyancy and high cocoa prices provided more cash for amenities and wages. The reforming British Labour government of 1945, building on a shift towards development that had already begun, expanded the civil service and public works in British African colonies and recruited more clerical workers and labourers to meet their requirements. The new urban population not only had money in their pockets, they had 'leisure time' and pursuits associated with leisure: cinema, sports, dance halls, shows and concerts. These were, to some degree, sponsored by colonial authorities anxious to regulate urban behaviour, but it was popular enthusiasm, local appropriations and entrepreneurial innovation that made them thrive. Cinema shows, first appearing in West Africa at the beginning of the twentieth century, had become regular features of social life in Dakar, Accra, Cape Coast, Lagos and other cities by the early 1920s. 'Bioscope' or 'cinematograph' shows often appeared in a mixed bill along with musical performances, comedy turns, magical displays and ballroom dancing. Though initially organised by and for elite social clubs, they attracted large popular audiences: in Cape Coast, the first screening at the new Cinema Hall in 1914 was 'packed to its utmost capacity' (*Gold Coast Leader*, 3.10.1914); in Lagos, an energetic expatriate on a hike into the city observed, 'Here is a cinema. From within comes the strident blare of a cornet ... Throngs of noisy Natives, talking in a polyglot of tongues, surge outward through the doors. On the wall is a placard showing Charlie Chaplin in a characteristic pose' (J. M. Stuart-Young, *Gold Coast Leader* 9.12.1922).

These new forms of entertainment were associated with the new rhythms of the city and the road. They occupied space in new ways.

They signified technological change, speed, progress, fashion and romance. It is noteworthy that the first movie and the first motor car arrived in West Africa in the same year, 1900. Films, like cars, transported people to unfamiliar places; cars, like films, signified modernity at its most opulent (Green-Simms 2010). Cinema became a reference and resource for a whole spectrum of local twentieth-century African popular genres. It had a double power: it was in itself an entrancing example of modern technology, and it could also portray many other technological inventions and social innovations – including skyscrapers, domestic gadgets, dance styles and fashions in clothing.

So what new local forms of popular culture were generated in these rapidly expanding cities, the ports and the commercial and administrative hubs? How did the emerging transport networks shape and facilitate their spread to every nook and cranny of the rural areas? How was the increasing buzz and pace of traffic – the commercial trucks, buses and bush taxis and the privately owned vehicles – imprinted on new cultural forms of colonial West Africa? We will look in detail at two examples: Ghanaian concert party and Nigerian popular literature.

Ghanaian Concert Party

Ghanaian concert party was a travelling popular musical theatre form which began in the British colony of the Gold Coast more than a century ago, and which has continually evolved and transformed itself up till today. A genre encapsulating popular concerns and aspirations, its evolution sheds light on the social history of the whole twentieth century in Ghana, particularly southern Ghana, where the concert party was based. We will focus on its formative years from 1930 to the early 1960s, when it assumed its most characteristic and enduring features as a popular genre plying the roads of the Gold Coast from one end to the other.

The small creolised society that grew up around the European coastal fortresses during the slave trade had a long history of Western-style schools and entertainments, including school plays and adult productions of Shakespeare. By the late nineteenth and early twentieth centuries, the 'concert', based on the format of a variety show or music hall, was well established in Cape Coast. It incorporated elements borrowed from American vaudeville, Charlie Chaplin films, Empire Day concerts, dance bands and church 'cantatas'. It was performed by elite amateurs in schools, social and literary associations and other voluntary organisations. The ticket prices were high – as much as a week's wages for a manual worker – and the prevailing language of the performance was English. The shows were made up of songs, sketches, tap-dancing, brass band music, poetic recitations, instrumental solos and so on, a format that was popular all along the Anglophone coast. In Accra, it was taken up by commercial entertainment entrepreneurs and staged in purpose-built halls, with graduated ticket prices allowing the less affluent to gain admittance, seated separately from the elite. But it was in Sekondi, the deep-water port, railway headquarters and communications hub for mining and timber enterprises, that young innovators first seized on elements of the concert and converted them into a professional travelling show playing to ordinary people. Sekondi in the 1920s was full of sailors and migrant railway workers who were away from their families, had wages in their pockets and wanted entertainment after working hours. There was an elite Optimism Club, but also a popular Palladium open to all. Here Ishmael 'Bob' Johnson and his friends Charles B. Horton and J. B. Ansah, who were all pupils at the Methodist School opposite the Palladium, would inveigle their way into the shows and then copy them in performances of their own. At first they performed for friends and asked only for food in payment. But very soon, before 1930, they had consolidated into a recognised 'trio' that charged 6d or a shilling for attendance. Their innovations included mixing some Fante with the English that was the norm in concerts and establishing a three-part dramatic structure for their shows, consisting of an 'opening chorus', a short duet or comic monologue, and then the main dramatic sketch built around the three stock characters represented by all the trios of that period: the affluent and apparently Westernised 'gentleman', the refined English-speaking 'lady' (played by a female impersonator) and the 'Bob', an illiterate but clever and subversive servant who showed up his elite or would-be elite employers. The gentleman and the Bob appeared in blackface inspired by American minstrelsy (see Figures 7 and 8). But perhaps the most significant innovation was the decision to take their shows on tour. Availing themselves of the roads and railways built by the colonial government, they travelled during their school holidays to villages and towns within a radius of thirty or forty miles from Sekondi, taking their own products, the fruits of their invention, from place to place. Soon many other groups had sprung up, all 'trios' and all adopting the same basic format. In

FIGURE 7 The Dix Covian Jokers during World War Two. Courtesy Catherine M. Cole, *Ghana's Concert Party Theatre* (2001).

the 1930s, many of these groups became professional, making their living by performing, and gradually building up a repertoire of narratives, songs, jokes, comic turns, topical allusions and other materials from a wide array of sources, from which they 'picked' what they wanted to use and 'made it their own'. In Catherine Cole's brilliant history of Ghanaian concert party, she emphasises the social background of these pioneers: almost all of them were children of migrant parents engaged in the new colonial economy, used to moving around in order to gain an income, and used to work, housing, food and entertainment all having a monetary price.

In the 1950s, there was a further major development in the concert parties' practice. E. K. Nyame, the leader of a highlife band and

FIGURE 8 The Akan Trio during an opening chorus, late 1950s. Courtesy
Catherine M. Cole and J. E. Baidoe.

composer of many of its songs, decided to expand his appeal by adding a concert party drama to his show. His Akan Trio, formed in 1952,
offered a play prefaced by a long session of highlife dancing; the dialogue and songs in the play were in Fante throughout, not English
with an admixture of Fante or Twi, as in the earlier trios; and unlike
the often rather simple English music-hall lyrics of the other trios, the
highlife songs incorporated into the plays often had extended philosophical, proverbial and narrative lyrics reflecting on the experiences
of modern life. Other highlife bands followed suit. The sensational
success of the Akan Trio also spurred existing trios to adopt Akan
languages and incorporate highlife music. The new troupes expanded
dramatically from three people into much larger ensembles, able to

deliver much longer and more elaborate narratives with many more characters. Whether they were a highlife band that had incorporated a theatrical component, or a theatrical troupe that had incorporated a highlife band, all concert parties now had this expanded, blended, vernacular form – though all also retained the curtain-raiser in which the older style of variety theatre turns was preserved like an arch-aeological layer. With the increasing size and professionalization of the troupes, their tours became longer and more carefully planned. They went to every part of Ghana, including the remote north. As they engaged in these long forays across multi-ethnic territory, they adapted by incorporating additional languages or fragments of languages. If a troupe member could speak the language of a non-Akan town they were visiting, he would translate key lines; several languages could be pasted together.

To carry out these extended 'treks', some troupes chartered lorries for the trip, which had the advantage of letting them do their pre-show 'campaign' around town in the vehicle rather than on foot, increasing its impact. Some hired a truck, but only to reach the town where they were to perform; others simply told the performers to make their own way by *tro-tro*, bus or motorbike. John Collins's fascinating reminis-cences about trips he made with the Jaguar Jokers concert party in the late 1960s is full of vehicles breaking down, troupe members making their way to the agreed venue only to find that it had to be changed at the last minute and the physical rigours of the road. Travelling, just getting there, finding the place and setting up the stage, was a big part of the story. They did not usually give more than one show in any town, which meant that after performing until the early hours of the morning, they would snatch a few hours' sleep and then get up early to pack the equipment and travel on to the next destination.

Catherine Cole, Efua Sutherland, K. N. Bame and John Collins have all written illuminatingly about the history of the earlier 1930s to '50s period of 'trios', but recordings and transcriptions of com-plete performances only exist for the full-blown 'troupes' period of the early 1950s onwards. These texts, and eyewitness accounts of perform-ances, show a 'highly disjunctive, topsy-turvy style' (Cole 2001:134), combining buffoonery and pathos, moralising and cynical irreverence, local knowledge and allusions to global events. Plots exhibited fre-quent flips and switches, sudden and only perfunctorily explained reversals of fortune, jumps and elisions in time and space, and muta-tions in the function of the characters, so that a foolish old man could become a moral arbiter and a wicked stepmother could have her own moment of pathos at the microphone. Cole has argued persuasively that concert party took shape in the 1930s and blossomed in the 1950s precisely because this disjunctive, loose-jointed, improvisatory style fulfilled a need to integrate disparate and conflicting elements of social experience that colonialism had produced: not by welding them into a seamless whole, but by holding them together in suspension. As Cole suggests, the art of improvisation, and of making borrowed materials their own, required a quick wit and resourcefulness, which were also the prerequisites for success in the unstable world of the colonial city.

Some of these concert party plays also bear, imprinted in their very idiom, a sense of experience itself as a kind of travel, a sense that personal and social fulfilment are in some way suspended between the alternatives of the city and the farming village. Characters constantly oscillate between the two, the plot depends on the contrast and the evaluative needle fluctuates: the city may be a site of opportunity or a place of waste, deception and loss; the village may be a locus of honest hard work or of poverty, a place of security or of oppression by cruel kin. They may even be both in rapid succession within the same play.

A play recorded and translated by K. N. Bame as 'The Ungrateful Husband' is poised on criss-crossing trajectories of movement through space which are like a cat's cradle of threads running through the characters' commentary on their experience. The blameless, generous heroine, Awura Akua, speaks the first words of the play, introducing herself in typical presentational concert party style: 'My story is that I am a lady who had travelled far and wide in this world without any gains. I have therefore come back home.' She then sings a plaintive highlife, presenting herself as 'a poor wanderer'. Home is where she hopes to find a husband and settle down, but she picks the first young man who comes by, a stranger called 'Father Yaw Ntow', who is a penniless, stammering oddity. He instantly agrees to marry her, and she says she needs to introduce him to her father 'in case you travel with me and any mishap such as death occurs, you will be in a position to send my body back home without any blame' (Bame 1985:132). It turns out that she's not actually at home when she meets Yaw Ntow: she's on a 'visit' and now wants to take him 'to go to my home and see my people'. But her father walks in – he has been summoned from his village to a meeting of the farmers, of whom he is the leader, in Accra, and has stopped by to see his children on the way. Yet when he leaves for Accra, the father tells her to look after the house while he's away, as if that was

where he, his son and daughter all lived. The unmarked shifts in time
in concert party, noted by Cole, are paralleled by shifts in place, as con-
trasts (between home and a place where you are 'on a visit', between
the small town where you lodge and the big city) succeed each other
without any displacement of the characters from the stage or even the
dramatic scene they are enacting. Rather than an Aristotelian unity of
time and place, this is a unity of displacements.

More allusions to journeys of displacement follow. People travel in
order to gain, and travelling without a purpose is equivalent to destitution, failure to gain anything. When Awura Akua is away, Yaw Ntow
brings in two women – 'harlots from Kumasi', as the comic Nigerian
houseboy correctly divines – who ply their trade in Takoradi but are travelling to Tema, when they spot Yaw Ntow gorgeously dressed in *kente*
cloth given to him by Awura Akua and think he is a rich man. To impress
them with his wealth, he boasts that he will take them both to the UK,
an invitation they accept: 'You see, we are just travelling and if you want
to go overseas with us, we are very grateful to you. We shall indeed go
with you.'

Meanwhile, Awura Akua and her father, on their way back from
Accra, are involved in a traffic accident, separated and left for dead.
Kind bystanders take Awura Akua to the military hospital to have her
injuries treated, and she now appears, bandaged and barely able to
walk, to find Yaw Ntow and the harlots dancing and flirting. She sings,
'Oh I'm tired of too much travelling / Oh my burden is heavy / I am
wondering how I can get home.' Yaw Ntow disowns her and literally
kicks her out, but her brother Joe Smart affirms his duty to look after
his sister; the others can jet off overseas, but not him:

> Let the lucky ones go
> I shall travel slowly to my destination
> No man knows what fate has in store for another man
> No man knows another man's destiny
> Fortunes come to men in turns
> To some in the morning, to some in the afternoon, and to others in
>   the night
> When is my turn? I have been left behind by all my mates; but need
>   I die on account of that?
> No! I shall travel slowly to my destination. (Bame 1985:172)

The harlots realise that Yaw Ntow in fact has no money, and one of
them sings, in a moment of pathos, 'I made this journey to make

money / If I have been unsuccessful in making money to take to my home town, then, as an orphan, bury me wherever I die' (179). Finally, Awura Akua returns, fully recovered and in blooming health; the father also returns, revealing that, after the accident, some kind helpers took him to Ayikuma to recover. The family is reunited and combines to drive Yaw Ntow out and send him back to his own town. The final song is 'Safe journey, my dear, safe journey' (190).

What a kaleidoscope of travels and returns, homes and aways! In this play, biographical experience is stretched like a skin over a framework of roads, sometimes linking significant sites of action (characters travel by road between the unnamed 'home' town, the big capital city Accra, where important meetings take place and runaways can hide, and Takoradi, a centre for the night life that springs up in industrial ports), but sometimes simply leading off into a wasteland of disappointment for aimless wanderers. The perils of road travel are the first things Awura Akua thinks of when explaining the need to formally introduce Yaw Ntow to her father, and it comes to pass: the accident on the road from Accra is the central pivot of the plot.

Travelling, then – and particularly road journeys by motor vehicle – provides both the narrative skeleton and the affective, philosophical ambience in this play. Not all concert party plays concentrated the theme quite so dramatically. But the synopses and play texts we have at our disposal show that in many of them, journeys on the ground are ways of conceptualising changes of fortune and sources of experience. In many cases, it is a journey from the country to the city that proves to be the narrative pivot. In 'The Jealous Rival', Akwaa and his two wives have 'come to town to work, earn money, and take it to our home town' (Bame 1985:104). In 'Treat Somebody's Child as Your Own', an old Asante cocoa farmer goes to Kumasi for the weekend, visits a nightclub, meets a strange woman and marries her; in a version of the Cinderella story, she mistreats the man's daughter by his dead first wife and favours her own two girls. In 'Think Twice' by the Golden Stars Band, a man and his nephew come to town from their farm with the cocoa harvest. Ignorant of town ways, the uncle is duped and fleeced by a smart operator, who takes everything, including the clothes he stands up in. The nephew, who has returned to the cocoa farm, now rescues him and helps him become rich once more. The uncle regrets staying behind to enjoy town life.

In some plays, however, going to town is the avenue to self-betterment. In the Jaguar Jokers' 'Orphan Do Not Glance' (Barber,

Collins and Ricard 1997), the orphan schoolboy Antobam, cruelly mistreated by his stepmother, is sent away by his father to Kumasi to stay with one of his father's friends. There he completes his education, does well in his exams and lands a job as a postmaster. He returns in a smart suit with an elegant wife to give money to his less prosperous relatives and demonstrate the moral, sung by his father, Mr Johnson, which is

> In this life if you don't succeed
> It may be best to leave and try elsewhere
> Antobam didn't succeed until he went to Kumasi
> As you can see my wife wants Sam to succeed
> So she is now letting him go away
> But in the long run only God knows who will succeed in life. (114)

Sam is the spoiled and profligate half-brother who, with his sister Abena Dansowa, has been drinking, dancing, flirting and 'roaming about' instead of passing his exams. These activities, typically associated with city life, are happening right at home, in a small town named on that occasion as Nsaba – the place where the performance recorded by Collins took place. So here the contrast between the values of the city and the small town has been reversed; home is the site of dissolute behaviour, the big city the site of self-discipline and progress. Travel is the avenue to a change of fortune. But Mr Johnson's philosophical conclusion, 'in the long run only God knows who will succeed in life', concludes the play on a plangent, poignant and resigned note typical of highlife.

Ghanaian concert party reached its apogee in the years immediately before and after Ghana's independence in 1957. Unlike the earlier trios, the full-blown concert party form was national and appealed to nationalists in several senses. Travelling all over the country, it could not exclusively represent the customs or culture of one region; it was polyglot, mixing English and Akan languages, playing with the languages of migrants (Yoruba, Hausa) and adapting to other Ghanaian languages when they performed in the north and east. The themes were chosen to represent the common experience of Ghanaians regardless of linguistic or ethnic group: common-denominator themes included family conflicts, the plight of orphans, the domineering wife, the perils of town life, and the importance of honesty, faithfulness and hard work. And as we will mention in the next chapter, they could also be explicitly nationalist, especially in the 1950s: some were vehemently pro-Nkrumah ('Kwame Nkrumah Is a Mighty Man'), and some were co-opted by Nkrumah's Convention People's Party to form 'Workers' Brigade Troupes'.

Transformations continued. In the 1980s and '90s, the format began to be extravagantly expanded – music was infused with rock, reggae and soul, though remaining highlife underneath; plays got much longer and more elaborate; extraordinary spirits, monsters and giants began to be indispensable; visually extravagant scenery and special effects became important. Offshoots, which were called 'drama' rather than 'concert party', began to appear – the main difference being that whereas female characters in concert party were played by young men, in drama they were played by women, which changed the whole dynamic and aesthetic. In the 1990s, however, it was still common for an audience to spend a whole night at a concert party: first listening to long sessions of band music, then watching the opening comic monologues or skits and then sitting through an enormously elaborate play, before finally closing with more music from the band before making their way home at four or five in the morning. In the plays I saw in 1990, the theme of travel was still the red thread that ran through the narrative: the plots were picaresque, and the hero or heroine would experience multiple encounters and adventures before returning home.

Popular Pamphlets in Onitsha

A striking example of popular print literacy that articulated the aspirations of would-be upwardly mobile 'new literates' is Onitsha market literature – the booklets and pamphlets produced in Onitsha in eastern Nigeria from the late 1940s to the 1960s.

Onitsha was, and is, a thriving commercial city on the banks of the river Niger. The railway from Port Harcourt on the coast to Kaduna in the north did not pass through Onitsha: it was routed through the coal-producing city of Enugu farther east. But the Niger was the principal transport conduit before the arrival of railways and motor roads. The Onitsha market was one of the largest and busiest in the region, noted with wonder by travellers in the mid-nineteenth century. And the river continued to carry goods and passengers between the coast and the hinterland well into the twentieth century. Like other West

African commercial, administrative and transport hubs in the colonial
era, Onitsha expanded spectacularly with the development of road
links to the railway and to other cities: from a small town of a little
more than 10,000 people in 1921, it almost doubled by 1931 and more
than tripled again by 1952–3; by the start of the Nigerian civil war
in 1967, it was a city of more than 100,000 people (Obiechina 1972;
Korieh 2004). This expansion was fed by migration from rural areas.
Before the colonial era, the Igbo-speaking areas had not been organ-
ized in large cities – unlike the Yoruba and Hausa – but the region
had long been densely populated. Tens of thousands of people came
from their village communities to settle in Onitsha, Enugu, Aba and
other Igbo urban centres. Partly pushed by increasingly stringent taxation policies, partly pulled by the concentration of schools, hospitals,
waged labour and white-collar jobs in the cities, they rapidly and
enterprisingly created vast expansions of existing urban nuclei.

As Onitsha grew, so did local artisanal and artistic production,
on the one hand, and a primary-school educated public, on the
other. Opportunities for small-business ventures, combined with an
exceptional concentration of schools (reputedly the greatest in eastern Nigeria, if not Nigeria as a whole), provided the conditions for
the creation and efflorescence of a new print genre. From the 1940s
to the 1960s, there was vigorous production of locally produced
pamphlets, printed on small presses by entrepreneurs who bought up
manuscripts from aspiring writers, modified them as they saw fit –
usually changing the title, but often also rewriting sections of the text
and even publishing under their own names – organised their printing
and distribution, and promoted them through local forms of advertising (Dodson 1973). They sometimes got their printing presses from
government or commercial firms which were upgrading their equipment after the Second World War, and they got some of the models
for what they wrote from Indian popular pamphlets which had been
brought back by soldiers who had served overseas, but they also
drew on all kinds of other sources. The pamphlets were often illustrated with an array of images ranging from male models in British
knitting pattern booklets to home-made (often strikingly attractive)
line drawings.

This was street and market literature. The New Market Road leading into the famous Onitsha market was lined with small printers'
shops. A whole section of the market itself was devoted to booksell-
ers' and stationers' stalls. From this hub, parcels of pamphlets were

distributed through road and rail to networks of towns across Nigeria, penetrating even small villages, carried for the last stages of the journey on bicycle or motorbike. As merchandise, value was placed on their novelty. Pamphlets that were perceived to be a few years old usually did not sell, so after a few print runs of a few thousand copies, publishers would drop them and turn to new ones. The authors were often not educated beyond a year or two of secondary school; the publishers and printers were artisans who also turned out calendars, almanacs, wedding invitations, posters and church programmes, and whose output was sensitive to immediate local fluctuations of taste and buying capacity. The people who bought and read the pamphlets had enough education to read relatively straightforward texts in local varieties of English. Obiechina, in his pioneering study *Onitsha Market Literature* (1972), describes the readers as 'the new literate class of elementary and grammar-school boys and girls, low level white-collar workers, primary school teachers, literate and semi-literate traders, mechanics, taxi-drivers and, above all ... the numerous products of ... adult education classes and evening schools'. Pamphlets were a way of both showing off one's literacy and increasing it by practice. The project of self-improvement was visible in every aspect of the pamphlet literature, and the overwhelming emphasis was on self-betterment or avoidance of moral and personal degradation, specifically in the city. The city and city life were, to a great extent, what these pamphlets were about.

Their subject matter and style were very varied. They included compilations of practical advice, as you can see from some of the titles: *How to conduct meetings* by I. M. U. Ibekwe; *How to write better letters, applications and business letters* by N. O. Njoku; *Pocket encyclopedia of etiquette and common sense* by S. O. MacDonald Bubagha. In many cases, the advice was to young men seeking romance or marriage: *How to get a lady in love* by F. N. Stephen; *How to write and reply letters for marriage, engagement-letters and how to know a girl to marry* by J. Abiakam. There was political history, for example, *How Lumumba suffered in life and died in Katanga* by O. Olisa and *The life story and death of John Kennedy* by W. Onwuka, and social and political criticism, for example, *The Age of Bribery* by B. A. Oji. There were many works of fiction – mostly romance, sometimes presented in the form of a drama, thriller or soft-core pornography serving as a moral warning. Famous examples are *Rosemary and the taxi-driver* by Albert O. Miller, *Mabel the sweet honey that poured away* by Speedy Eric, *The*

Game of Love by R. Okonkwo and, above all, *Veronica My Daughter* by Ogali A. Ogali, which was so popular that it bucked the trend and went through numerous reprints after its initial publication in 1957, reputedly selling more than 60,000 copies overall. Finally, one of the most common genres was advice explicitly about coping with modern life in the city, revolving around money and women, also taking in drinking and other dangers: *How to become rich and avoid poverty* by J. C. Anorue, *Money hard to get but easy to spend* by O. Olisa, *How to avoid enemies and bad company* by F. N. Stephen, *Why harlots hate married men and love bachelors* by C. N. O. Money Hard, *Beware of Harlots and Many Friends – the world is hard* by J. O. Nnadozie, *Why boys never trust money-monger girls* by R. Okonkwo and *Drunkards believe bar is heaven* by S. O. Olisah.

Their styles varied from chatty and down-to-earth to wildly ambitious and grandiloquent. Strikingly apt phrases and comical coinages were driven by a vehement sense of urgency to put the message across. What Thometz (2001) calls 'mad English' bounded across their pages. Within a single pamphlet you could find several different kinds of text combined together. Consider *The Game of Love* by R. Okonkwo, which is subtitled 'a classical drama from West Africa' and is presented as a play with characters interacting and conversing – but then the stage directions begin to get longer and more elaborate, until they are describing events, experiences and feelings not shown on stage, and even include quoted speech, as in a novel: 'Edwin received this telegram with all happiness. He bought every necessary thing in order to meet the occasion. Before the proposed time, he dressed up and moved to the taxi park in grand manner and movement. But before he reached it, AGNES had been already waiting for him. Immediately EDWIN saw her he moved towards her and embraced her. Both of them smiled and EDWIN said to her; Dear me, I am sorry for having not come in time. Please forgive me. They entered another taxi and drove away' (Obiechina 1972:59). The lovers exchange letters, to the point where the text begins to resemble an epistolary novel, and the play ends with a 'poem of love', apparently separate from the drama, as it is not spoken by any of the dramatis personae. This mixing of genres is a pervasive feature of the Onitsha authors' creative and experimental approach to assembling texts.

Onitsha market literature, then, was produced by an artisanal, small-scale process turning out small batches of unique and highly varied products. It contrasted maximally with the contemporaneous

mass-market fiction being produced in Europe and the US, such as
Mills and Boon romances. While Mills and Boon books were mass-
produced and highly standardized, prefabricated in accordance with
rigid rules about plot, characterization, length, structure, setting and
vocabulary – to the point of being manufactured *by* the editorial
process – Onitsha market texts were scarcely edited, and, to the extent
that they were, the editing was erratic bricolage rather than the imposition of standard forms. They were apparently written without any
sense that there are existing conventions of genre, grammar and plot
that have to be followed. Successful formats were copied, and thus
new conventions were established, but piecemeal and partially: there
was no uniformity, and authors continually did new things, either
because they wanted to experiment or because they did not feel in any
way bound by what had gone before. Because of this heterogeneity
and room for experiment, there could be no hard and fast boundaries
to this category of literature. Cyprian Ekwensi, a 'young pharmacist
with a flair for story-telling' (Obiechina 1972:8), began as a market
literature writer in 1947, with *When Love Whispers*; he went on to write
several acclaimed novels, published in the Heinemann African Writers
series, that have featured ever since in university literature courses
and literary histories. There is strong continuity between them. *People
of the City* and *Jagua Nana* are about city life, money and sex, represented with a down-to-earth vividness that is characteristic also of the
Onitsha pamphlets. Ogali A. Ogali, doyen of popular pamphleteers,
also combined two pamphlets to make a well-known novel, *Coal City*,
and he went on to write other novels which inhabit the borderland
between popular pamphlets and more officially sanctioned novels.

The city's pleasures and dangers, opportunities and risks are central themes in almost all the pamphlets. The reader is addressed as a
lone individual, typically someone who has left the security of his or
her village community and come to the city to try his or her luck. All
the things taken for granted in the village have to be paid for in the
city – food, lodging, recreation, even water. Everything is convertible
into money, and money is slippery. The city is a place full of strangers
who might be intending to defraud you: 'Money hard to get but easy
to spend'; 'How to avoid enemies and bad company.' And in the city
there are temptations that might ruin you: 'Drunkards believe bar is
heaven.' The biggest danger and temptation is woman, who can drain
a man of all his wealth and then dump him. With education, urbanization and massive expansion of commerce under colonialism, gender

roles were changing. Women dominated local trade; women who acquired schooling were also able to compete with men for white-collar jobs (whereas division of labour by gender was fairly clear-cut in more rural settings). There was doubt and ambivalence about women. On the one hand, education and new forms of employment empowered women and enabled them to challenge the dominance of their fathers and elders of the family. This was good for the young men – they could get the young women as companions and lovers, instead of seeing them monopolized by the girls' fathers' friends. So some of these pamphlets championed the girl's autonomy, her right to choose her own husband. The flagship text in what became a popular subgenre of market literature was Ogali A. Ogali's famous 'romantic play' *Veronica My Daughter*, which he described as 'an attempt to spotlight in playing form, the obstructionist role which some fathers in our traditional society like Chief Jombo, play in the love and marriage affairs of their daughter'. As Stephanie Newell points out, in these texts the old patriarchy is surreptitiously replaced by a new patriarchy: the old illiterate man is replaced by the young, educated, 'enlightened' one, and the young woman is expected to defer to the latter instead of the former (Newell 2002b). But there is a zestful liberation involved in this imagined transfer of power, and the young couple are portrayed as companions, engaging in rational discussion as well as passionate embraces. What is most striking is the disdain the young people feel for the older generation – not primarily because they are old, but because they are 'bush': backward, illiterate, stuck in the old ways. Their pidgin English is mocked and their traditional values are depicted as stupid. It is striking that this literature, which flowered in the period just before and after Nigeria's independence, is largely untouched by the elite intellectuals' project of preserving, sanitizing and revitalizing traditional heritage. To the Onitsha writers, what matters is modernity and progress, encapsulated above all in education, urban amenities and personal autonomy.

But, the pamphlets warn, modern women can also be a danger. Many of the pamphlets focus not on the enlightened, educated young couple, but on the loose women who apparently abound in the city and lay snares for unwary young men. The city, for all its amenities, has given bad women free rein to exploit and defraud young men. The answer is not to return to village customs, but for young men to be vigilant, self-disciplined, prudent and frugal. Each is responsible for his own fate. Women cunningly use men to get money, but if men

FIGURE 9 Onitsha market pamphlet by J. C. Anorue.

use their money to get women, they are fools. 'Women like money too much', warns J. C. Anorue. 'A woman's love for a man is money ... A woman cannot love you if you cannot spend.' He goes on, 'Money maketh a man! Dresses Maketh a woman!' and therefore, 'Please my dear young man, If you want to become rich and live long life. Beware of Harlots. Things are not what they are and there are many changes in the world today' (Anorue n.d.: 7, 11, 27).

'The city' is not only the setting but the theme of many pamphlets, and they often refer not to urbanism in general, but to specific named cities: Lagos, Enugu, Onitsha itself. And the cities are connected by road and rail. Miller O. Albert's *Rosemary and the Taxi Driver* (the complete text of which is reproduced in Thometz 2001) is a fabulous

MONEY AND WOMEN

    This is the picture of the Boy *Ghanna* giving money to
a hotel girl. Harlots gave him this big name because he can
spend. Please do not be like this foolish boy, who does not
think of himself. He must suffer at last.
    Women like money too much. A woman's love for a man
is money. When you get plenty of money you get plenty of
women and by then you become Mr. Somebody. But where
there is no money, you become Mr. Nobody. A woman cannot
love you if you cannot spend. And when you do not spend
for them, they will hate you and begin to call you money miss road.
    When a woman answers you sir and calls you master, know
that she wants your money.
    Women like sweet things and talk too much. They are like
empty gallons that make the greatest noise.

7

FIGURE 10 Onitsha market pamphlet by J. C. Anorue.

evocation of fast-moving city-hoppers seeking pleasure and fleeing
the law. The stunningly seductive Rosemary has been 'chasing around
the romantic seaport of Lagos, with her flareful flush of romance',
but 'It was time for love to roar on the air, and equally, the time for
Rosemary to travel on a journey from Lagos to the East' (Miller in
Thometz 2001:7). The journey becomes never-ending. Rosemary
goes by train to Enugu: 'After it was just midnight the train could be
noticed rumbling through the land, making its harsh, grimy noises.'
While 'enjoying the slow gallops of the train', she decides not to board
the bus to Onitsha from Enugu straightaway: 'she resolved to divide

her journey in order to trace out one to marry, or to fall in love' (10). The man she picks is Okoro, a taxi driver who, however, pretends to be a businessman with a private car (having erased 'the annotations terming the car a taxi'). Now he has to drive like a maniac to escape the taxi owner whose car he has absconded with; in a highly cinematic car chase, they speed from Enugu to Onitsha, from Onitsha to Owerri, from Owerri to Aba, committing more robberies and frauds along the way. Rosemary, it turns out, is herself an ex-cop turned robber. After a final splendid night of enjoyment on stolen money, they part company; Okoro heads for Port Harcourt, while Rosemary (who betrays Okoro) takes 'the limited train off to Lagos' (39). Both escape the law and disappear. Thus the story switches between two kinds of scene: urban dance halls and frantic car chases from town to town pursued by implausibly active police. Movement along the road at breakneck speed ('finishing the speedometer') is the criminal counterpart of the 'high life' of boozing, romancing and dancing. Rosemary executed 'the latest South African acrobatic style of patha-patha, the highest ever fashioned' (17) and 'danced like an Indian dancer and knew the top most style of highlife. She knew the toeing style and the most eyes catching foot demonstration ever, danced with a slide, by any star high life specialist' (38). Both the nightlife and the road races are thrilling because they exhibit speed, energy, zest, style and skill. It is significant that Okoro knew what to do in one crisis because he 'was a film goer' who knew 'the English method of bringing confusion into crime'. In this text (which is written in such exhilaratingly 'mad English' that it is at times incomprehensible), the city and the road, danger and pleasure, sexual attraction and mutual exploitation, are fused into one uproarious story.

Wider Views

This chapter has looked in some detail at two examples – popular musical theatre and popular print culture – from Anglophone West Africa. It has traced the impetus for these new genres in the experience of rapid urbanization and massive expansion of transport networks. The concert party troupes and distributors of Onitsha market pamphlets were part of the commercial life that buzzed up and down these arteries and congregated in the buoyantly expanding cities that were linked by them. They were produced by energetic entrepreneurs who were close in experience and outlook to their audiences and who continually experimented to capture these audiences' attention. Without formal training or (except in rare cases) any form of official support, the concert party troupes and author-editor-publishers of the popular pamphlets operated like other small businesses in the West African informal sector. An expanding urban population, dependent on wages or income from entrepreneurial activities, separated from the cyclical festivities of the village, striving to make a living and improve their situation, and needing recreation, were a ready audience for these new forms of entertainment. The point is not just that these changing conditions provided the seedbed for new forms, but that the plays and pamphlets were permeated through and through with reflections on the experience of city life and travel between villages, towns and big cities. And as the concert party troupes and the bundles of printed texts travelled by truck, taxi, motorcycle and bicycle along the expanding network of roads, their mode of dissemination moved through space in the same way as their narratives did.

I chose these two examples because they are exceptionally well documented and have given rise to an extensive body of commentary and historical contextualization. But there are similar examples everywhere in Africa. New popular cultural forms associated with rapid urbanization and expansion of transport networks sprang into existence across the continent at different times. Popular travelling theatres flourished in Nigeria from the 1940s onwards, in Togo in the 1960s, in Malawi and Tanzania in the late 1970s and 1980s. Locally published popular fiction was sold on the pavements and roadside stalls of many cities. In Dar es Salaam in the late 1960s and the 1970s – a little later than the heyday of Onitsha market literature in Nigeria – young entrepreneurial writers created a thriving business in 'pulp fiction' in Swahili. This was one of a number of African-language written literatures which emerged across the continent, stimulated and sustained, like the English-language publications, by the expanding number of primary school leavers with basic literacy. The young writers of Dar es Salaam collaborated to develop plot lines and edit each other's work, and relied on an urban network of friends employed in offices, printing presses, stationery shops, bookstalls and motor parks to help them get their texts typed, printed and distributed. Emily Callaci suggests that their aim was not just to write, but to produce and move something material through the city, and thus contribute to the making of urban life, and build up their own reputation, through their participation in this everyday traffic (Callaci 2017). Nairobi, too, became the centre of a wave of popular urban fiction in the 1970s, after the traumatic fight for independence had been won – novels in which the city was not only the site of production and the location of most of the audience, but also the principal theme. In the Nairobi novels, the city is a darker place than the city of the Onitsha market literature, a place of drunkenness, degradation, unemployment and corruption, and without the euphoria that buoys up even the most powerful warnings against the immorality of city life in Ghanaian concert party and Onitsha market literature.

In almost all cities in colonial sub-Saharan Africa, new genres of popular music were pioneered: highlife in the Gold Coast, juju in western Nigeria, Congolese rumba, *dansi* in Dar es Salaam, *marabi*, *kwela* and *isicathamiya* in South Africa. Increasingly, in the mid-twentieth century, the movement of popular music gained an extra dimension: radio, and later television, gave it longer reach and more rapid travel. New popular styles surged across national boundaries, and new songs took over audiences across whole regions with extraordinary rapidity. But underlying this there remained live bands travelling from town to town and records, later cassettes, being distributed along the roads and the railways from one city to another and from cities to smaller towns and villages. There remained a sense that new styles were being forged in specific urban centres and travelling out, adapting as they went, to other places.

Thus urban space and networks of commercial traffic on the ground remained both the means by which cultural products were disseminated and, often, the inspiration for their creation.

CHAPTER 5

The Crowd, the State ... and Songs

The Crowd

It was when disturbances happened that 'the people' became manifest in political histories of Africa. The record bristles with revolts and rebellions of many kinds: rural uprisings, millennial movements, industrial strikes, boycotts, marches, market women's protests, mass rallies, urban riots. Against the background of the slow burn of obstruction and sabotage fuelled by long-lasting resentment, there were sudden eruptions of outrage and defiance that flashed up and died down quickly. It was at these flashpoints, when embers in the undergrowth took fire, that 'the people' had most directly to be reckoned with. Flashpoints often took the authorities by surprise. They could not be wholly predicted from the existing state of affairs: they were the wild card that sometimes changed the game. Even when the immediate objectives of the moment were not achieved, as was often the case, flashpoints could release energies that continued to work in unforeseen ways. They could live on in popular memory and become starting points for future action.

Some popular uprisings were instigated and partly steered by formal organisations – a union, a local committee, a civic or religious outfit – but then they would very often spread to the population at large. At flashpoints, heterogeneous congeries of people with overlapping interests could coalesce temporarily and unite in pursuit of an objective. This unity might subsequently dissolve, but the fact that it had existed changed things. Other popular uprisings seemed to have no visible organisational structure. Colonial authorities saw them as the senseless actions of a deranged mob. Yet the authorities found, to their bafflement, that there was an effective mode of cooperation and communication operating below their range of vision. People had ways of making things work. They drew on the informal practices of everyday life unknown to the colonial authorities – ways of assembling, passing messages and recruiting support – to orchestrate new forms of collective action. Popular resistance and protest thus depended on a shared popular culture of habits and performance skills. And within this cultural repertoire, one particular performance genre is remarkably salient: popular song. Songs were a feature of virtually every popular uprising. Songs mobilised and inspired people to action – they drove home the key messages. As a participatory genre, they unified people emotionally; as an oral genre, they were accessible to all; as an improvisatory genre, they lent themselves to rapid response on the frontiers of social change; and as a poetic and musical genre, they were vitally memorable, meaning they could spread rapidly across a population and live on in people's minds for decades after the event. There was also the possibility that they could be used more coercively: getting people to sing from the same hymn sheet could involve various kinds of pressure, whether or not the cause was just.

African political leaders – of both liberation movements and repressive regimes – comprehended the power of popular culture, and particularly song, and attempted to harness it to serve their cause or their ends. After independence, new African governments often attempted to reach the population through cultural means: by sponsoring music groups and concert parties, by controlling radio and television programming and by staging spectacles such as the Black and African Arts Festivals in Dakar in 1966 and in Lagos in 1977. When co-optation fell short, many regimes added censorship and, in some cases, outright persecution of cultural producers.

This chapter focuses on how, in situations of crisis and confrontation in the colonial and post-independence eras – in riots, protests, uprisings and wars of liberation – people created and used popular cultural genres, and especially songs, as a key element in their arsenal of creative practices. It then goes on to look at state attempts to co-opt, channel and direct popular expressive forms, above all popular music, and how popular musicians and their fans responded to these attempts.

Our focus will be on the period that started after colonial rule had been definitively established. But resistance had begun well before this. The earlier phases of Africans' encounters with encroaching European forces, up to the beginning of the twentieth century, had unleashed waves of reaction and resistance all over Africa. Some of these events were taken up as touchstones by subsequent generations: their leaders became icons of nationalist historiography, and key episodes were recreated in multiple popular and elite art forms. For example, in West Africa, Sarraounia, the Azna-Hausa warrior queen, led her forces against the French colonial army at the battle of Lougou in 1899. Her legend lives on in a novel by the radical trade unionist Abdoulaye Mamani, which was later turned into a heroic art film by Med Hondo. In East Africa, the Maji Maji movement of 1905–7 brought together an army spontaneously formed from numerous linguistic and ethnic groups, uniting under the charismatic leadership of Kinjeketile to confront incipient German colonialism. This inter-ethnic, anti-colonial cooperation was taken up later as a symbol and precursor of Nyerere's African Socialism, and Kinjeketile featured as the protagonist of a famous play in Swahili by Ebrahim Hussein. Other iconic movements were more ambiguous and provoked varying interpretations: in South Africa, the call by Nongqawuse, the girl prophetess, for the Xhosa to sacrifice their cattle to purify the land and put a stop to the relentless incursions of whites into Xhosa territory led to the disastrous cattle killings of 1856–7 and the definitive defeat of the Xhosa. This dramatic but difficult story has been revisited again and again by Xhosa writers, from W. W. Gqoba's narrative of 1888 to J. J. R. Jolobe's 1959 poem to David Yali-Manisi's oral praise poem of 1970 to Zakes Mda's novel *The Heart of Redness* in 2000. And popular uprisings of the past may be sanctified by nationalist politicians who show little patience with current grass-roots protest.

A Tax Protest, a Strike, a Riot and Two Boycotts

Unlike these early confrontations between opposing forces not sure of each other's strength or long-term plans, popular uprisings after the First World War were faced with an entrenched colonial state. To

Nongqawuse, Sarraounia and Kinjeketile, it had still seemed possible to drive the colonial invaders out. After the First World War, popular resistance was more likely to be targeted at specific grievances within the colonial domain and to enshrine definite demands.

Early colonial regimes had a permanent problem: getting enough labour without creating an insurgent, organised working class. In the earliest days of colonisation, colonial governments and white commercial interests resorted to forced labour and indentured workers imported from abroad, but this was not found to be a satisfactory solution in the long term. After the First World War, taxation was introduced, not only to fund the scanty colonial apparatus, but also to force self-sufficient subsistence farmers to join the waged labour force, or to produce cash crops for export. Cheap, daily-paid wage labour was the predominant form of employment on colonial infrastructural projects (roads, railways, docks), while above them a smaller structure of salaried civil servants was erected. For the majority, these two factors – taxation, and poor pay and conditions in government employment – were among the most powerful triggers of popular rebellion, and a third trigger lay in the array of regulatory instruments by which colonial governments sought to control economic activities and urban space.

Historians of popular uprisings in Europe have made a distinction between pre-industrial riots based on a popular 'moral economy' and organised industrial action by labour unions. This distinction does not work all that well in Africa, where industrialisation was limited and patchy and agriculture remained the majority occupation. In West African cities, the vast majority of the urban workforce belonged to the informal sector of petty traders, artisans and self-employed people. Even in South Africa, the most highly industrialised region, industry never employed a majority of the total population. Everywhere, the unionised workforce was a small fraction of the labour force. Yet it was a significant fraction, initiating actions, setting standards and framing demands which influenced the larger population. There is no doubt that the continent-wide wave of organised industrial strikes in the later colonial period had a major impact on the colonial powers. Between 1935 and 1948, there was a major series of strikes in Northern Rhodesia, South Africa, French West Africa, the Gold Coast, Nigeria and Kenya. These concerted uprisings frightened the French and British governments. Confronted with the spectre of loss of control, they started the decolonisation process sooner than they had planned. Nonetheless, industrial action was not the only or even the dominant mode of colonial contestation. Popular forms of protest that had little to do with the industrial workplace continued to flourish. At other times, industrial action could coincide with wider unrest, which might partly mesh with the workers' campaign and partly diverge from it, making separate demands and using different methods. In these circumstances, popular culture genres, particularly songs, could form a bridge between strikers and the wider population of insurgents.

Our first case study is a tax protest by women in rural and small-town areas of Eastern Nigeria: the famous 'women's war' of 1929. This was an insurgency that drew on long-standing local forms of association and mobilisation and had no links with industrial unions. It was sparked by rumours that taxation was about to be extended to women; this combined with other grievances. Women's resentment of colonial rule in Nigeria had been building for some years: artificially created 'warrant chiefs' were abusing their new-found power; economic and social changes were eroding women's position and status. Trouble began in September 1929 in the Igbo village of Oloko, where the warrant chief appeared to be assessing women's wealth. Immediately, a group of women converged on the village chief's house singing abusive songs. Instead of admitting wrongdoing, this man, Chief Okugo, set his male household members onto the women, and eight of them were injured. This ignited a widespread reaction: thousands of women surged in from neighbouring towns to besiege the District Officer's office and demand the chief's deposition. The D.O. tried to placate them, but rumours of taxation continued to spread and women's protests sprang up across an ever-widening area. In December 1929, 1,000 women attacked the native court at Owerrinta, damaging property and destroying documents. At Aba, women not only attacked the native court, but also looted Barclays Bank and some European companies' warehouses. The action spread beyond the Igbo-speaking area into Calabar Province, and in Utu Etim Ekpo, women attacked the native court, a warehouse and clerks' houses, where government troops shot and killed eighteen women. At Opobo on the following day, thirty-nine women and one man were shot dead and another thirty-one women were wounded. The insurgency then died down, though with occasional flare-ups, and two commissions of inquiry followed. Women as well as men testified. Chief Okugo was deposed and jailed (Matera et al. 2012).

The uprising was an expanded version of a village procedure known locally as 'sitting on' or 'making war on' a wrongdoer by besieging his or her compound. In the village setting, a mass of women would converge on the house of the target – preferably in the dead of night – strip themselves semi-naked, sing improvised, abusive songs and dance with exaggerated sexual gestures all night long or until the target capitulated. The performance carried a ritual charge (Green 1964). In the women's war of 1929, the same procedure was adapted to meet the new purpose and was carried out on an unprecedented scale. Bands of women, in ritual dress of palm leaves and chalked faces, would surge into a village from elsewhere, gather information about warrant chiefs and male elders associated with the colonial order, target their houses, ritually sweep their compounds and perform songs about them. The sight and sound of the massed women were said to have been frightening. Their songs were full of menace.

> What is the smell?
> Death is the smell!

sang a thousand Ibibio women converging on the Resident's house at Essene in Calabar Province (Akpan and Ekpo 1988). In a number of episodes of the conflict, the women would present a string of demands, many of which were focused on the need to restore women's customary economic and social rights. The colonial institutions that they targeted were all ones that were perceived as circumscribing or excluding women: warrant chiefs' compounds, native court buildings, colonial commercial and administrative buildings, railway and telegraph stations and European shops, banks and warehouses, which, unlike the open, circulating marketplace dominated by women, were seen as secretive and unjust. All of these institutions were seen as foreign abominations that affected the fertility and purity of women's bodies.

The longer-term outcome has been disputed. Some see it as a defeat for the women: taxation was indeed introduced, European government and commercial institutions remained, and women's ritual and cosmological status continued to be eroded by conversion, schooling and economic change. Others argue that the impact of the uprising at the time was considerable, leading to changes in the implementation of colonial administration – not least the inclusion of women in local government. Beyond this, it is argued, the uprising furnished a long-lasting model for future female insurgency in the region, which continued throughout the twentieth century and into the twenty-first. Women protesting against oil spillage and environmental destruction in the Niger Delta use symbolic action reminiscent of the songs, dances and ritual gestures of the 1929 'women's war'.

Though early colonial accounts of the 'women's war' saw it as a riot, the actions of a senseless mob, it was in fact well coordinated, efficient and controlled, and the apparently 'barbarous' and 'obscene' actions of the women came from an established repertoire of procedures for calling wrongdoers, both male and female, to account. It is notable that the physical attacks were carefully judged. They were not on people, but on property, and property of a particular sort. The women assaulted colonial administrative offices and judicial buildings, invaded warrant chiefs' compounds and ate their yams by the barnful, but they did not attack spaces women and children frequented – churches, hospitals and schools. Moreover, what we see here is a situation not only where women used a distinctive symbolic performance genre to mobilise fellow women into taking political action, but where the performance genre itself actually *was* the political action; the abusive songs, 'obscene' dances and gestures and ritual dress were what the thousands of insurgent women brought to bear upon the colonial authorities and their appointees and institutions, with intimidating effect.

A second case study shows how a workers' strike and a popular urban uprising meshed together – and shared a theme song – in Freetown, Sierra Leone, in 1919. The colonial government had offered a bonus to railway workers, but only to those of higher grades who received monthly salaries, not to daily-paid mechanics and labourers, even though the latter in some cases had worked many years on the same job and had similar responsibilities to those on monthly salaries. Protests from the daily-paid mechanics and labourers escalated into a strike in July 1919; some categories of workers for the Public Works Department came out in sympathy. Four days after the start of the strike, an urban riot broke out because of a threatened food shortage. Extra consignments of rice, imported by the government in the expectation of a poor harvest, had allegedly been bought up and hoarded by Syrian middlemen. Different classes and interest groups combined: elite Creoles who had suffered from mercantile competition from the Syrians, jobless migrants from the hinterland, the railway and PWD employees and large numbers of ordinary urban residents all joined in a city-wide protest. The authorities were baffled by the efficiency and control with which their actions were orchestrated. Strikers went in procession; despatch runners on bikes carried news and instructions from one section to another; there was a system of signalling with flags; picketing was carried out effectively. As in the women's war of 1929, the apparently wild actions of the rioters were in fact judiciously targeted: they looted the shops and warehouses where rice was believed to be stored, but did not attack other property, let alone human beings. Break-ins and looting erupted simultaneously in different parts of town, giving the impression that the riots had been coordinated from below (Abdullah 1994). And running through the action, uniting strikers and rioters, was the 'bonus song', composed in Krio, the Freetown patois, by a popular entertainer who more often performed for elite social clubs. This song, with humorous stridency, commented on the unfair distribution of the pay rise:

> White man all get Bonus
> Dem get pass Ten pounds
> We want we small Bonus
> Bonus, Bo-Bonus,

affirmed unity:

> Strike don cam for Bonus
> We unite for Bonus,

threatened the Syrian traders with expulsion:

> When all dem Coral go ['Coral' was a nickname for Levantine traders
>   because part of their stock-in-trade was plastic 'coral' beads, much
>   cheaper than real coral]
> Then Bonus, Sweet Bonus,

compared the strike to the influenza epidemic that had devastated the town in 1918:

> Last year we say ner Flu
> This year we call am Strike

and commented on the policies of the colonial officials who were attempting to deal with the situation:

> Milner say pay Bonus
> Barker say bit first

Maude say make Red-belleh shoot
Bonus, Bo-bonus. (Spitzer 1974:161)

Sung by strikers and rioters alike, the song combined the perspectives of both. On the one hand, it rallied the strikers to demand their
'small Bonus'; on the other hand, the strike was seen as an event affect-
ing the whole of social life, akin to the influenza epidemic that swept
Africa in 1918 – which sounds more like a rioter's perspective than a
striker's. Though it did not originate with either group – the composer,
Mr W. Mends, appears to have been a fringe member of the Creole
elite – the catchy, colloquial song was able to help bring the two groups
together for a brief period of joint action. It was remembered decades
later as the leitmotif of the turbulent events of the summer of 1919 in
Freetown.

This kind of liaison between industrial strikers and the wider urban
population could, in some cases, benefit from a larger-scale popular
cultural institution than a concert party song. A well-known example
is the Beni dance associations, a cultural innovation of colonial Eastern
Africa which involved team dancing based loosely on military brass
bands, similar and related to the Kalela dance described in Chapter 3.
The Beni dance associations provided a real organisational backbone
for political and industrial mobilisation. They had a hierarchy of titled
office-holders, functioned as welfare or friendly societies as well as
performance groups and formed regional networks of competing
teams. In Mombasa in 1934, the Beni dance associations provided the
organisational backbone for a major dockworkers' strike in the days
before the workforce was unionised. Labour at the docks was daily
paid and casual: workers came and went, and were selected from the
available hands on a daily basis. The shipping lines relied on licensed
stevedoring firms to recruit labour; these in turn relied on *serangs*,
or headmen, to collect workers, organise them into gangs, supervise
them and receive and distribute the lump sums paid to the gang. The
serangs were semi-autonomous: they stood as patrons to the gang
members, who gave them their loyalty in return for a steady supply of
work when they needed it. The interesting thing is that members of the
same gang were often also members of the same Beni dance society,
and the *serang* was often the 'king', or leading title holder. In their bid
to become Beni leaders, *serangs* called on the support of their gangs;
and conversely, the dockworkers' solidarity as social and recreational
units increased their capacity for collective industrial action. It is notable that the strikers held their mass meetings in Mwembe Tayari, the

same place where Beni dance competitions were staged at weekends and where labour hiring took place (Ranger 1975; Cooper 1987).

A fourth example is the South African Alexandra bus boycotts of 1944 and 1957. South Africa has been the site of more intense and sustained popular struggle against the state than anywhere else on the continent. Confrontation dates back to the earliest days of the Dutch settlers' violence against the Khoikhoi in the Cape in the 1650s and runs through the subsequent relentless white expansion into the hinterland in the eighteenth and nineteenth centuries, the conquest of the independent African kingdoms, the twentieth-century policies of land dispossession, segregation and movement control, was formalised as full-blown apartheid by the National Party after it came to power in 1948, and reached its apogee in the draconian imposition of states of emergency in 1985 and 1986, when hundreds were killed in police violence, tens of thousands were detained, and curfews, banning orders and censorship ratcheted up to the breaking point. Soon after these final convulsions of white minority rule, the National Party government began negotiations with the African National Congress (ANC), which led, eventually, to the end of apartheid and majority rule in 1994. Participation in the struggle came from multiple disparate sites: from formal political organisations (the ANC, the South African Communist Party, the Pan-African Congress and the Black Consciousness Movement), from local action committees mobilising around specific issues, from trade unions, from intellectuals and independent grass-roots radicals, from school pupils, from the urban populace resisting pass laws, from agricultural, industrial and domestic workers at the end of their tether. In the eyes of activists, pervasive simmering discontent would be ignited into action as soon as people recognised the true causes of their oppression, a theme seen in the pioneering film *Mapantsula,* which shows a tsotsi gangster, in the last frame, finally declaring 'No!' to the apartheid authorities. In the 1970s and '80s, all expressive forms were mobilised. 'Culture is a weapon of struggle', according to the ANC, and fiction, visual art, theatre, poetry, dance and music were all taken extremely seriously by political activists.

Running through a multitude of protests and acts of defiance were immediately recognisable slogans and songs. *Amandla*! (Power!), *Mayibuye*! (Bring back Africa!) and *Asinamali*! (We have no money!) were slogans that, perhaps forged in the heat of one flashpoint, became the rallying cry of many subsequent ones, linking separate episodes of the struggle across time and space. These condensed kernels of historical memory were also embedded in songs, which could travel from massed gatherings of protestors to popular recording artists, to the radio, and back to the people on the street.

The Alexandra bus boycotts were the response of Johannesburg workers whose precarious survival was threatened by a one-penny increase in bus fares. In the 1940s and '50s, the demand for industrial labour, already intense, sharply increased with the rapid expansion of manufacturing in response to the shortages of the Second World War. This, combined with the devastation of the rural economy, led to a massive influx of migrants into the cities. The fear of a settled urban working class, which had led to the pass laws, was in tension with the manufacturers' need for a stable, permanent workforce and the migrants' lack of alternatives. The result, as we saw in Chapter 3, was the rapid expansion of extensive, overcrowded, unsanitary informal settlements, which the municipal authorities attempted to control without fully acknowledging them or providing basic amenities for them.

In November 1944, the company operating the buses from Alexandra, a township outside the centre of Johannesburg, where most of the township's residents worked, raised the fare from 4d to 5d. This was an increase the people simply could not pay. For seven weeks, the entire population boycotted the buses: 15,000 people walked nine and a half miles to work and nine and a half miles back every day, until the bus company dropped the fare increase. The slogan of the boycott was '*Azikhwelwa!*' (We will not ride!). The slogan was expanded into a song, and the song was picked up by the jive vocalist Mabel Mafuya, elaborated on, recorded by Troubadour Records and played on the radio. Thirteen years later, in 1957, the Public Utility Transport Corporation – set up by the government to run the buses following the 1944 boycott – again tried to raise the fare to 5d. 'Like a single shot fired', in the activist Ruth First's words, 'the people refused to board the buses.' This time the boycott lasted for three months and involved far more people, from Sophiatown and Newclare and some districts of Pretoria as well as Alexandra, even extending to sympathy boycotts in distant towns, such as Port Elizabeth and East London, that had suffered no fare increases themselves. At the height of the boycott, a total of 60,000 township residents refused to ride the buses to work. Sympathisers in the white districts through which the long procession of walkers passed turned out to offer lifts. Others demanded police action to disperse the crowd. A committee was set up in Alexandra to negotiate with the bus company, the employers (represented by the Chamber of Commerce) and the Johannesburg City Council. This committee was formed of representatives of the local landlords' and tenants' associations, the Workers' League, the ANC and several splinter groups that had broken away from the ANC. It organised democratically run mass meetings to inform the boycotters of developments in the negotiations, to take decisions and to maintain popular enthusiasm. But disagreements between the different interest groups that made up the committee weakened its effectiveness. It was the marchers themselves who remained determined and united, rejecting compromise offers until the 5d fare was once again dropped (Lodge 1982). Here we see a popular insurgency partly shaped by, but partly independent of, formally organised political groups. The ANC sought to generalise the specific opposition to the fare increase and link it to wider insurgency. To a considerable extent they succeeded, but in the end the marchers remained united only because they were wholly focused, no matter what the suffering, on a single concrete objective.

The bus boycotts became iconic events in ANC history. And the slogan and song '*Azikhwelwa*' from the 1944 boycott came back in 1957. It was 'one of those terse, succinct, "magic" catchwords that epitomizes a whole legion of African demands, a concept of struggle, an entire campaign', wrote Ruth First (First 1957:55). The 'boycott song' was heard everywhere in 1957 – even on the radio, until SABC banned it. In 2012, the 100th anniversary of the Alexandra township's foundation and the 55th anniversary of the 1957 boycott, the Department of Arts and Culture sponsored a musical '*Azikhwelwa*' to celebrate both.

The galvanising, inspiring and unifying power of song was not confined to rallies, marches and demonstrations. It could work in more unexpected ways, sometimes even against the ostensible intentions of its creator. Gibson Kente was a composer, impresario and theatrical entrepreneur who became famous for his musical theatre drawn from black township life and played to township audiences, starting with Soweto, where he lived. Though his was the first musical theatre to reflect the everyday life of township populations, he generally took a cautiously populist and non-political line. Only between 1973 and 1976 did he become briefly identified with black political struggle. After his play *How Long?* was banned while he was making a film version in 1976 and he spent some months in prison, he reverted to uncontentious musicals with escapist or anodyne moral endings. His glamorous lifestyle, combined with his plays' messages of patience and endurance, angered some radical critics, and he was condemned by South African Student Organisation (SASO) and Black Consciousness Movement (BCM) intellectuals. Even the more overtly critical plays were ambiguous. *Too Late* (1974–5), for example, showed clearly that the suffering of black township populations was caused by the apartheid state, yet it still emphasised the need for Christian faith, hope and endurance rather than violent insurrection. ('Too late' meant something must be done before it's too late to prevent revolutionary violence.) But the contradictions and hesitancies in Kente's plays were overridden by his youthful township audiences, first because they identified wholly with the young radical characters whose position the plays themselves rejected in favour of the more moderate elders, and second because the music of the plays transcended and overpowered any verbal formulations. Kente's musical compositions were thrilling. Kente recalled in an interview that an apartheid official had warned him that 'your message, whatever it is – you make it stick. People carry it home, they sing about it because it is musical. It's very dangerous. We are watching you' (Solberg 1999:84). The music became 'the most powerful vehicle for the expression of the emotional or spiritual elements of the plays'; it was 'able to fuse an audience of separate and divided individuals in an experience of intense cultural identity' (Kavanagh 1985:139). The words of the songs, often hymn-like, appealed to people's faith, hope, patience and capacity for endurance, but the thrilling *sound* of the songs, which were in African languages and combined Xhosa music with gospel jazz and other popular township genres, went beyond the ostensible verbal message and stirred collective defiance. The audience's experience of hearing the songs together, in a packed, emotionally charged community hall, transcended everyday doubts and differences.

Since the end of apartheid in 1994, the exacting ideological style of cultural analysis that prevailed in the years of struggle has gone out of fashion, and the popular radicalism of Kente's plays, even though muted, can now be recognised, as can the possibility that at some level the majority of township audiences (unlike the BCM and SASO) may have actually embraced the Christian counsel of patience and dignified suffering. Nonetheless, it is apparent that there was something about the music of Kente's theatre which inhabited a different dimension from his plots and dialogue. It is this potential of song to transcend the preoccupations of everyday life, to bring people together in

FIGURE 11 Olive Masinga and cast of Gibson Kente's *Can You Take It?*
(1977).

consciousness and tune them up to collective action that runs like a
red thread through all the examples we have looked at.

The preceding examples show some of the ways in which popular
creativity can play a part in popular uprisings. The Eastern Nigerian
'women's war' demonstrated people's capacity to form effective col-
lectives without formal leadership roles, and it showed how political
action could take the form of traditionally sanctioned ritual song and
dance performances. The uprising in Freetown showed how organised
labour and popular urban riot could coalesce rather than be historical
alternatives. It also showed how a song could become freed from its
original context to take on resonance for wide sections of the population not included in its initial intended audience: a humorous song
composed by a concert party leader on the periphery of the highly
exclusive Freetown elite was adopted and adapted by both strikers
and the mob and became their joint manifesto. In the Mombasa dockworkers' strike, a dance society provided the organisational framework for industrial action. And the Alexandra bus boycott, along with
Gibson Kente's music, illustrate the power of song to encapsulate and

stimulate the passion of the moment and extend its effects over time and space. All the examples show how songs can live on in popular memory – able to be reactivated in future actions.

In these examples, it has become apparent that the mysterious and volatile 'masses' that lurk behind African colonial history are, in fact, people with a long experience of fixing up social arrangements, making informal agreements stick, navigating highly heterogeneous and unpredictable social landscapes, and communicating rapidly and inconspicuously over long distances. These eruptions are not aberrations, but rather outcrops of an underlying geology of social forms (for getting by, and getting on) laid down by experience and practice. Everyday practices established the rhizomatic networks through which 'matter happens'. And creating performances – of songs, dance and dramatic and ritual actions – was integral to those practices.

There is a congruence between the way songs work in these situations and the nature of political flashpoints themselves. Songs have a double effect. On the one hand, they can stir powerful momentary emotions which lift people out of their habitual inhibitions and social divisions. They can do this because their words are inherently polysemic, open to different interpretations by different participants, thus appealing to all, while at the same time the music issues a compelling, unifying call. On the other hand, they linger in the mind after the episode of collective action has passed. If episodes of intense collective action continue to have effects long after the moments in which they happened, so do the songs associated with them: they stay in the memory and may indeed become the central peg on which narratives of the past action are hung.

Songs of the Liberation Wars

In the context of the liberation wars in Kenya and Zimbabwe, songs were deliberately given a central role as an instrument of radicalisation, education, communication and rapport-building.

Let's look at the *chimurenga* songs of Zimbabwe. '*Chimurenga*' is a Shona word said to mean 'struggle'. In Zimbabwe, the struggle was above all about land. Cecil Rhodes's British South Africa Company (BSAC) had entered the area in 1890 expecting to find gold. When this did not materialise, whites began to appropriate farmland in Ndebele country, clearing the way for further expropriation by conquering the kingdom of Lobengula and subsequently, in 1896, crushing a rebellion in both the Matabele and Shona areas. In Shona territory, resistance had been led by a woman called Charwe, the medium of the royal ancestral spirit NeHanda. Charwe, along with the medium of another ancestral spirit called Kagubi, was captured and publicly hanged in 1896. On the scaffold she prophesied, 'My bones will arise.' White occupation of the land proceeded apace, institutionalised by a series of laws passed by the settler government, which had taken over from the BSAC in 1923. By the 1950s, they had appropriated fully half of all cultivable land – taking far more than they could actually cultivate. African subsistence farmers were pushed onto Reserves, later named Tribal Trust Lands, and forced to divide and redivide their plots until overcrowding and overcultivation brought them to the verge of destitution. Expropriation was a deliberate strategy to force Africans to undertake waged labour on white farms, in the mines and in other white-owned enterprises, while, in the classic manner of African migrant labour economies discussed in Chapter 3, the cost of reproduction of the labour force was borne mainly by female labour on the reserves. The African farmers resisted from the beginning; they had actively chosen the 'peasant option' in preference to migrant labour, and they stubbornly clung to their farms through the Depression and subsequent intensified government expropriation. Ranger (1985) emphasises that their unwavering aims throughout the twentieth century were, first, to get back their 'lost lands' and, second, to throw off government interference in their methods of cultivation. Following Ian Smith's Unilateral Declaration of Independence in 1965, which defied British and international attempts to induce majority rule as a precondition of independence, the political resistance of the black urban elite began to take the form of armed struggle. The first battle took place at Sinoia in 1966; there followed thirteen years of bitter guerrilla warfare against ruthless but overstretched government forces. The liberation movement's ultimate victory and the resulting independence in April 1980 would not have been possible without the widespread support of the rural population.

However, collaboration between the peasants and the guerrillas was not a foregone conclusion. There have been disagreements among scholars about the nature of the relationship between them. Terence Ranger and David Lan explain that the guerrillas were young men and, as a matter of military policy, were never local to their areas of operation. Many of them had grown up in exile in the front-line states, and all of them had been trained outside Rhodesia: the mainly Shona army of the Zimbabwe African National Union (ZANU) in Mozambique and Tanzania, the mainly Ndebele army of the Zimbabwe African People's Union (ZAPU) in Zambia. The young soldiers were taught that their mission was to enlighten, instruct and conscientise the peasants about ZANU's and ZAPU's structure, the history of colonial exploitation, the nationalist anticolonial struggle and the socialist state that would replace settler capitalism. The villagers understood the causes of their exploitation, and their goal was to regain their land. But their sources of authority and conceptions of a better world diverged from those of ZANU and ZAPU. Traditional chiefs had lost their credibility among the people because they had been co-opted by the white regime. But the royal ancestors, the *mhondoro* spirits, had not: they represented the authority of the pre-conquest dispensation. The *mhondoro* were benign. They were inseparable from the land, for their burial sites were sacred spaces, and their beneficence had to do with ensuring rainfall and the fertility of the earth. After the conquest, they alone had the authority to lead the people, and the means of communication was through spirit mediums – men, and more rarely women, who, after a long period of testing and experience of possession, became recognised and accepted by the community as vehicles for particular royal ancestors with influence over particular territories. The mediums were a powerful symbolic focus of anticolonial resistance because they rejected everything in any way associated with whites: food, cars, trains and, above all, white employment. This inspired resistance but sat uneasily with the liberation movement's goals of modernisation and development.

After initial failures, the liberation armies quickly realised that they needed to enlist the aid of the spirit mediums – both for the benefit of their practical knowledge of the territory and for their authority with the local population. The spirit mediums became key figures in the struggle. Some went into battle alongside the guerrillas; the ancient female medium of NeHanda – who, as prophesied, had returned to the fray – was believed to be directing operations, and when it became unsafe she was carried on a stretcher to Mozambique, where she continued to instruct the soldiers until her death in 1973. Not only this, but the guerrillas took on board some of the perspectives and behaviour of the villagers and their spirit mediums. They relied on the mediums' local knowledge and trusted in the spirits' protection. The mediums taught the guerrillas ritual techniques, including how to read omens, how to avoid sexual pollution and how to use invisibility and anti-bullet medicines. By adopting these practices, the guerrillas became more like autochthons and therefore more capable of assuming leadership roles alongside or instead of the mediums (Lan 1985:165).

Norma Kriger (1992), contrary to Ranger and Lan, emphasises the element of coercion in the guerrillas' relations to the villagers. Testimony from villagers in the north-east of the country, where she did her research, described the guerrillas' resorting to beating, humiliating and killing villagers they perceived as non-compliant, and their violent extraction of food and money from poor communities. Kriger also maintains that local struggles within village communities – between men and women, parents and children, chiefs and subjects, richer and poorer peasants – were a stronger motive for getting involved in the war than national liberation. Youth, for example, gained power from their association with the guerrillas, and this enabled them to dominate their parents.

This view is darker than Ranger's and Lan's, but all of these scholars focus on the fact that the guerrillas did succeed in forging a relationship with the peasants and that this was a crucial factor in the outcome of the war. All also identify a central mechanism by which the relationship was cemented: the *pungwes* or *moraris*, nocturnal meetings between guerrillas and civilians, held in the bush outside the village. In these sessions, the guerrillas would seek to educate and enthuse the villagers about the war. The guerrillas would 'talk for half an hour, then teaching the masses songs for an hour, then talking for another half hour and so on, so that people did not get bored', as one former guerrilla put it (Lan 1985:127). Villagers said that they quickly forgot the content of the speeches; what they remembered was the slogans and songs (Kriger 1992:99).

Both ZANLA and ZIPRA armies had liberation choirs based outside the country. Their rousing songs, in Shona and Ndebele, were banned in Rhodesia, but were broadcast into the country from Maputo and Lusaka. Within Zimbabwe, and especially in the Shona-speaking areas, these songs formed the basis of the repertoire that the guerrillas sang with the villagers. They were of various types. They were based on indigenous musical and song forms, or sometimes on hymn tunes, but they were always given new lyrics. What is interesting is that the words sometimes articulated the ZANU ideology and sometimes made appeals to the ancestral spirits for protection. The most commonly used indigenous song form was the 'mosaic' type (*kudeketera* in Shona), where participants contributed their own improvised lines, which were interwoven to form a composite text. It might be that this format was attractive because it lent itself to the juxtaposition and slotting-together of elements from the two contrasting ideological repertoires:

> Oh, Takawira, our guardian spirit
> NeHanda our ancestral spirit
> Protect us as we fight our way back to Zimbabwe.
> Our guardian spirits we
> Pray to you to please watch over us.

> We appeal to you Mugabe
> We appeal to you our revolutionary leader
> Lead us until final victory
> We also appeal to our guardian spirits
> Protect us from the enemy. (Pongweni 1982:51–2)

The *chimurenga* songs showed how the composition and performance of songs could be the chosen crucible in which a shared ideology was supposed to be – and to some extent was – forged and disseminated. But as the reference to night-long programmes of 'talking' and 'teaching the masses songs' suggests, the two sides of the encounter were not equally balanced. The guerrillas' agenda was the driving force. If they absorbed and adopted some of the local people's perspectives, including an acceptance of spirit mediums, they more systematically imposed and enforced their own. In songs, they had chosen a powerful means of driving home their message and making it memorable.

In the towns, away from the guerrilla war, there flourished a different kind of *chimurenga* song. The 'home artists', popular urban musicians performing for entertainment, could not deliver the explicit messages of the *pungwe* and liberation choir songs: it was too dangerous. When Thomas Mapfumo formed Blacks Unlimited in 1978 and sang openly political songs, he was banned from government-controlled radio, thrown into prison camp without charges and only released after mass popular demonstrations. Most home artists instead concealed coded allusions to armed struggle in their songs. An example is Zexie Manatsa and the Green Arrows' song 'Musango Mune Hangaiwa', which stayed at number one on the Rhodesian charts for a record seventeen weeks. It camouflages a message of support for the guerrillas with mild ornithological imagery:

> Dear Lord, we have a request, help us
> We need rain please,
> But it must not fall in the forests,
> There are some pigeons there
> Birds that have run wild
> They are dedicated to our ancestral spirits;
> Don't trap them if you see them,
> You get NeHanda's permission first,
> The chief guardian spirit of Zimbabwe. (Pongweni 1982: 140-1)

After the end of the war, *chimurenga* songs were performed in celebration of independence and majority rule, and home artists, prominent among them Thomas Mapfumo and Oliver Mtukudzi, became superstars. But as the ZANU government's problems began to pile up, Mapfumo turned the *chimurenga* genre into criticism of Mugabe, leading eventually to his flight from Zimbabwe and exile in the US. *Chimurenga* became the name not only for the armed struggle against the white settler government, but also, more broadly, for the struggle to create a better and more just political, economic and social order. At the same time, the liberation choirs continued or were revived to perform official *chimurenga* songs at Heroes' Day celebrations and at the funerals of liberation leaders. As the ZANU government increasingly moved towards forming a one-party state, liberation was increasingly represented as a Shona victory, and the ZANLA *chimurenga* songs were celebrated to the detriment of those of the ZIPRA choirs. *Chimurenga* music thus took on multiple contradictory attributes. It could evoke memories of unity in heroic struggle; be adopted as a recreational celebration of peace by urban youth; assist in the rewriting of the outcome of the war as a Shona victory; provide a justification for a more authoritarian style of ZANU rule and for draconian land reform since the 1990s; and serve as a vehicle for political criticism of the regime and evocation of a better future.

States, Political Parties and Cultural Policy

In the lead-up to independence, nationalist leaders of all political stripes were aware of the capacity of popular cultural genres to connect with the 'grass roots'. Kwame Nkrumah formed a concert party to popularise his vision of an independent and progressive Ghana. Thomas Sankara was a popular guitarist before he became a leader and then the first president of independent Upper Volta (now Burkina Faso). Heads of state in Zambia and Mali invited popular Congolese jazz bands to play at their independence day celebrations, in a gesture of populist pan-Africanism. The MPLA, from 1977 onwards, patronised the vigorous and ancient tradition of carnival in Luanda; by fixing it to a date commemorating the liberation of Angola rather than to the church calendar, it attempted to strengthen the weak state by capturing a popular base.

After independence had been won, leaders of new African nations had a number of urgent objectives which popular genres could be made to support: the consolidation of national identity, arbitrarily carved out in diverse, multilingual territories; the promotion of rapid development – education, cash-crop farming, industrialisation; and, not least, the desire to maintain themselves in power. It is the last of these objectives that has perhaps been most noticed outside Africa: President Hastings Kamuzu Banda of Malawi was famous for getting teams of women bussed in from the countryside to sing and dance his praises at every national festival and for every visiting dignitary (Chirambo 2013); Mobutu Sese Seko in Congo/Zaire, one of the most long-lived and successful tyrants (1965–97) in a vast territory that stretched the state's capacity for governance to the breaking point, harnessed the popularity of Congolese rumba (White 2008). He sponsored popular bands, built powerful radio transmitters to beam their recordings out and took Franco, the most popular Congolese musician, on international trips with him. (However, this reportedly backfired on one famous visit to Uganda, when he discovered that the massed crowds awaiting their arrival at Entebbe airport were there to welcome Franco and not him! [Salter 2008].) And dictators had their sycophants among popular musicians. When Idi Amin expelled the Asians from Uganda, he received unqualified support in Christopher Ssebaduka's vitriolic song 'Mali ya Nyoko': 'I will first applaud the liberator, together with those who assisted him. Sir, Dada, thank you for fighting that hard. You will be remembered even by the grandchildren of the fourth generation for chasing the exploitative Indians … They multiply like locusts, deliver every year and sometimes twins. They come as a couple but in ten years they are already a village! They masquerade the towns, sleep in storied houses as we the owners are chased to the villages ... Sir Amin, thank you for fighting hard, thank you for fighting that hard.'

In some ways, post-independence states' interventions in everyday culture took a leaf out of the colonial book. For though the rhetoric of African governments tended to emphasise the cultural repression and censorship exerted by colonial and missionary authorities, and hence the importance of their own nationalist programmes of cultural revitalisation, they shared with their colonial predecessors the idea that government could and should shape popular culture from above in order to achieve changes in public attitudes. Colonial regimes had provided film shows and dance halls in the hope of steering urban crowds towards harmless leisure activities; missionaries had provided reading matter for popular edification; government Literature Bureaus in the 1930s to 1950s offered prizes and publication opportunities for modern African-language fiction, with a view to fostering a realist style consonant with modernisation and 'progress' (an intervention which played its part in the impressive explosion of Hausa, Yoruba, Swahili and other African-language novel-writing: see Furniss 1996, Frederiksen 1994). But for many post-independence governments, the scale and urgency of cultural transformation that they sought to bring about was much greater than for colonial governments.

African leaders were acutely aware of the importance of the media both as an instrument of government-led change – to promote development, education and national unity – and as a potential channel for dissent and rebellion. Military coup-makers' first move was always to seize control of the radio station. Governments therefore kept a tight grip on radio, television (where it existed) and the press, and kept them strongly centralised. But they needed to use these quintessentially modern technologies to construct an 'authentic' national culture drawing on local oral traditions and performance arts. Most African governments thus paid tribute to indigenous cultural heritage and associated its preservation or revival with assertions of national identity. The problem, however, was how to combine this with a commitment to modernisation and development. In many countries, governments paid only symbolic and superficial attention to the role of culture in the life of the nation. A striking exception to this was Tanzania under Julius Nyerere. Cultural issues in Tanzania, not least because Nyerere's Tanganyika (later Tanzania) African National Union government foregrounded them in both theory and practice, have been unusually well studied. We have a rich corpus of studies of popular theatre (Lange 2002; Edmondson 2007), theatre for development (Mlama 1991) and popular music (Askew 2002, Perullo 2011).

One of the achievements of these Tanzanian studies has been to flesh out a detailed and nuanced picture of the intersection of cultural policy and popular cultural production. They move beyond the binary and top-down model that sees national consciousness as being forged by educated elites and spread to the populace via education and print culture, and which posits a one-way march in the direction of 'nation-ness'. In the top-down model, the idea of belonging to a nation not only was exported from Europe to the colonised world, but also was disseminated within the colonised world from the elites to the masses. The Tanzanian case study we look at here focuses rather on the two-way process, often compromised and partial, often hesitant, through which people 'on the ground' in some ways embrace official cultural policy, in some ways subvert or appropriate it and in other ways simply ignore it. The state, in this picture, also has to compromise, adapt to popular tastes, absorb popular perspectives, collaborate and make concessions in order to get a working relationship with enough people to make their policies effectual. By looking at performance as well as print – and at unofficial street print rather than the publications of official publishers – one can see that ideas of national belonging are *also* constituted from the bottom up. Laura Edmondson calls attention to 'the dynamic nature of Tanzanian national performance in which the state borrowed from popular culture and vice versa in an ongoing cycle of shadowing, adaptation, and, indeed, co-creation' (Edmondson 2007:18). The state, like the populace, was improvisatory and creative, and the alternatives are not popular acquiescence versus popular resistance, but a whole spectrum of mutual borrowings and adaptations taking place between policymakers, officials, performers and audiences at many levels.

Tanzanian Music and Cultural Policy

Tanzania is a good example of a state that had a definite conception of the role of culture in nation-building and public enlightenment. The dominant and later sole political party, the Tanzania African National Union, took popular culture seriously and tried to prescribe its functions, recognising and sponsoring some types and denouncing others. However, its views changed and adapted over time. And popular performers and writers also had ideas about the civic and political importance of their art which were subtly different from government policies on culture, education and development.

After Tanganyika's independence in 1961, Nyerere, like many other African leaders, espoused cultural nationalism, promoted the rediscovery of the people's authentic indigenous heritage and rejected what he identified as foreign. Five years later, Nyerere's view of the role of culture was recast: in the Arusha Declaration of 1967, which unveiled Tanzania's programme of African Socialism, culture was given foundational status not as traditional customs for their own sake, but as the embodiment of an indigenous spirit of cooperation, which was named *ujamaa*.

Pride of place among cultural forms was *ngoma*, the word for any performance involving drum, music and dance of a 'traditional' type (including Beni, despite its relative modernity). Distinctive local forms of *ngoma* were associated with all of Tanzania's more than 100 ethnic groups. These genres had been suppressed by missionaries and colonial authorities and were therefore associated with anti-colonial struggle and resistance. And *ngoma* performers had indeed formed networks which enabled them to communicate across ethnic boundaries, and had been able to encode subversive messages undetectable by the colonial eye. So after 1961, *ngoma* was taken up and championed by the government as an assertion of national culture. This led, as in many African countries, to the creation of a composite mosaic representation of national culture. While seeking to be inclusive, the policy of representing each cultural area or ethnic-linguistic group by its 'typical' music and dances was based on an idea of equivalence of forms: every 'tribe' had to have its 'own' distinctive *ngoma*, but each had to occupy the same kind of slot in the overall picture. Picking particular styles of music and dance to represent each group led to a schematic and selective emphasis on a few key characteristics that differentiated them from the others and, at the same time, proclaimed their parallel and equivalent roles. But in order to transcend ethnic divisions and promote a shared national culture, state-sponsored *ngoma* groups were also supposed to learn how to perform the dances and music of other ethnic groups. This led to further homogenisation and stereotyping. Such efforts were sponsored and subsidised by the Ministry of Culture, but not very effectively. Although the performances were supposed to be national and to deliver progressive messages, the performing groups often stuck to older patterns of inter-group rivalry, caricaturing one another's ethnic characteristics.

A second form, extremely popular but disapproved of by the government, was *dansi*. Derived from Western social dancing, it was seen as urban, modern and the prerogative of the aspiring classes. In the 1920s and '30s, *dansi* music had accompanied ballroom dancing by the educated Christian elite. After the Second World War, it was popularised, absorbed massive influences from Congolese rumba and became a syncretic guitar-based dance music played in urban halls across Tanganyika. Participants embraced *dansi* to demonstrate their 'civilisation' and cosmopolitan modernity. But more traditionally minded people felt it opened the door to drunkenness and loose behaviour on the dance floor. In a poetic debate in the Swahili-language monthly paper *Mambo Leo* in 1953, one contributor wrote, 'Dansi is a worthless dance ... a dance for loafers, you can't see respectable people dancing ... Into the dance-floor, showing off your thigh / With alcohol and beer in your head, you feel in paradise / Dansi is a worthless dance, to the wise,' while another countered with 'Dansi is a modern dance, its origins in Europe / Just imported here, to be danced in Africa too / So that Tabora and Pangani residents can embrace each other / Dansi is a pleasurable dance, and it's absolutely attractive' (Suriano 2011:45). Both sides thus saw *dansi* as thoroughly non-indigenous. Though the lyrics at times articulated political positions, after independence, *dansi* was not recognised by the Ministry of Culture, because it was 'foreign'.

A third major form, also initially frowned upon by the Nyerere government, was *taarab*. This was a poetic and musical genre of coastal origin. In Zanzibar, it was played by male orchestras and sung in Arabic, and it adhered closely to the elaborate metrical and rhyme schemes of its Egyptian model. But in the 1920s, Siti binti Saad, a woman singer of slave origin, had appropriated the genre, composed lyrics in Swahili and gradually infused into it the rhythms of women's local *ngoma* on the mainland. Women's *taarab* clubs sprang up, and Tanga, on the mainland, became a centre of diffusion for the new style. Throughout this process of popularisation, the singers retained the hallmarks of the genre: its personal and romantic themes, its stanzaic and metrical complexity and its highly allusive, metaphorical style. The lyrics sometimes functioned as veiled criticism and sometimes as a mode of dispute resolution. It developed into 'a quietly oppositional form that by its mere existence celebrated the cosmopolitan,

FIGURE 12 Siti binti Saad.

mercantile Swahili coastal region that was largely excluded from dominant renderings of the nation' (Askew 2000:37). If the 'traditional African values' that were supposed to underpin *ujamaa* were the hard work and cooperation of rural farming communities, there was no place for the syncretic, urban *taarab* genre, and, like *dansi*, it was classified by government agencies as 'foreign music'. But *taarab* was so popular that it found its way into government-sponsored events nonetheless. It became the most popular item in the variety shows that spread in the 1980s. Performed by troupes initially established and sponsored by parastatals, these shows – which could last a whole afternoon at weekends – included skits, short plays, comic monologues, *ngoma* dancing, singing, conjuring tricks and even acrobatics learned from China in accord with Tanzania's political affiliations. But it was *taarab* that drew the crowds, so to keep audiences in their seats, the troupes had to put the biggest *taarab* stars last in the programme; once they had performed, the audience would leave (Lange 2000).

FIGURE 13 Taarab singer Fatuma Kisauji with Babloom Modern Taarab, Tanzania. Courtesy Kelly M. Askew, *Performing the Nation* (2002).

Eventually, *taarab* was even played at state events such as dinners for dignitaries.

Kelly Askew's *Performing the Nation* explores with great subtlety the interaction of central government policy, local officials' implementation of the policy and performers' responses to popular music genres in Tanzania, tracing the cultural life of these three main musical genres in Tanzanian colonial and post-independence eras. Her argument is that ideological contestation and change was not carried out purely at the level of policy and propaganda, new national ideologies were not simply invented by elites and passed down intact to the population and the sense of national belonging that emerged was not homogeneous. Rather, ideology was negotiated at the interface (always porous) between the state and the people. At this interface we find local petty government officials – cultural officers without resources – sitting in their empty offices, and visiting dignitaries treated to musical performances that the state ideology did not approve of. And she shows that these negotiations happened not only through words, but through modes of organisation (*ngoma* networks), symbolic lifestyle affirmations (*dansi*) and indirect and non-verbal as well as veiled verbal gestures (*taarab*). All of these effects arise from the act of performance. Music in all these genres is political.

Conclusion

The focus of this chapter has been on the role of popular culture, and especially song, in contestations between the crowd and the state. Though apparently amorphous, both urban and rural populations had an unnerving capacity to act together and to manage their protests 'from below'. Both colonial and post-independence governments feared the moments when the heterogeneous populace coalesced into a determined mob. Such protests were often assembled out of congeries of disparate participants with different agendas – trade unionists, the urban poor, women, intermediate strata whose privileges were under threat – so that their ability to forge a permanent common agenda was limited. Nonetheless, the flashpoints of collective action had a lasting effect, by showing what was possible and by engraving this in popular memory. The songs that so often ran through popular uprisings were not only a unifying rallying cry for action at the time, but also its mnemonic later on. When people recalled the struggle, they often did so by remembering the songs. And in this way, the song could become the focus of a renewal of the struggle.

After independence, nationalist leaders in many cases disowned the popular groups that had supported them and deliberately blocked their capacity for formal organisation. But neither colonial nor post-independence states were fully able to harness popular culture to their policy objectives. They saw the power of popular genres and tried to utilise them to promote development and modernisation, forge a sense of national belonging transcending regional and ethno-linguistic differences and consolidate their own authority. But policies did not always yield the anticipated results. Most states' attempts to construct a pan-ethnic mosaic of traditional cultural elements resulted in the evacuation of local particularity and meaning and the reduction of 'traditional dances' to token showpieces. The state's interventions, however well-intentioned, always changed what they sought to preserve.

And as the example of Tanzania showed, even those states that had a well-developed cultural policy of active sponsorship and intervention could not entirely direct popular taste. People on the ground – including the local intermediaries appointed by central government to push cultural policy among the local population – interpreted cultural initiatives and emphases in their own way. They seized upon genres like *dansi* and *taarab*, which originated as elite 'foreign' forms, and popularised them; government disapproval made no difference, and eventually government policy had to bow to popular taste or appropriate popular forms for their own purposes. In the meantime, people went on working with what cultural resources they had at their disposal, preserving some elements, adapting others, generating new ones, borrowing from here and there. Official cultural policy rarely got right into the generative sites where new things were continually being created – in the bar, on the street, in church. Though African governments' efforts to foster a sense of national belonging often took the form of the creation of a national dance troupe or the staging of huge spectacles showcasing traditional arts from every region, local populations often had other ways of forging common identities. In Angola, for example, during the liberation struggle against Portugal, popular syncretic dance music provided an autonomous space outside the formal political domain where Angolans could come together and imagine the nation through its very cosmopolitanism (looking *beyond* the Portuguese right-wing state to other, alternative political dispositions). 'Music was where the nation was imagined and even lived' (Moorman 2008:7). The long civil war that followed independence in 1975 left a vacuum in state control, with the MPLA leadership, based outside the country, attempting to instil in its followers a sense of national allegiance based on shared commitment to a progressive ideology. But Marissa Moorman argues that this effort at shaping national consciousness fell on stony ground. What people liked was the cosmopolitan sound of popular dance music, as they gathered around the radio or came together in urban halls in the mixed, multi-ethnic shanty towns where 80 per cent of residents were first-generation migrants. This newness and heterogeneity, this capacity to work out a modus vivendi and forge a sense of commonality with people of varied backgrounds through participation in shared musical tastes, was how a sense of being Angolan grew up. A top-down call to pay homage to the idea of the nation was ignored: 'nation-ness' emerged from the bottom up.

Clearly, direct interaction between state and populace constitutes only a small fraction of the ways in which popular culture can be said to be political. Religious movements, drawing on and creating rich performance repertoires, often seek to establish an alternative to the state and to define personal and social objectives in different ways from government policy. Popular moralising, articulated in fiction, drama and songs, often understands the source of societal ills as ultimately resting with individual personal morality, especially sexual morality: the body politic is rotten because men and women exploit and betray one another in their everyday lives. In very repressive situations, popular culture does not need to protest or put criticism into words to keep open a small space, a 'moment of freedom' (Fabian 1998): the act of creating something is in itself an assertion of the capacity for self-realisation on terms other than those prescribed by the dominant power. If culture is a weapon of struggle, as the ANC's Cultural Desk affirmed at the height of the struggle against apartheid in the 1970s and '80s, it is not always a weapon brandished on the battlefield in face-to-face combat. People in intensely difficult circumstances were making what sense they could of their situation, often compromising, often ideologically inconsistent – but by writing, singing, joking, by creating at all, they were affirming their humanity and their capacity to be a source of new things.

CHAPTER 6

The Media: Globalisation and Deregulation from the 1990s Till Today

Since the early 1990s, there has been a surge of new research and writing on African popular culture, mostly focusing on mediatised forms. This was no accident. It coincided with a transformation in African popular culture brought about by economic and political liberalisation, deregulation of state-owned media and the increasing availability of digital media technology which could be operated by individuals – bypassing the state and creating networks of transmission with audiences or consumers locally and around the world. Various forms of African popular culture became available and understandable to audiences outside the continent as never before, drawing on internationally circulating imagery, using familiar formats and accessible online. At the same time, the intuition that in Africa imported forms were being transmuted into something different – that the global was being appropriated to express distinctive local understandings of experience – inspired many researchers to document and explore what was being said in the new genres made possible by the media.

As we have seen in previous chapters, it is not the case that the media is something new in Africa, an alien technology that entered the scene and had a major 'impact' on local culture only in the last few decades. Successive generations of media technology have been thoroughly assimilated into much local cultural production in Africa for more than a century. They are not generally seen by local users as external and foreign. When new genres were created in response to new experiences – of schooling, conversion, urbanisation, migrant labour, national and local politics – most of them drew on ideas

130

from the media, or were boosted by media broadcasting, or incorporated elements of media technology into their live oral and performance modes. This started with print, from the mid-nineteenth century; then photography, film and gramophone from the late nineteenth and early twentieth centuries; radio, from the 1930s onwards; television, from the 60s; audio cassette recordings in the '70s; and video recordings in the '80s. In Nigeria, the live, improvised drama of the Yoruba popular theatre drew on print fiction as well as oral narratives as a source of plot and theme, and passed back into print when plays were photographed for presentation in 'photoplay' magazines (Barber 2000). In Mali, music was shaped by the possibilities of electronic amplification, which created spaces for new categories of performer, and by radio broadcasting, which involved addressing, and thus constituting, new audiences that were of a scale, scope and nature not previously encountered (Diawara 1997). Even within the severe constraints of apartheid, which shaped South African media until the 1990s, the creators of African-language radio programmes found ways to give voice to everyday popular concerns, as Zulu radio drama demonstrates (Gunner 2011). Across the continent, popular painting was stimulated by portrait photography, film posters, advertisements and magazines to explore new ways of representing the world with 'realistic' two-dimensionality. Popular painters of the Democratic Republic of Congo not only use photos from magazines as a starting point when creating images, they also keep albums of photographs of their own past work for prospective customers to select models from (Jewsiewicki 1997).

Nor is it the case that the 'alternative worlds' represented by the media have only become significant in the last few decades, as is sometimes thought. As we have seen, people have avidly consumed or dreamed about the styles of life evoked in American and European written literature, film and recorded music since the early years of the twentieth century. Jesse Weaver Shipley draws attention to the antecedents of 'hiplife' – a combination of highlife and hip-hop – which is merely the last in a century-long rapport during which 'black diasporic popular culture has had a particularly potent influence on Ghanaian aesthetics' (Shipley 2013:4). The intense extraversion of South African township culture, which we looked at in Chapter 3, is another vivid example. In the context of incipient apartheid and homelands policies, the youth of Sophiatown rejected anything 'tribal' or 'traditional': 'Give us jazz and film stars, man! We want Duke

Ellington, Satchmo, and hot dames! Yes brother, anything American' (Nixon 1994:11). To a lesser extent, 'cosmopolitan' styles, drawn especially from African American popular mediatised culture, were popular all over Africa in the run-up to decolonisation after the Second World War, as a wave of optimism and the prospect of new opportunities opened up.

So media are not new in Africa. Nonetheless, there has been a step change in the way much popular culture has been produced, circulated and consumed since the early 1990s. Deregulated, privatised media and new personal media technologies have eroded the boundaries between public and private space and given people a new platform, new ways of reaching new kinds of audiences and new means of expression. The digital revolution has also made foreign, imported media products both more easily accessible to African people and less easy to disentangle from home-made cultural forms. The possibilities of freer access to media space and opportunities for lavish cultural appropriation excited many people but alarmed others, who feared that distinctive, much-valued oral and live performance traditions would be superseded by shallow, standardised clones of global trash. The new wave of research on media and popular culture in Africa, which focuses overwhelmingly on the period beginning around 1990, has recognised, and is insightfully exploring, what amounts to a new and intensely active era in popular culture's history.

In this chapter, we look at the new forms of popular culture that the transformation in the media landscape has enabled. But we also counteract the suggestion that all popular culture in Africa is now the same thing as media culture. Even today, this is far from being true. Media formats may stimulate new live forms of storytelling, jokes and song; conversely, much of what gets 'into' the locally produced media comes from street talk, stories, jokes and adaptations of oral traditions. There are also many performance genres that are only marginally entangled with media, if at all. The generative approach taken by this book makes it essential to look beyond media formats to see the everyday creativity that feeds them.

African Cities in the Neoliberal Era

Structural adjustment policies imposed on African countries from the mid-1980s onwards combined an emphasis on democratisation with an insistence on privatisation, massive cuts in state provision and the relaxation of import controls. At the heart of these policies was a faith in the power of the 'free' market to solve all problems, combined with a belief that the political counterpart to the free market was the 'free' society, in the form of multiparty electoral democracy and liberal conceptions of individual civil and political rights. The economic consequences were devastating. The political consequences, though uneven and frequently hijacked by powerful vested interests, were generally cautiously welcomed, not least by activists who had been campaigning, often at risk of their lives, for the elimination of military dictatorships, civilian one-party states and presidents for life.

All this took place in the general context of globalisation: the speeding up of transport and communications, so that time and space appeared to shrink; the deterritorialisation of both industrial production and international finance, as manufacturers took advantage of concentrations of cheap labour or specialist skills and capital took flight to wherever conditions were most favourable; and the extensive commoditisation of culture, lifestyle and ideas. One of the stated aims of the IMF and World Bank policies was to integrate 'emerging' or 'developing' economies into this global system of mobile interconnectedness.

In reality, the movement of information and goods has been highly uneven and unequal, and globalisation has been patchy. James Ferguson depicts Africa in terms of a number of hot spots of communication, plugged into worldwide circuits but surrounded by deserts of poor infrastructure and slow communications (Ferguson 2006). In Brad Weiss's Tanzanian example, youth are connected to global imagery but unable to buy global cultural goods, producing a frustrating experience of simultaneous inclusion and exclusion (Weiss 2009). Within cities, wealthy walled enclaves with generators, satellite dishes and tarmacked access roads are surrounded by miles of unplanned, impoverished squatter settlements without basic amenities. Some aspects of the communications revolution are proceeding at breakneck speed, while others remain sluggish: smartphones are spreading like wildfire, and the proliferation of satellite and digital technologies has given viewers access to a vastly expanded range of television programmes from within and beyond the continent, yet only about one-third of the African population today has access to grid electricity, the basis of most civic and industrial development. Most residential areas have neither pipe-borne water nor adequate waste-disposal systems.

As Francis Nyamnjoh puts it, 'Silent majorities in villages and urban ghettoes are still groping in the dark, seeking footpaths and footholds in the era of satellite television, digital revolutions and the information superhighway' (Nyamnjoh 2005:4).

Structural adjustment forced African governments to sell off public assets and cut back their investment in social provision – education, hospitals, water, electricity and housing. This resulted in a loss of jobs and a drastic reduction in living standards and life chances for most of the population. It forced governments to lift the trade tariffs that had been designed to foster local manufacturing, and to open their doors to foreign goods; the result was the shrinking of local production and a further loss of jobs. Agriculture declined and increasing numbers of people migrated to the cities, so that massive new population influxes coincided with the massive reductions in jobs and services. The results were widespread unemployment and underemployment, casualization of the labour force, rising prices, falling wages, greater inequality and the rapid expansion of peri-urban shanty towns without sanitation or services. Structural adjustment became the target of bitter jokes. In Ghana, people said that they were wearing 'Rawlings's chains' when their collarbones and spines began to stick out from hunger; in Sierra Leone, they quipped 'OAU for you, IOU for me' when structural adjustment drove them into debt.

These were conditions where people had to eke out a living through a combination of hustling, entrepreneurship and legal and illegal services. In most African cities by the start of the twenty-first century, 75 per cent of basic needs were provided informally, and the informal sector absorbed at least half of the urban workforce (Simone 2004:6). Even in South Africa, where the newly democratic post-1994 state combined neoliberal market economics with strong state intervention in an attempt to provide welfare, housing and work opportunities to the black population (James 2015), the informal economy has grown exponentially and the state is unable to ensure that basic needs are met. In other African countries, migrants to cities often saw them as staging posts in longer-range migration aiming at Europe or the more economically buoyant regions of Africa, above all South Africa. But most would-be migrants' escape is blocked and they remain, constantly planning, perpetually striving to find the money and the contacts to make another attempt (Andersson 2014), or imagining 'elsewheres' whose outlines are superimposed on the flimsy provisional here and now (Malaquais 2007).

A vibrant scholarly literature on the culture of the African city post–structural adjustment explains that to thrive, or even to survive, requires a desperate inventiveness, a willingness to combine different repertoires of skills and seize on any little opening that presents itself. Social smartness and a flair for self-presentation increase a person's chances and can become ends in themselves. The fluid urban population of entrepreneurs generates a culture of the street in which economic survival and cultural ingenuity are inseparable. In Dakar, where 65 per cent of the population is under thirty years of age and more than 40 per cent are unemployed or underemployed, the youth invest immense energy into procuring fashionable clothing, which may be rented, borrowed, bought on credit, bought with others, swapped, shared or stolen – as long as they have the appurtenances to make their status as successful entrepreneurs credible. Style – expressed through dress, music and language – is both means and end: simultaneously an economic pursuit, a tool for self-advancement and an expressive creation (Scheld 2007). In Abidjan, 'bluffing' – pretending to be wealthier or better connected than one really is, in order to impress members of the opposite sex and thus extract money and status from them – is the norm in relations between young people. It is a 'mimetic performance of modern urban identity' that 'collapses oppositions between appearance and reality' (Sasha Newell 2009:379) – a kind of drama where both parties are aware of the artifice, and yet continue to perform. Numerous popular songs and plays in West Africa are built around the theme of the fake lover who is only pretending to be rich, or the fake preacher whose immaculate white robes disguise a confidence trickster or thief. Urban hustling, especially by youths who feel themselves to have been abandoned by their elders and put in a position of having to survive on their wits, often crosses the border between legitimate entrepreneurship and theft, deception, fakery or violent crime.

Recent studies evoke a world where the dissolution of boundaries between appearance and reality is experienced as all-encompassing. Nothing is what it seems: 'Fraudulent identity cards; fake policemen dressed in official uniform; army troops complicit with gangs of thieves and bandits; forged enrolment for exams … There is hardly a reality without its double. Hence acting efficaciously requires that one carefully cultivate an extraordinary capacity to be simultaneously inside and outside, for and against, and to constantly introduce changes in the reading and usage of things, playing, in this way, with the structures and apparatuses' (Mbembe and Roitman 2002:114–15). These

FIGURE 14 Cityscape mural by Cheri Cherin, in a bar in Kisangani, Kinshasa, 1983. Courtesy Katrien Pype.

terms (being simultaneously inside and outside, constantly introdu-cing changes, playing) evoke the alert creativity needed to get by in the phantasmagorical city. It can be a dangerous doubling: the Kenyan film *Nairobi Half Life* (2012) strikingly captures the mental split and sense of unreality experienced by an impoverished, bewildered but smart migrant to the city, who is forced to become a member of a gang of car thieves and simultaneously realises his dream of becoming an actor by getting a role in an elite drama production. In rehearsal, he confides to a fellow actor, 'It seems confusing, this strange double life. It seems like I am two different people every day.' (The fellow actor, misunderstanding, breathes, 'I know what you mean', and tries to grope him!)

Whether or not people living their daily lives in such cities really experience them as being so continuously and dramatically fluid and uncertain, what is striking is the efforts they make to fix and stabilise them. Imagination and will are called up to create order out of noth-ing. Born-again Christians pray with relentless, incessant energy to fix positive outcomes for a myriad of undertakings. In Kinshasa, street boys carefully create domestic spaces out of stretches of pavement or vacant lots, dividing their patches into parlours and kitchens and maintaining their invisible compartments (Geenen 2009). Deceptive and chimerical as the city may be, people find ways to operate in it. What people may name as 'confusion' is an environment constructed by innumerable imperceptible operations as they trace routes, form links and find or create usable form out of the apparently inchoate (Guyer 2015).

We should not romanticise the creative side of survival in the modern African city. The relentless stream of everyday obstacles and indignities encountered by the poor can generate outrage, despair and even individual or collective violence. Improvising does require imagination, but as Simone observes, the city is also a place where 'enormous creative energies have been ignored, squandered, and left unused' (2004: 2). The present-day African city is a place of luxury and excess jammed up against dire want. The big man in his gold-plated Mercedes may squander thousands of dollars on Champagne, but the real and tragic waste is the waste of human potential and human talent among the poor. The aspirations of millions of young people to shoulder family and communal responsibilities, and to build a life through productive hard work, are thwarted by a prolonged con-dition of 'waithood'. Without work or prospects of any kind, they are condemned to a long-drawn-out life in limbo (Honwana and De Boeck 2005; Masquelier 2013). Nonetheless, people do figure out how to get by ('When banks collapse in Africa, citizens figure out new modes of banking. When institutions of governance or justice are in crisis, citizens find detours around them' [Gikandi 2010:xiv]), and in the process people fashion new subjectivities and new means to express them. Hard times may stimulate invention.

Media Deregulation and the Digital Age

In the early 1990s, the combination of economic privatisation and political liberalisation made deregulation of the media inevitable. Constitutional changes across the subcontinent paved the way for a wave of new private newspapers, radio stations and television stations run by local and international commercial interests, religious groups, politicians and NGOs. Though state-owned media outlets continued to exist, they were eclipsed in both numbers and popularity by private stations and publications.

Deregulation of formerly state-owned 'big' media in the 1990s was followed by the increasing availability of 'small' digital media technology in the 2000s, which individuals could buy and operate without licences or state controls. Mobile phones transformed interpersonal communication. Smartphones and laptops not only opened up access to the Internet, but made it possible for people to make audio and video recordings for themselves and then post them on the Internet or pass them along to television or music producers. Internet cafes opened in every city to cater to people without the means to buy laptops. Digital beat-making and recording technologies which could be operated by a solo music producer in a small room led to the emergence of a host of competing music-production studios catering to a host of young, aspiring musicians.

Deregulated 'big' media was intertwined with the new 'small' media, each depending on the other for its impact. The result was to give a much wider range of people access to public space on their own terms – or nearer to their own terms – than had previously been permitted.

Radio is a central example. It took off spectacularly after privatisation: by the end of the first decade of the twenty-first century, some African countries had more than 100 radio stations on air. With privatisation came new formats, oriented more to entertainment and engagement with listeners and less to the dissemination of public information, education and nation-building promoted by the state-owned media. In both Kenya and Ghana, new FM radio stations introduced a new, loose-jointed and accommodating structure: a daily 'breakfast show' running for several hours, anchored by a presenter who brought in all kinds of items, including music, news, panel discussions of political topics, comic skits, advertisements, traffic updates and conversations with invited guests in a freely flowing assemblage. As Sika Ahadzie has noted, it was impossible to ascertain the timetable for the segments that made up the assemblage – either it was not published, or the published times were not adhered to. Instead, you just had to tune in and see what came up (Ahadzie 2007). The key component in this potpourri of programmes was the talk show and phone-in segment. Listeners piled up to call in on their mobiles, often with long discourses to deliver, and presenters anxious to accommodate them all would often run over the notional time allotted for the segment. This freewheeling interactivity was deliberately highlighted, and the monologic authority associated with official state media presenters was sub-verted. In Kenya, Kiss FM introduced a fictitious joker character who never reveals his true identity but asks ignorant questions and disagrees with everything his partner, the serious presenter, says. Then callers are asked to phone in and take sides. Easy FM went further, sending the joker character out into the street to canvass opinions from passers-by, who would be unaware they were on the air. Thus, Christopher Odhiambo argues, the audience became the main performers, adjudicating between two playfully opposed opinions and adding their own (Odhiambo 2011).

In Ghana, private radio immediately opened itself to the language of the street, characterised by slang and continual code switching and linguistic mixing of English, Akan and other Ghanaian languages. Presenters translated English-language news items for the benefit of listeners, and callers phoning in spoke in everyday registers, which in the past had been rigorously excluded by the state-run GBC. Disguised, ambiguous language became a central trope in several popular programmes. Radio Gold's *'Konkonsa'* ('Gossip') featured a narrator who strenuously tried to make listeners believe that everything he said was well-researched and factually correct, whereas listeners knew that the word *konkonsa* implies untruths. Their 'Good Morning Mr President' was a fifteen-minute monologue by a drunkard character who, in his inebriation, is bold enough to admonish the president of Ghana. Adom FM ran 'The Diaries of Mr Chu', in which 'Mr Chu' reads his diary in fake Chinese and the presenter asks him questions about it and then 'translates' the answers for listeners. The disguise in both, as drunkard and Chinese man, provides a kind of licence – it is not the presenter or any identifiable real person speaking (Ahadzie 2007).

The fascination with translation, mediation and the borderland between fiction and deception is very striking. In both the Kenyan and Ghanaian programmes, authority is questioned through clowning and impersonation, which invades the space of topical political and social discussion previously controlled by monologic representatives of government. There seems to be a joy in destabilising the hierarchy and even the fundamental order of the radio format (as when panellists on one discussion programme in Ghana came to blows and the panel ended in disarray). The much-described uncertainty, precariousness and unpredictability of modern urban Africa therefore do not seem to be experienced as an entirely negative condition; in Kenyan and Ghanaian radio, at least, both presenters and listeners seem to take great pleasure in making an art of the fakery, ambiguity and undecidability that scholars have depicted as so pervasive in modern urban life in Africa.

Media deregulation and privatisation had political consequences. Politicians listened to public views expressed through phone-ins and sometimes responded. Listeners' opinions expressed on the Kenyan programmes described by Odhiambo had an impact on government policy on more than one occasion (Odhiambo 2011). Political leaders gained from the opportunity to display tolerance and responsiveness. In Kinshasa, Katrien Pype tells us, a television programme focusing on complaints generated by ordinary citizens plays a central role in legitimising the rule of Joseph Kabila, unpopular in the city for his perceived remoteness from citizens' concerns. The Journal Télévisé en Lingala Facile, hosted by Zacharie Babasawa, was created at the invitation of Joseph Kabila himself, but only after Babasawa had a previous programme shut down for its outspoken criticisms of politicians in the local argot, Hindubill. The new programme, in everyday Lingala, Kinshasa's lingua franca, was built around the 'proximity report', in which citizens would draw attention to problems in their neighbourhoods – lack of electricity and running water, a fire, lethal road accidents, potholes in the road, an outbreak of thefts and so on. Testifiers would speak emotionally to the camera and would exhort the president or other agents of the state to fix the problems. And the president made sure that his generous response was also filmed and broadcast. Soon, local residents began summoning JT Lingala Facile to document their problems and began to do their own documentation with smartphones or digital cameras, which they handed over to the producers for inclusion in the programme. Thus the increased access to public space, in this instance, worked both ways: people sent their complaints to the programme because they believed that the president and his wife watched it and were moved by the suffering it showed, and often they did get redress; the president, conversely, got positive publicity as a caring head of state without having to institute citywide or nationwide programmes of reform (Pype 2011). Here we see media brokering a reciprocal obligation of responsibility between the state and the citizens – an idea developed by Harri Englund in his study of a Chichewa-language radio programme in Malawi (Englund 2011). But liberalisation did not necessarily mean liberation: privatised media could represent reactionary international commercial

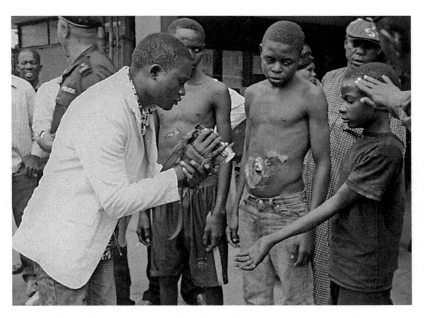

FIGURE 15 Reporter from JT Lingala Facile documenting a complaint in Kinshasa. Courtesy Katrien Pype.

and political interests, local ethnic and religious intolerance, and abusive 'hate' journalism (Nyamnjoh 2005).

If the state's capacity to regulate and censor the 'big' technologies of radio, television and the national press was weakened, though not eliminated, by privatisation in the 1990s, its capacity to regulate small-scale technologies that could be operated by individuals or small groups at relatively low cost was almost non-existent from the start. Digital music technology made it possible for local studios not only to mix and record high-quality sound, but also to print CDs and DVDs for a mass market at low cost and high speed. Even less investment was needed to save a musical performance on a memory stick and distribute it through social media – a way of gaining popular recognition, albeit without immediate financial returns. Piracy was easy and rife, but while it threatened musicians' rights, it also speeded up dissemination of their work. It was a free-for-all, with numerous small outfits competing and experimenting with formats and styles; these opportunities stimulated and provided accommodation for a host of new entrants to the commercial music scene (Shipley 2013).

And small-scale personal technology gave access to the huge, amorphous, transnational domain of the Internet, which no national entity has succeeded in controlling anywhere in the world. The domain of the unregulatable became increasingly central to popular culture as more and more people became connected. Early Internet users had to set aside time and money to visit Internet cafes in the city, but after 2000, more and more people acquired smartphones and could access the Internet instantly via mobile phone networks as they walked along the street and went about everyday life. This ease of access meant that participants could launch and elaborate on cultural tropes collectively through informal, instant exchanges. In Kenya, according to Dina Ligaga, this played a major role in further disrupting the highly politicised media space previously controlled by the Moi regime (which, despite the introduction of nominal multiparty democracy in 1992, remained in place until Moi was finally voted out of office in 2002) (Ligaga 2012:4). While the interactive programming of private FM radio stations had, as we have seen, already questioned the authority of state-owned broadcasting, it was still the case that radio and television were under the editorial control of the broadcasting professionals. The Internet, by contrast, was virtually uncontrolled. This, Ligaga states, 'destabilised the information infrastructure that had been built around the nation-state, creating a space for categories that before had been "floating" in private and individualised sites, uncategorised, unacknowledged, and therefore easily dismissed' (ibid.). Internet space, simultaneously public and uncontrolled, allowed the oral-based creativity of the street to be audible in virtual space, in discussion forums, blogs and chat-room dialogues, and take up a place alongside formal and authoritative written texts. Anonymity lifted the fear of censorship, online moderators were lax and discussion 'traversed boundaries and borders, constructing a new Kenyan diasporic public' – a diaspora both outside and within Kenya. As an example, Ligaga describes the phenomenon of Makmende, an imaginary Kenyan hyper-masculine superhero introduced in a music video by a Kenyan band, and then taken up by Internet users as the peg for a whole stream of Makmende quips revolving around his invincibility: 'After eating garlic Makmende doesn't smell like garlic but garlic smells like Makmende ... Makmende can look at your photo and know you are lying ... Nobody knows what would happen if Chuck Norris and Makmende met, but one thing is for sure: Makmende would still be

FIGURE 16 Makmende cartoon. Courtesy Victor Ndula.

standing ... Always look before you leap. Unless Makmende is chasing you. Then you had better just jump' (Ligaga 2012:5). Makmende has a counterpart in Nigeria: Akpos, a folkloric trickster-hustler who appears in a Nigerian-built phone app called Akpos Jokes (Yeku 2016). Akpos jokes poke subversive fun at Nigeria's politicians and offer a 'humorous interpretation of social life in Nigeria':

> Three prominent politicians in Nigeria boarded the same flight from Abuja to Lagos.
> The first Politician started, "I can throw one N1000 note down and make one person laugh [i.e. make him/her happy]."
> "I can make two persons laugh with just two N500 notes," the second politician replied.
> The third politician retorted, "With just five pieces of N200 notes, I can make five people laugh."
> The pilot then looked at the politicians and added, "I'm the pilot here, meaning I can throw all of you down and make more than 150 million Nigerians laugh."

Much more extensive narrative genres were also launched on the Internet. In Tanzania, the media entrepreneur Eric Shigongo serialises his own Swahili epic novels in his five weekly tabloids, while a group of young authors have set up Kona ya Riwaya (The Novel Corner) on Facebook to overcome distribution problems: they post three episodes per day but do not complete any novel, instead providing readers with a mail-order contact to buy the printed book (Reuster-Jahn 2016). A fascinating example of online fiction from Lagos is 'Chronicles of a Runs Girl', revisiting the long-established theme of the urban African good-time girl attempting to exploit rich men but often ending up exploited herself. The 'Chronicles' are a continuous first-person narrative in the voice of a university student trying to stay afloat in a competitive and materialistic world. Running to twenty-nine episodes, the narrative is hilarious, touching, gripping and – unlike its much earlier print precursor, *The Life-story of Me, Ṣẹgilọla* (Barber 2012) – furnished with a romantic happy ending.

The rapid adoption and spread of these technologies did more than provide local cultural producers with new means of production and dissemination. It created a new environment where more people felt empowered to use innovative tools of artistic creation, more people had entry into a segment of public space, the public and official was no longer clearly distinct from the private and unofficial, and local, national African and international spaces overlapped and interacted. It altered the relation of local cultural artefacts to global ones. If you go to a video rental store in Lagos, you will see on the same shelf, or adjacent shelves, Hollywood, Bollywood and Nollywood, the World Cup final, Rihanna and Youssou N'Dour. They are produced in the same technical format and are inserted into the same slot in the VCR or DVD player. If you go online in Birmingham, Benares or Banjoul, you can get African music performances and video dramas on YouTube, blogs, Facebook pages, streamed evangelical services and today's daily newspapers from numerous African countries. Ease of access and relations of equivalence foster the sense that African popular culture is globally connected and intertranslatable.

The new technologies also, conversely, brought within reach of African cultural producers a vastly expanded range of globally circulating imagery which they could 'remediate' – appropriate, adapt and recontextualise at will. In a dazzling series of ethnographic snapshots across the continent, Matthias Krings has shown the enormous variety of ways in which 'copies' of global cultural forms are transformed so as to generate new meanings: images of the Titanic, for example, inspired by the blockbuster Hollywood film but fragmented into a greeting card in Kenya, transmuted into a pictorial romance novella in

Tanzania and referenced in a Congolese popular song to describe the triumph of one band over another (Krings 2015).

Multidirectional connections at negligible cost made possible new forms of political mobilisation and commentary – both to incite hatred and to call for moderation, as happened in the Kenyan election crisis of 2007–8, when blogs and mass Short Message Service (SMS) tools were used both to stir up ethnic antagonisms and to appeal to Kenyans to declare 'I Have No Tribe … I am Kenyan' (Goldstein and Rotich 2010). But the networked spaces opened up by social media were never neutral. The technology itself is shaped by multinational corporations with vested interests. The media space in which ordinary people can have their say is a space colonised by commercial-, political-, religious- and development-oriented motives (Nyamnjoh 2005).

Many NGOs began to intervene in cultural production more actively than before. Learning from past failures, they adopted an approach in which participation in expressive forms became a means to win hearts and minds. Building on a longer history of Theatre for Development, NGOs began to sponsor live and mediatised shows and music groups, and delivering their messages became an opportunity for unemployed youth. The role of NGOs in Africa was heightened further by the worldwide HIV/AIDS pandemic. A rich case study is Fraser McNeill's description of an educational project on AIDS in Limpopo Province in the far north-east of South Africa (McNeill 2011). It describes how NGOs trained 600 young women to serve as peer group educators. They were given basic biomedical instruction and encouraged to compose songs exhorting the use of condoms, drawing on existing musical repertoires including ANC struggle songs, church hymns, beer-drinking songs and the rich Venda traditional music. McNeill concludes that the campaign failed to achieve its educational goal, but hundreds of young women got some work experience, gained some status and contacts, and in the process engaged in a novel form of musical creativity.

Pentecostal churches were among the most ambitious providers of alternative structures where the state was lacking. Seeking to constitute new communities based on faith rather than family or place of origin, and built around charismatic pastors, long sojourns in faith villages and participation in mass services and vigils, Pentecostal churches were extremely dynamic innovators in media and popular culture production. They exploited the possibilities of desktop publishing to produce pamphlets and tracts, often written in the slick style of American televangelists. They videorecorded their services and broadcast them globally. They made gospel songs and other Christian-inspired music genres so popular that musicians who had previously made their names in secular social and recreational music took them up. Pentecostal groups bought up television airtime and created channels devoted to sermons and services. In Kinshasa, evangelical groups assumed the role of public educator, organising and sponsoring all the most successful drama troupes which performed live and on television (Pype 2012).

But evangelical churches were not the only religious organisations seeking to take over the cultural space vacated by the shrinking state. Muslim reform movements also produced new popular cultural forms and generated new modes of addressivity through media. In Mali, women reformers created a new form of female community and a new public place for themselves through prayer and discussion meetings, and through vigilant attention to religious observances. Like their Pentecostal counterparts, they were active in using media to constitute a public that extended beyond the face-to-face. They recorded audio cassettes of sermons by women leaders and circulated them beyond their own circles (Schulz 2012). In Nigeria, some Islamic reform groups rose to the Pentecostal challenge by producing their own video dramas and television programmes. In Senegal, women adherents of Sufi sheikhs created a 'new tradition' by adapting secular praise singing to express their devotion (McLaughlin 1997). Both born-again Christian organisations and reformist Muslim organisations stepped into state space in another way too: as well as making provisions for community welfare, education and edification, they also exercised control and censorship. Pentecostal groups rigorously monitored and rejected anything deemed 'ungodly', from blue movies to family members who were contaminated by residues of paganism. In the predominantly Muslim north of Nigeria, an enormously popular video actress, Rahama Sadau, was banned for life after she fleetingly embraced the popular rapper ClassiQ on screen in a music video (*The Guardian*, 19.10.2016 p. 21).

Commercial and political interests also shaped media space. The popular 'Mr Chu' programme in Ghana was sponsored by a Chinese herbal remedies importer; the JT Lingala Facile programme in Kinshasa was sponsored by President Joseph Kabila's party. Popular musicians in Ghana and Rwanda were eager to win commercial sponsorship through competitions organised by beer manufacturers

(Shipley 2013; Grant 2017). But these examples show that aspiring performers and articulate citizens alike had some room to manoeuvre: if
they needed patrons, the patrons also needed them. The commercial
free-for-all of the neo-liberal economy in situations of scarcity made
opportunism unavoidable. The forms of mutual accommodation that
artists and businesses arrived at did open up possibilities for innovative and creative expression, as well as blatant dissimulation.

Nollywood

The phenomenon of Nollywood films shows how small-scale media
technology, originally intended for personal and domestic use, can
be adapted and eventually generate a massive global industry. It also
bears out the claim that studies of 'globalisation' should look not only
at cultural flows from north to south, but also at the vigorous spread
of cultural forms between south and south, and from south to north.
      Nollywood responded to a desire for a locally produced popular cin-
ema that had been growing for decades. Cinema was one of the oldest
and most influential imported media forms across Africa. Audiences
became adept at interpreting foreign film language. Indian films began
to be screened in northern Nigeria in the 1950s, their resonance with
Hausa Islamic culture making them immensely popular. Their format,
themes and musical style were absorbed into locally produced Hausa
music, fiction and, later, video film-making (Larkin 2004, 2008;
Furniss 2006). In Lamu, on the other side of the continent, the most
enthusiastic of the young female audience members watched so many
Indian romantic musical films that they acquired an understanding
of Hindi and could interpret for their friends (Fuglesang 1994). But
even when audiences did not know the language, their familiarity with
the film conventions enabled them to 'read' the visual imagery and
soundtrack and follow the plot. I watched many Hollywood B-movies
in Nigeria in the 1970s and '80s, and was always impressed by the
alacrity with which the youthful audiences seized the point, got the
jokes and even anticipated the plot turns – well before I did. They were
thoroughly steeped in Hollywood cinematic conventions. But there
was a craving for African films with local settings, in African languages
and portraying recognisable situations.
      African-made art film shot on celluloid predated Nollywood.
Colonial governments saw the potential of film for public education.

After independence, film-makers who had been trained in colonial film schools began to make feature films. In Francophone Africa, there was an efflorescence of art cinema in the 1970s and '80s. The beautiful, profound films of Souleymane Cissé in Mali (*Yeelen*, 1987), Idrissa Ouedraogo in Burkina Faso (*Yaaba*, 1987), Gaston Kaboré in Burkina Faso (*Wend Kuuni*, 1982) and Jean-Pierre Bekolo in Cameroon (*Quartier Mozart*, 1992), among many others, won international renown. These films used African languages, were shot in the West African landscape, drew on local oral traditions and often used amateur actors drawn from the local community. The doyen of Francophone African film-making, Sembène Ousmane, turned from writing novels to making films in order to reach a popular audience (*Xala*, 1974; *Camp de Thiaroye*, 1987). Nonetheless, in its enigmatic purism and austerity, Francophone cinema was essentially an international intellectuals' film tradition. Its central platform and show-case was the annual FESPACO film festival in Burkina Faso, which attracted film buffs from all over the world, gained international media coverage and promoted international distribution. Nollywood was something different.

Nollywood started with the arrival of video cameras and VCRs in Nigeria in the mid-1980s. Inventive entrepreneurs began to use these for commercial purposes, recording weddings, funerals and other social events to sell to the celebrants. Very quickly, this skill was extended to the production of video drama, meeting the craving for local film which Nigerian cinematographers such as Ola Balogun had not been able fully to satisfy because of the expense, infrastructure and technical training needed to shoot on celluloid. The video drama enterprise quickly absorbed actors from the moribund Yoruba popular travelling theatre and from television and university theatre arts departments. The early video dramas were partly scripted, partly improvised by the actors in front of a single fixed camera, using basic sets (usually a living room in a borrowed house) intercut with stock shots of glamorous cityscapes. They were edited on personal computers and copied onto cassettes and later discs for sale and rental. Some were in Yoruba, some in English. All delivered narratives of personal and social conflict, with a strongly moral and usually conservative resolution. Even the earliest experiments in this form extended the live popular theatre's range in two directions: socially, they could move upward into the realm of the professional, educated classes and the dilemmas of social mobility, and could evoke extreme glamour and wealth; supernaturally, they could represent occult spiritual forces with unprecedented visual effects. But the distinctive form now recognised as 'Nollywood' is said to have been defined by *Living in Bondage* (1992), performed in English by Eastern Nigerian actors, and with a sensational plot ending in Christian deliverance from Satanic bonds. The key characteristics of Nollywood were established: excesses (stupendous luxury, dazzling glamour, ghastly penury, the horrific ravages of madness and disease), stark narrative opposition (villainy versus purity, punishment versus vindication), shocking revelations about the nature of sexual and occult transgression and, finally, a powerful emotional appeal to the audience's capacity for moral outrage, sympathy and desire for edification.

Despite this tendency towards extravagant sensationalism, Paul Ugor has argued persuasively that at the core of Nollywood lies ordinary people's experience of marginality and their assertion of their own power to speak. In a detailed reading of some of the most influential Nollywood films, he shows how, in representations of youth vigilantism (in *Issakaba*), urban dispossession (in *Maroko*), campus-based consumer competition (in *Face of Africa*) and transnational sex trafficking (in *Glamour Girls*), the lurid idioms of Nollywood give expression to an ambiguous but heartfelt social criticism and cry of anguish. The occult horror in the most famous film of all, *Living in Bondage*, he suggests, is connected not only to 'rising inflation, youth unemployment, existential uncertainty', but also to 'the almost paranormal nature of the contemporary global late-capitalist economy' (Ugor 2016:98). While Ugor sees Nollywood as a youth genre, others have observed its broad appeal across class, gender and age lines.

Perhaps the most striking thing about it, given the dominance of young men in most popular cultural production in Africa, is the prominence of female stars in Nollywood. The video drama's precursor, Yoruba travelling theatre, unlike the Ghanaian concert party, had always featured woman actors, and many of the plays had strong female roles. But in Nollywood, the scope for female stardom greatly expanded. Some of the most famous films of the 1990s were built entirely around women characters. *Glamour Girls* (two parts, 1994 and 1996) followed the misfortunes of five young educated women trying to survive – and get rich – in Lagos at a time when economic hardship and instability following structural adjustment were at a peak. Their

FIGURE 17 Nollywood – scene from *Face of Africa*.

methods of self-enrichment all revolve around sex – securing men as sugar daddies, stealing from them or blackmailing them – but their plight is made worse by their rivalry and mutual betrayals. In part two, the story shifts to international sex trafficking; the mastermind behind the criminal ring is Doris, the most successful and predatory of the five women. *Face of Africa* (three parts, 2005) is set on a university campus in Lagos and is structured around the rivalry between two female students, one rich, the other poor. The poor student, dazzled by the spectacle of her wealthy classmates' opulence, with their cars, mansions and designer clothes, and humiliated by their determination to exclude her, embarks on a secret career as a sex worker. Through prostitution and theft, she amasses wealth and buys the car and the mansion and the latest fashions, but is caught and ends up in jail. In both of these multipart dramas, the male characters are secondary: all the action is driven by the desires of the women. As you have probably already guessed, the representation of wealth and poverty is highly ambiguous. The bar is high: the 'poor' girl in *Face of Africa* arrives on campus looking groomed, chic and elegant and speaking 'refined' English; only her cheap 'Ghana Must Go' carrier bag betrays her inferior status. But the camera dwells lovingly, almost pornographically, on the appurtenances of the really fashionable, stratospherically wealthy girls. The poor girl gets her comeuppance, but while the film seems to condemn, or at least warn against, her methods, it does not seem to distance itself from her desires.

As Moradewun Adejunmǫbi suggests, one reason for Nollywood's popularity with virtually all strata of Nigerian society is its capacity for offering direct access to the world of inordinate wealth, excessive consumption and otherwise unimaginable luxury (Adejunmǫbi 2004). That this imaginary is carried by the trajectories of female characters in these two iconic films is in one sense simply a continuation of the long-standing habit of thinking of urban wealth and women's sexuality as parts of a single equation; but the outright condemnation of this equation found in Onitsha market literature and other colonial-era forms has given way to a more accommodating view, which may include criticism not only of the girls' morality, but of the dire circumstances arising from the postcolonial commodified economy. The lines of class difference and what counts as economic necessity are both redrawn: the characters are jobless, but they are university graduates; fashion is essential to their struggle for survival; they inhabit a cosmopolitan, outward-oriented world where they represent not Nigeria, but 'Africa', and where Europe is an outpost of a Lagos criminal ring's operations.

The pioneering Nollywood films were followed by an astonishing surge of video drama production. At its height, more than 1,500 new titles were produced every year, making Nollywood the second-largest film industry in the world in terms of numbers of films produced (Jedlowski 2013:25). They were exported all over Africa and its diaspora, aided by further technological innovations: satellite television and the Internet (Krings and Okome 2013:1). Within Africa, they were widely accepted because of their 'Africanity' and the familiarity of the scenes and issues presented, but also because of their glamour and the exotic differences that audiences elsewhere in Africa perceived – Nollywood set fashions for new styles of dress, speech and even architecture. Audiences read the Nollywood texts according to their own local preoccupations. Thus Namibian and Capetonian viewers liked Nollywood for its representations of what they saw as authentic traditional African life (even though scenes set in pristine villages were in fact comparatively rare), while audiences in Kinshasa saw the films as audiovisual Christian parables, and for the African diaspora they provided a link with 'home' (Ẹsan 2008; Becker 2013; Pype 2013). Appropriation and assimilation of Nollywood films could amount to wholesale remediation, as with the amazing Tanzanian 'video narrators', who not only did live translations of the dialogue of English-language Nollywood films into Swahili, but also explained the story, commented on the characters, drew comparisons with Tanzanian experience, gave details of the stars' lives, underlined the moral and generally brokered the Tanzanian audience's reception, all while the film was in full swing (Krings 2013).

Nollywood films not only were exported to other African countries, whether digitally or by travellers and traders who carried physical copies from Nigeria, their presence also stimulated the production of local variants of the industry, as either new start-ups or heavy adaptations of existing genres, in Ghana, DRC, Northern Nigeria, Tanzania and Kenya (Krings and Okome 2013). Thus acts of remediation were occurring on several levels. Nollywood was adapting its productions to make them more exportable; audiences in Cape Town, Windhoek, Kinshasa, Dar es Salaam and Nairobi were seeing different things in them according to their own historical situations; local interpreters were translating and re-narrating them; local video producers were assimilating key elements of Nollywood into new productions of their own, which in turn were translated into their own terms by fresh audiences; and in Europe and the US, expatriate Nigerians were collaborating with people at home to produce videos about African experiences overseas and their continued links to their homeland.

Hip-hop All Over the Shop

Rap, alongside Nollywood, is the other popular culture form to have taken off in the 1990s and taken root all over Africa in multiple variant forms. Unlike Nollywood, its origins were definitely African American, and the early rappers in Africa were elite kids who had access to imported media. Hip-hop style in the US was a combination of rapped music, breakdancing, graffiti and dress (typically baggy trousers, T-shirts, baseball caps, trainers and shades): an aggressively masculine youth style associated with anti-establishment anger. The earliest African rappers copied US techniques and styles, including American English. But the neo-liberal removal of import controls made possible an influx of not only hip-hop video and audio recordings, but also the new technology required to produce it at home. Hundreds of small studios, equipped with keyboards, computers and music software, were set up in African cities. Thousands of hip-hop groups were formed across the continent (1,500 in Dakar alone in the early 2000s). They would pay the producers for a backing track and for recording their vocals, then take the recorded piece and pay the burgeoning private radio stations to play it (a system referred to as 'payola'). Contacts as well as funds were needed, and only a few rappers became big-time celebrities. Those who did were able to set up their own websites, attract commercial sponsors, feature in mass concerts and travel overseas with their groups.

But for many young men, rap was a way of life rather than a source of income. Moulard-Kouka describes the days spent by young Dakarois rappers: still in a condition of 'waithood' and living with their parents, they established an alternative temporality by staying up all night and sleeping all morning. Then they would repair to their meeting place and brew tea – like the young men in Masquelier's Niger study – before beginning their day's practice. David Kerr has described the 'underground' rappers of the informal settlements of Dar es Salaam who did not have the means to record their music. They established *maskani*, informal meeting places, on street corners, marked sometimes with graffiti on the walls, sometimes merely by the temporary positioning of things to sit on. There they would hang out all day when they were not at work (many were unemployed, underemployed or waiting for work). They would try out their compositions, critiquing and adding to each other's efforts, philosophising and passing the time. Occasionally they would organise a bigger event, a *kampu*, which involved blocking off the street, setting up a stage and inviting rappers from neighbouring quarters of the city. No one was paid (the organisers were presented with a piece of cake in recognition of their contribution!), but a larger public was reached, especially given the very high volume of the all-night sounds (Kerr 2018).

Early in the history of rap in Africa, performers began to use African languages: in Ghana, Reggie Rockstone (who was actually brought up in the UK) returned home in 1994 and pioneered the Akan-language blend of hip-hop and highlife that became known as hiplife. Rap in Swahili, Luganda, Wolof and Zulu appeared. Performers began to exploit the extremely flexible and accommodating format of rapped music to incorporate all kinds of locally relevant sequences. The rappers of Dakar thought nothing of segueing into sketches, dialogues, comic narratives and spoofs of radio talk shows in mid-performance, and juxtaposing Wolof oral traditions with globally recognisable references (Moulard-Kouka 2008).

It was a form, in other words, that had an instantly recognisable global brand identity but at the same time was highly adaptable and open to local languages, genres and concerns. Witness the contrast between the aggressive hip-hop youth style and the moralising lyrics, which often strike a mature, responsible note as they call politicians to account and demand greater civic consciousness. This is attributable only in part to sponsorship by NGOs and other agencies with public messages to impart; more important is the rap artists' own self-image as authoritative moral spokespersons. In Dakar, rappers took the moral and political high ground, calling on their elders to clean up the city both literally and metaphorically. Contemptuous of the older generations' *mbalax* dance music, which blended romantic and praise lyrics, they composed texts meant to be seriously attended to, often referencing intellectuals they had come across at school or through self-teaching – Senghor, Césaire, Fanon (Moulard-Kouka 2005). In Tanzania, Professor Jay's dramatic monologues lampoon a big-man politician who makes impossible promises to the electorate ('I want to turn Tanzania into Europe / The first thing I will do is eradicate poverty / Students will do their science experiments on the moon / I will provide hospitals with as many drugs as there is sand in the sea') and use the voice of an HIV/AIDS sufferer to warn the public to practise safe sex ('I confess that I have been infected with AIDS / My journey has come to an end, and I am suffering greatly… After taking a test I knew I was not okay / Now I have a role to notify the entire population') (Ntarangwi 2009:71, 108). Nor are the political implications of African rap songs always radical. *Binadamu* (Human Being), a Swahili-language collaboration between the Tanzanian artist AY and the Ugandans Maurice Kirya and Hamdee, articulates one of the oldest and most conservative moral responses to poverty, a response ubiquitous in Africa: a blend of philosophical resignation to the world's contempt for the poor and an exhortation to work hard so as to avoid this fate:

> Never bring suffering on yourself
> For if you don't have money
> You'll be lonely like a tree in a desert
> You'll be nothing in people's eyes
> You'll become a burden
> No one will give you a hand …

> Mother, don't cry, these are the trials of this world
> There'll come a day when everything will be OK

You may even forget everything you've gone through
They'll love you when you have [wealth]
So go and work.[1]

Because of the new technologies of production and dissemination, hip-hop artists did not have a single, definite, identifiable target audience. Especially after digital technology became dominant, their productions spread from flash drive to laptop, from website to smartphone. They could as easily reach the African diaspora in Europe and the US as local listeners. Some groups dealt with the challenge of multiple constituencies in ingenious ways, like the Tanzanian group X-Plastaz, who devised a dual form of self-presentation on their website: for a Tanzanian audience, they produced Swahili-language promotional materials which highlighted their Dutch sponsor and their international networks; for a European audience, they produced English-language materials which highlighted their street cred, their status as poor youth in an upcountry town, Arusha, their traditional or semi-traditional style and their fusion of Maasai and hip-hop music. Katrina Daly Thompson draws attention to the inherent ambiguity of their self-presentation. Their hybrid image, in which Maasai cloth was combined with imported trainers, involved 'simultaneously rejecting and relying on exoticism', or having it both ways (Thompson 2008).

In South Africa, the trajectory of hip-hop bore the imprint of the momentous transition from the apartheid to the post-apartheid era and the enormous efforts of reconstruction and cultural reconceptualization that this entailed. Hip-hop culture started in Cape Town, and the political conditions of the time – the state of emergency, riots and racial oppression – gave the early rappers a strong sense of affinity with the aggressive radicalism of the 'conscious' brand of US rap. From the beginning, there was also a second strand to Cape Town rap – that of grass-roots educators and activists, who used hip-hop culture as a means to engage the youth (Pieterse 2010:435). But both strands remained a minor part of the popular music scene until after 1994. Then hip-hop spread to Johannesburg, Durban and other cities, began to rival the more eclectic *kwaito* dance music style hugely popular in the townships, achieved some commercial success (with the first

---

[1] English translation of Swahili text taken from video subtitles. *Binadamu* (accessed at www.youtube.com/watch?v=jzSolNRhBDM on 12.8.2016).

hip-hop CD reaching gold in 2003) and diversified into numerous variants (Künzler 2011).

Some twenty-first-century South African rappers retained the politically conscious stance of the early 1990s generation, but many focused on personal identity, material success and international connections. Post-apartheid youth, dubbed 'Generation Y', had an urgent need for self-making and self-stylising in the uncertainties of the new South Africa, where everything had shifted and yet few of the struggle's utopian visions had been realised (Allen 2004; Nuttall 2009). Ethnicity, political alignment, class, economic and educational status were all in dissolution and reformation, and ghetto gangs shared musical tastes with the rapidly expanding young black middle class, yet a bedrock of inequality remained. The private and personal had to be rediscovered, revalorised after decades of sacrifice and commitment to the public cause; anger had to be redirected or diffused. Advertising targeted new upwardly mobile consumer groups, and the new availability of imported goods intensified promotion of, and identification with, commercial brands. Some rappers embraced conspicuous consumption almost as much as the *kwaito* stars did with their in-your-face bling; others were selective or disdainful of materialism. The disjunctures and fluid combinations of both *kwaito* and rap may have been good for expressing an attitude of non-hierarchical inclusiveness, at the same time permitting the contradictions of post-apartheid experience to be expressed without resolution. Some rappers rejected the 'rainbow nation' rhetoric of post-1994 reconciliation, others embraced it and many aligned themselves with several positions at once. The 'open discourse' of hip-hop 'allows the contradictory and complicated politics of identity, community, belonging and aspiration to be surfaced in all its unresolved rawness' (Pieterse 2010:437).

Innocentia Mhlambi's analysis of a South African rap song, Zuluboy's 'Hail to the King' (Mhlambi 2014), is a vivid demonstration of the way this 'open discourse' can work to layer global and local registers in a non-linear patchwork assemblage, in an open-textured appeal to multiple fragmented audiences. The king of the title is Shaka, the Zulu war leader of the early nineteenth century; the album was released in 2006, the hundredth anniversary of the Zulu uprising known as Bambatha, which was only put down after protracted resistance. The song consciously invokes this heroic Zulu past, in which the remnants of the Zulu empire were pitted against the relentless encroachment of the British empire and then the white South African state. It signals

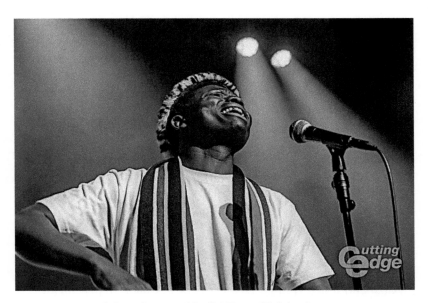

FIGURE 18 Zuluboy. Courtesy Mxolisi Zuma (Zuluboy).

the authenticity of this past by incorporating a performance of Zulu
royal praise poetry by a traditional bard (Mhlambi 2014:84). But
this evocation of Zulu authenticity is mediated and recycled at several levels: the song is introduced by a Jamaican rap artist vouching
for the significance of Zuluboy's 'Zulu empire', and in fact the Zulu
imagery had long been part of the global black repertoire. One of the
most famous pioneers of the American rap genre, born to Caribbean
parents in the South Bronx, called himself Afrika Bambaataa and his
group the Universal Zulu Nation. Thus the inspiration coming from
African American rap already contained within it an appropriated
version of Africanity. Furthermore, the Shaka tradition available to
Zuluboy had been converted into post-apartheid tourist heritage – a
past safely over – on the one hand, and into the rallying cry of the
resurgent, militantly ethnic-nationalist Inkatha political movement – a
dangerous future – on the other. Mhlambi suggests that Zuluboy, by
mobilising fragments of these conflicting dominant representations, is
able to evoke an alternative black subjectivity, suppressed in the official rhetoric of the inclusive, post-racial rainbow nation. Her point is
that the non-linear, segmentary, fragmentary mode of hip-hop music
corresponds to new modes of opposition to the new 'empire' of global

capitalism – opposition which can erupt anywhere from within that all-encompassing empire, and can link with other points of protest and critique through networks of new global media communications.

This account does raise some questions about the distinction between a meaningful and a meaningless jumble – about what meaning *means* in this genre, and to whom – and about the ethical implications of a style that can play host to a violent ethnic-nationalism alongside evocations of progressive black internationalism. But it also draws attention to a common feature of the rap phenomenon all over the continent. It seems plausible that the ability of hip-hop to mix and combine disparate repertoires and references with extreme freedom, leading to a disjunctive, fluid kaleidoscope of sensory, aural and ideational impressions, was one reason why it was seized upon by young people all over Africa. The juxtapositions of hip-hop lend themselves to constantly shifting perspectives, to irony and ambiguity. Hip-hop is composed of quotations sampled from a wide range of existing musical and visual sources overlaid with rap texts, which themselves are often fluid, freewheeling flights through multiple scenes and zones of the imagination. What is 'quoted' may not be fully endorsed; what is juxtaposed may produce gaps where contradictions are left unresolved but implicit critique may lie. Listeners need to bring social knowledge to bear, but no listener can read all the possible routes through these multiform texts. This makes it possible for rappers to take up radical critical stands while at the same time profiting from commercial sponsorship and state or NGO patronage; to align themselves on the side of global justice and gender equality while denouncing loose women; to affirm their roots in what they see as traditional African culture while quoting radical critical theorists; and to aspire to commercial success while referencing local and international black liberation discourses and pan-African visions of the future. As the South African rapper Proverb proclaimed in 2005, 'I have a dream of platinum sales minimum gold ... / I have a dream that African hip-hop is the future' (Künzler 2011:39).

Zuluboy's emphasis on ethnic assertion is not typical of hip-hop elsewhere in Africa. Much more prevalent is a multilingualism that reflects and promotes the emergence of a new 'common' language among urban youth: language not to proclaim ethnic nationalism, but to demonstrate command of a range of cultural resources and agility in hopping between them. In Eastern Africa, the mix of Swahili, English, Sheng and fragments of other African languages serves as a lingua franca across the whole region. Ethnic and even national identity may not be the primary referents: 'By virtue of the language and content of their music, the relative ease with which this music travels across national boundaries, increased collaboration in producing and performing songs, and their ... shared political and economic experiences, it is hard to limit or even link them to a specific national or ethnic location' (Ntarangwi 2009:116–17). Hybrid urban youth languages avoid ethnic compartmentalisation; new, inclusive registers forged out of slang, code-mixing and code-switching replace both the languages of ethnic groups and the official national language imposed from above.

But if the media revolution has helped foster a new polyglot youth culture, it has also made possible the instant communication of messages promoting ethnic exclusion and violence sparked by political and social competition – witness the use of the Internet and cultural shows to galvanise ethnic groups during the 2007 Kenyan elections and the upsurge of ethnic nationalism and xenophobia in South Africa. In Johannesburg, media were used to target not only 'foreign' immigrants such as Zimbabweans, but also non-Nguni and non-Sotho speakers from within South Africa. Hip-hop, among other popular genres, provides the conventions of an art form where both an emerging consciousness of a shared supra- or non-ethnic urban identity can be expressed and reassertion of ethnic aggression and intolerance can be given new forms.

Creativity in the Street

This chapter has presented studies that suggest that the widespread deregulation, trade liberalisation and privatisation (collectively referred to as neo-liberalism) from the late 1980s onwards did two things at once in Africa. On the one hand, they made life worse for most ordinary people by increasing unemployment, removing social services and driving rural populations into hand-to-mouth existences in the shanty-towns of bloated conurbations. On the other hand, they brought new goods, new connectedness, new access to international media technology, which enabled the predominantly youthful urban population to occupy, if only provisionally and precariously, a kind of virtual global space. Since the youth often had access only to images of consumer goods and not to the things themselves, performing the self in this space involved a kind of make-believe. But in this it was no different from the strategies of everyday life, where appearance often counted when substance was absent. The effects of misery and mediatised connectivity are linked. Dire conditions of uncertainty, which mean hustling to survive, generated a ferment of inventiveness; and for the first time, many ordinary young people had the means to express this creativity to a potentially wide audience through access to media.

Media have their own dynamics. They are not just 'spaces' into which people, in unprecedented numbers, can have a voice in public discourse or a moment in the public eye: they foster particular ways of representing the self and social relations. If modernity in general is associated with the multiplication of representations (Mitchell 2000), then the proliferation of media in Africa suggest the evocation of modern personhood as supra-ethnic, globally networked, street smart and eclectically mimetic. Celebrity, evoked in Nollywood and popular music videos through images of excess, is created by mediatised images and sustained by their repetition and proliferation: 'celebrities make themselves famous by announcing their own success' (Shipley 2013:82). The successful, charismatic pastor, politician, footballer, comedian and singer share the same imagery and may sometimes convert one kind of success into another.

But 'life on the ground', the starting point for the approach taken in this book, remains the key. What people see and hear through media feeds into everyday narratives, jokes and other performances; what people themselves put out on media is drawn from everyday repertoires.

Recent innovative research has begun to look at the circulation and mediation of cultural forms from the perspective of the person literally on the street – in the *matatu* or *tro-tro* that rushes and lurches along the roads, creating a mobile debating chamber, a site of music consumption, a pulpit for evangelical preachers, an opportunity for improvised stand-up (or, rather, sit-down) comedy, a platform for extended narratives of personal experience, a showcase for displays of style and a place for flirtation – a place which participates in a material and literal way in the circulation of cultural goods and ideas (Wa Mungai 2013; Quayson 2014). Ato Quayson advises that in exploring the formation of new urban African identities, it is a mistake to focus only on the relationship between images and media technologies, because these things pass through 'variegated discursive environments, some of which have nothing to do with technology'. Working within local traditions, people select and combine them so that they 'coalesce into inventively syncretic new wholes' (Quayson 2014:129). He focuses

FIGURE 19 *Tro-tro*, Ghana. Courtesy R. Lane Clark.

especially on mottoes and slogans, which, when they are about things
central to urban life, tend to circulate across several popular genres
and platforms – painted on the sides of *tro-tro* vehicles, voiced in popular songs, adopted as the names of kiosks, scrawled as graffiti. Jesse
Weaver Shipley gives some memorable examples of such circulating, semi-detached formulations arising from hiplife songs, a musical
genre well known for its rich eclecticism, effortlessly combining proverbial oratory, folk tale allusions, hip-hop sampling, scratching and
rap. Sidney the 'Rap Ninja' released a solo album in 2002 titled *Scenti
no!!* ('the scent'), referring to body odours of big men: 'The scent,
the scent / Is everywhere / When the honourable removes his shoes /
it's the socks' (Shipley 2013:153). The song became wildly popular
and the phrase passed into common currency to refer to the stink of
corruption. The title 'acted as a proverb in its detachability, potential to provide indirect and metaphoric commentary, and ability to
quickly reference multiple registers in the song and in new contexts'
(ibid.:155–6). For example, a well-dressed woman customer in the
market who was annoyed at the seller's inflated prices commented
loudly, 'Scenti no!', drawing laughter from the crowd and insults
from the seller. MPs who saw the song as offensive tried to get it
banned but failed, which made it still more popular. President Kufuor

was cannier: in 2004, he bought the rights to the song for his electoral campaign advertising, reinterpreting the 'scent' to mean the sweet
aroma of ubiquitous progress and development.

As Quayson observes, such sayings are 'everywhere', not only because
they are carried around in the incessant traffic of the urban streets, and
not only because they pass through multiple media, genres and contexts
and are interpreted in multiple ways, but because it would be pointless
to seek their source. It is as if we are in a field of allusions and quotations without an original – which, incidentally, is exactly how popular
orature worked before the intervention of media technology (Barber
2007:ch. 3, 7). The formulation could come from a proverb, a song, a
media programme, someone's coinage in the course of conversation,
a concert party's verbal exuberance: everyday conversation is often a
palimpsest of quotations, commanding recognition while artfully giving
the words a new twist. 'Street talk' is picked up by the press, radio and
television (Otiono 2015, Obadare 2016), just as fragments of media performances are captured in street talk. Ephemera, the passing allusions,
are not to be ignored: 'rumors and urban myths are the transactional
glue that hold African urban societies together' (Quayson 2014:241),
and they become the ingredients of further songs and performances.

Media genres can inspire original inventions on the ground. David
Kerr, during fieldwork in Dar es Salaam, used to frequent a *maskani* on the edge of the USwahilini (lower-class) district. Every afternoon a group of acquaintances – mostly taxi drivers from the taxi
rank opposite, car-wash guys who plied their trade in a football field
over the road, and middlemen and businessmen dropping in from
the main road – would while away the time chatting and exchan-
ging news. From this vantage point, they often witnessed a spontaneous performance by a man who called himself 'Quaresma', after the
Beşiktaş and Portugal footballer, though in fact he was an Arsenal
fan. Quaresma had a shoeshine stall in the nearest corner of the field;
he also mended clothes and broken shoes and sold mobile phone
vouchers. In the evening, after dark, when business had died down
and conversation was building up, he would announce dramatically,
'Breaking news! Breaking news!' He would then tell a story, in Swahili,
in the form of a parody of a Tanzanian Broadcasting Corporation
newsreader, but always with a personal or local focus. According
to one of his stories, which he titled 'Grand Larceny' (he did not
speak fluent English, but often included English words for effect),
a local politician had come to him and entrusted him with a bundle
of cash to pass on to another party, for a fee. Quaresma identified

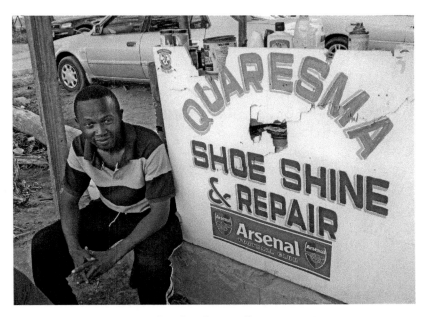

FIGURE 20 Quaresma at his shoeshine stall, Tanzania. Courtesy
David Kerr.

this transaction as *rushwa*, corruption, and though he named neither
the politician nor the recipient, the story provided food for extensive commentary and debate in the *maskani*. Sometimes conversation
would ebb and flow; Quaresma would join in for a while, and then
he'd start his performance again (David Kerr, interview, 30.8.2016).
Thousands of Quaresmas, in every city in Africa, must be inventing,
quoting and elaborating 'little genres of everyday life' that circulate in
and out of the public imagination.

In African cities characterised by insecurity, uncertainty and 'confusion', by the perception of the illusory and the fake, where the 'invisible city' is always present beneath the apparently visible one, arts may
have a particularly insistent presence, for art is essentially to do with
creating form. Art is a matter of making things and putting them 'out
there' such that they can be apprehended by others. What makes them
available in this way is the fact that they are formed: they manifest
a readable shape or pattern. In this way, art defies confusion while
drawing on its rich resources of ambiguity, deception, mutability and
appearance. And this supposition may be borne out by the fact that,
in these times of increased and widespread precariousness in African
cities, there has been such ubiquitous creativity.

CHAPTER 7

Conceptualising Change in African
Popular Culture

What, then, does this history of African popular culture look like? Across the variegated, uneven, temporally staggered and constantly mutating histories that we see in sub-Saharan Africa – histories of new genres, new modes of appropriation and combination, new expressive devices – several big historical arcs and overarching themes have emerged.

Production, Consumption and the Constitution of Meaning

The approach of this book has been a generative one. That is, it starts from life on the ground and seeks to understand how particular genres, forms and ways of thinking emerged in particular situations. The history of Africa has been packed with rapid and far-reaching transformations, especially intense in the two centuries for which, as it happens, we have detailed evidence about popular cultural forms. From the aftershocks of the slave trade to the fallout from enforced structural adjustment programmes, African people have borne the brunt of global transformation, and it is the ordinary, unprivileged people, whose experiences are so rarely documented and whose opinions are so rarely sought, who have been the most hard-pressed and also the most creative.

A ground-up approach puts the emphasis on production rather than consumption of cultural forms. It focuses on how things are made. This is entirely in keeping with African people's own views of what is involved in creative expression, which is often conceptualised in artisanal terms and uses small-scale artisanal methods: assemblage, trial and error, making use of whatever comes to hand and collaborative creativity. Popular genres, being often more informal and less constrained by conventions stiffened by vested interests than official and canonical genres, are more open to innovation, experimentation and novelty. This goes with an aesthetic of a work always being in progress, always being revisited and expanded, raising the question of a given work's relation to a larger corpus or tradition. Every iteration of a work renews and remakes it. When Kelly Askew explained to Tanzanian musicians that she was a trained performer, not a composer, she was met with incredulity: to perform is to create (Askew 2002:117). Audiences, too, usually do not think of themselves as consumers, but as producers of meaning: the artists supply the material, but it is they, the spectators, readers or listeners, who consciously participate in the constitution of the text by completing proverbs, grasping allusions or anticipating plot turns. Readers of Ghanaian popular fiction, for example, would take sides with the character whose social position was most like their own, and in this way would confirm their opinions about men's and women's domestic roles (Newell 1997). At Yoruba popular theatre performances, audience members used to assert, 'Other people come to the show just to laugh, but I come to pick a lesson to use in my life.' The audience takes responsibility for its own edification. Nor is it only textual meanings – 'lessons' – that people productively extract. Tanzanian film audiences 'didn't mindlessly imitate what they saw on screen, but they did quite consciously mine the movies for music and moves they could incorporate into their art and leisure activities' (Fair 2010:114). This metaphor of mining suggests that these audiences saw the films as a resource which, if worked, could yield useful raw materials for further production. In the Congo, Vincent Bouchard tells us, film audiences would not only interact with characters on screen, but also impersonate those characters off screen, adopting their catchphrases and mannerisms, and even elements of their costume. And during a screening, some viewers could take over the role of entertainer and 'get up to improvise an interpretation that is based on their familiarity with the film's plot or characters', an interpretation that is 'validated – or rejected – by the audience' (Bouchard 2010:100). Not only do audiences use what they see and hear to generate their own further cultural productions, they may also, in many locally produced genres, shape the work or the genre as it evolves: by writing letters to authors or editors, phoning in to radio programmes, responding to live shows or commenting on a Facebook site where a novel is serialised, they may bring about changes in form or content.

Not enough work has been done with popular culture audiences in Africa; most researchers have relied mainly on their own readings of popular texts. But a theme that keeps cropping up across regions and genres is the observation that an audience will listen intently to the words, or pore over images, and bring a world of historical memory and narrative recognition to bear on them. Pioneering work on popular painting in Zaire/DRC drew attention to the patient and intent scrutiny that viewers brought to apparently repetitive stock scenes. The image 'refers to a story and emits a narrative, even when the story is not explicitly represented in the picture space' (Jewsiewicki 1997:107). Many of the pictures, especially those collectively labelled 'Colonie Belge', served as a reminder of a traumatic collective history, but the story they prompted had to be furnished from the viewer's memory and shared discourse (Szombati-Fabian and Fabian 1976). Thus the viewer was participating in the creation of a total work that was composed not only of visual signs, but of a related verbal narrative supplied by him- or herself. The interdependence of visual and verbal registers is underlined by the artists themselves, when they incorporate written text into the actual pictures, a tendency particularly pronounced in the work of the internationally renowned Congolese artist Chéri Samba, whose written commentary sometimes takes up almost as much space as the painted image. But if this is an attempt to direct the viewer's interpretation, it may, on the contrary, simply provide more layers of material for the viewer to work on.

To see this work of interpretation in action raises fundamental questions: how are cultural forms held to have meaning – where is meaning believed to come from? It is rarely the case that popular culture participants describe meaning as inherent in a particular object (whether composed of words, images, sounds or movements). Meaning is not necessarily thought to be 'there' in the work, available to whoever looks. Rather, there are layers of meaning, some obvious and accessible, some known only to privileged insiders; and sometimes meaning is thought of as being attached to the object by the interpreter rather than needing to be extracted from within it. Thus 'consumption' is actually a work of production. In turn, most popular culture production is at the same time a kind of consumption, as it incorporates and refashions materials from a variety of sources.

Consider the example of the Congolese singer Mpiana, who incorporated a reference to the *Titanic* into a song. The allusion is a veiled criticism of a rival band, implying that he, Mpiana, is a survivor, while Werrason is a sinking ship (Krings 2015). But to get this allusion, the audience needs be aware of the backstory – Werrason used to be in Mpiana's band, but then split off and challenged his former leader for preeminence in the Kinshasa music scene. Only those in the know can attach this history to the otherwise unmoored allusion to the *Titanic* disaster and apply the relevant dimension of the metaphor – the ship's failure, rather than, for instance, its spectacular grandeur or the mass human fatalities caused by its sinking. This way of attributing specific and locally known interpretations to texts is very characteristic of older oral traditions, with which present-day popular genres are so often in continuity. By hijacking the story of the *Titanic* and giving it a new function, Mpiana is simultaneously *consuming* a globally circulating image and *producing* a specific and novel significance out of it. We are not looking at a linear passage from production to consumption, in which completed cultural objects pass from an originator to a receiver, but rather at a continuous proliferation and dissemination of creativity in which ideas, words, images and sounds are constantly remade by artists and audience members, all of whom can function as nodal points in networks of meaning-making.

The audience members, then, do not just decode what is there in the message – or even 'interpret' it. Often, they bring novel meanings to it. The text is 'out there', fair game for attachment of locally relevant and changing signification. An example from Malawi under President Hastings Kamuzu Banda describes the way many performers internalised, or pretended to internalise, the ideology promoted by Banda's repressive, systematic and efficient cultural apparatus. But this made the ability to 'turn' texts, to inflect them in particular ways, all the more important. In the 1950s, at Chintheche in the Nkhata Bay district, a musician called John Banda (no relation to the president) composed a song against those people who had allegedly been bribed by the colonial government to support the Federation of Northern Rhodesia, Southern Rhodesia and Nyasaland, which most of the African population opposed. The song warns the pro-Federation minority that the anti-Federalist majority in Nkhata Bay would drive them away from their lakeside fishing site into the hills: 'You're going to live in the hills ... Money that you've received / Has brought you trouble ... Because of money, you're going to live in the hills.' This was fine as far as President Banda was concerned; after being elected in 1963, he led Malawi out of the Federation. But in the 1970s, inhabitants of the Chintheche area were moved away from the lakeshore to the hills to make room for a paper factory and other development projects. These projects never materialised, and by the late 1980s the people said they wanted to move back to their old site. The government said no. Now the song was given a new meaning: President Banda had deceived people into giving up their life near the lake for the unproductive hills, in exchange for compensation money. Money that they received had brought them trouble. Note, however, that the president and his office were as adept at the art of interpretation as the villagers: they deduced the new meaning, and John Tembo, of the national radio station MBC, queried the music group that performed the song. This was enough to stop further public performances, for fear of reprisals (Chirambo 2013:119–20).

Cultural productivity, then, is not confined to particular gifted individuals. It is shared ground, a creative commons all can draw on and all, in different ways, contribute to.

We the Poor

The approach of this book also starts 'on the ground' in a societal sense. Popular culture is generated or, at the very least, circulated, and in the process modified, by people in the street, in the market, plying the roads, down the mine or sitting in a makeshift meeting place waiting for work. In the course of this history, we have met – at different periods and in different places in Africa – the affirmation of the experiences of 'us', the poor, as against 'them', the wealthy, privileged and powerful sections of society. The plaintive lyrics of AY and Maurice Kirya that we saw in Chapter 6 were a continuation of this long-standing theme. The orphans who populate Ghanaian concert party, the bereft, mistreated, impoverished characters who continually reappear in so many genres across time and space in Africa bear witness to a solidarity of 'us' in the face of the expropriations and excesses of 'them'. As a haunting Swahili verse from Remmy Ongala, the Tanzanian popular musician of the 1980s, says:

A bicycle has no say in front of a motorcycle
A motorcycle has no say in front of a car

> A car has no say in front of a train
> The poor/weak have no rights.
> I am poor, I have no right to speak
> Poor and weak in front of the powerful
> Weak as long as the powerful likes
> A hare has no say in front of the lion
> A rat does not promenade in front of the cat
> The walking stick of the poor is paid by God
> The poor have no rights. (Graebner 1989:250)

But only in exceptional cases were the expressive genres of Africa sealed off between social strata. Much more common was the free migration and diffusion of forms between social layers. Historians of early modern Europe have shown that, rather than having a wedding cake–like structure with clear space between the cultural forms of each social stratum, genres, themes and motifs circulated continually: aristocratic courtly cultures took up and reworked folk materials, while elite genres were popularised in simplified form in chapbooks and ballads. As we noted in Chapter 1, an even greater porosity is seen in African cultural strata, given that modern class structures are highly permeable, entry to the middle class is often open to those who can equip themselves with enough schooling or wealth, and families often straddle class lines.

But what is interesting is that in Africa, when elite forms were popularised, instead of being simplified, they were quite often rendered more elaborate. Elite highlife songs in the mid-colonial period in Ghana often had simple lyrics accompanying big-band dance music, for example E. T. Mensah's delightful 'Tea, tea, tea, tea, Oh mamma pour me out another cup of tea'. When highlife was taken up by lower-class itinerant acoustic guitar bands or soloists and sung in Akan languages, what emerged was extended, complex philosophical, political or humorous poetic narratives. Melancholy poetic reflections on orphanhood and death were given poignant expression:

> Lone miserable orphan, look at my end
> The child of a ghost, this is me
> Something has fallen into my eyes
> Darkness has reached me in the afternoon. (Van der Geest 2004:429)

This gives the lie to the common assumption that popularisation necessarily means simplification of a more developed, superior form.

If popular culture not only emanates from non-elites, but also often expresses a sense of what the non-elites have in common – sorrow, fellow-feeling, exclusion – it has also become apparent in the course of this history that some of the key generative points within this broad social field are people who are displaced, interstitial or in motion. David Coplan stresses that the new urban genres of South Africa were generated by liminal, unrooted people. The musicians in the shebeens of 1920s Johannesburg and the innovators of competitive dance and song in Durban belonged neither to traditional nor Christian school–educated categories, but were an in-between, mobile population locally described as 'cultural driftwood' or 'vagrants' (Coplan 2008:113, 84). More generally, many of the new popular genres of the twentieth century emerged in the interface of orality and literacy and were created by people who were partially displaced from the village communities of their parents, but without a secure social status in the town.

Continent-wide Historical Transitions

Throughout this discussion, recognition of local specificity and heterogeneity has had to be combined with alertness to wider historical trends or transitions that can be seen across the continent. Let me now outline four of these, all of which would reward future research.

The first is a general transition from an aesthetic style that was predominantly abstract or highly stylised to one that looks like realism. Across the continent, we see the emergence, in the first half of the twentieth century, of a form of lifelike representation focusing on the details of everyday life. Realistic representation was certainly not unknown in precolonial cultural traditions – witness the Ifẹ bronze and terra cotta heads of the eleventh to the fifteenth centuries, with their serenely human expressions, or the sixteenth-century Benin bronzes depicting Portuguese soldiers – but the dominant mode was schematic. Masquerades, for example, are notable across Africa for their stunningly impressive geometric or fantastic forms; they do not *depict* spiritual beings so much as provide a locus that spirits can occupy on their visitations to the human community. Sculptures representing human beings, similarly, usually selected and emphasised key features indicating status or ontological state rather than attempting to produce a surface copy. They could be seen as lifelike in a deeper sense than realism. The carvers of the Ọlọjọnwọn lineage in Yorubaland are saluted 'Ọmọ pagida sọgi deniyan': 'Those who transform a piece of wood and turn it into a person.' The carver creates a living being; when the image is completed, with eyes, mouth, fingers and toes, it strikes the viewer with wonder, and this gives it powers. The aim is not to make it look like an actual person you could meet in the street, but rather to evoke the essence of the object and create a source of agency. With its schematic and geometric forms, African traditional art was ahead of the European modernist painters, and it is no wonder that West African masks inspired Picasso's cubism.

In the twentieth century, ordinary people, everyday life, became the principal subject matter, and the mode of representation focused on lifelike detail. *Lifela* spoke of the Sotho miners' quotidian experiences – travelling on a train, arriving at the mining compound, longing for home – describing them vividly in accessible language, in contrast to the older poetic genre *lithoko* (praise poetry), which concentrated on a narrower range of heroic and aristocratic themes and was highly obscure and allusive. Onitsha market literature provided models for love letters and scripts full of slang and chitchat for schoolboys to woo girls, in contrast to the imaginative world of folktales and the distanced world of gods and heroes in oral legends. Protagonists in early twentieth-century African-language novels were commoners – and, in many cases, commoners of low status who needed to make their own way in the world without family or money to support them. The first novel in Zulu was *uJeqe insila kaShaka* by J. L. Dube (1930), which told the story of the travels and adventures of Jeqe, Shaka's body-servant. One of the earliest novels in Shona was *Murambiwa Goredema* by Solomon Mutswairo (1959), which, like Dube's novel, has a picaresque plot but is set in contemporary Rhodesia; its hero is an ordinary boy who travels to Salisbury, has his pocket picked, works in Castle Breweries and lives in the township before setting out on further adventures. The first novel in Yoruba was *Itan Igbesi Aiye Emi Sẹgilọla* by I. B. Thomas (1930), which told in graphic detail the story of the lurid life and death of a Lagos 'harlot'. Yoruba popular theatre, which began as a stylised choral form of Bible opera in the 1940s, transformed with astonishing rapidity into a genre that specialised in lifelike representations of everyday social and family relationships between husbands and wives, landlords and tenants, orphans and their relatives, bosses and servants, good and bad friends. Characters in these plays were not established by a narrator or presenter, but entirely through their own actions and speech, which poured out in idiomatic, lifelike torrents

complete with repetitions, hesitations and interruptions. Bar art across
the continent depicts young men and women in modern clothes dancing, drinking beer and flirting. The Congolese painter Chéri Samba,
already mentioned, dwells with forensic accuracy on every detail of his
subjects' appearance: their clothing, shoes, hairstyle, wristwatch, the
chair in which they are sitting, the parlour in which the chair is placed.
Something about the experience of everyday life and material actual-
ity had come to the centre of the field of representation.

Though this representational style 'looks like' realism, we cannot
assume that its function is necessarily to show real life for its own
sake. In many cases, the vivid evocation of the commonplace tended
to function to drive home and render incontrovertible a powerful moral lesson. The more lifelike the narrative, the more difficult
to imagine the protagonist escaping the consequences of his or her
actions. Across the continent we find a tireless didacticism based on
exemplary instances. So one avenue for future comparison and historical contextualisation is the emergence of the quotidian in artistic
representation, and what it means.

A second big historical arc is the emergence of a kind of audience
thought of as a 'public'; that is, as a constituency that is, in principle
if not in practice, of indefinite extent and made up of anonymous
and interchangeable units. This way of imagining an audience was
in conscious contrast to the intimately known, face-to-face audiences
of older oral and communal performances. It was made possible by
print and later by electronic media, but it was also built upon the
experience of the urban crowd and represented shifts in the way sociality was construed. Popular culture producers experimented with
styles of address and often imagined their public on different scales
from moment to moment, recreating an intimate face-to-face style
addressing known and knowing interlocutors and then switching to an
address that hailed an unknown public extending to 'the four corners
of the world'. Many genres are constituted so as to exclude some sections of society while convening others, and audience members play
their part in adopting or rejecting the role of addressee.

These changing and proliferating modes of address are a crucial hinge in the relationship between popular culture and society.
According to Bakhtin, addressivity – how the text 'turns to' and thus
convenes its audience – is a defining feature of every genre (Bakhtin
1986:99). As popular creators invented new forms of address and
new relations to their listeners, readers or viewers, they were also

constituting new genres. And new genres are needed when new experiences exhaust the capacities of old genres to speak of them. The history of audiences and how their local constitution and conceptualisation changed over time in Africa is a huge comparative question which, as far as I know, has yet to be addressed.

A third historical change that has been mentioned in almost every chapter, but without detailed analysis, is the emergence of women in genres formerly dominated or exclusively owned by men, or women's creation of new genres parallel to those of men. We saw that the male Sotho migrant workers' poetic genre *lifela* had a counterpart in the *seoeleoelele* poetry chanted and danced in shebeens by women workers and travellers. In some cases, the incorporation of women into a formerly male-only genre contributed to the broad shift from stylised to lifelike representation: the exclusively male concert party troupes in Ghana, for example, eventually began to employ women performers instead of using female impersonators. This change, which brought about a profound change in the aesthetics of the concert party theatre, was encouraged by television studio managers and by NGOs seeking to harness the concert party for development campaigns. In other cases, the rise of women performers in a formerly male genre could be a key factor in its popularisation and demoticisation – witness *taarab* music, which, as we saw, began in Zanzibar as an orchestral and sung genre performed exclusively by men, but was made popular on the mainland by a supremely gifted woman singer. Her influence was greatly extended and enhanced through radio and records. Media, more widely, did open new spaces for women performers and new scope for them to become stars. We saw in Chapter 6 how Nollywood films could give women more spectacular and more pivotal roles than they had enjoyed in Nollywood's precursor, the live Yoruba popular travelling theatre. An even more striking shift in the balance between male and female performers is seen in Malian popular music. In the older traditions of epic and praise song, the central figure was the male bard, who sang accompanied by the *kora* lute; a group of women would sing the refrains or short songs that interspersed the narration. But when traditional music began to be performed on stage, to a new kind of public, and especially when it began to be recorded and disseminated through radio, records, cassettes and CDs, audiences' preference for melody and female vocal qualities gave some women performers a chance to achieve superstar status, and men became their accompanists (Durán 1995). The new fictional genre of romance in northern Nigeria provided an opening which Hausa women writers seized upon; they became prominent in the production of *soyayya*, romantic novels, which in turn became the basis for many of the Hausa video dramas of the 1990s and 2000s. Women members of media-using religious movements, both Muslim and Christian, also seized the opportunity to enter digital public space through testimonies, preaching and religious songs.

All of these transformations in gendered performance spaces took place against a background of rapidly changing gender roles across the continent. The opening up of new possibilities for women was seen by many people as a threat of disintegration of social values. Popular culture in Africa has long been bristling with anxious and angry debates about marriage, sexuality and seniority. Denunciations of promiscuous and exploitative woman have been reiterated in many popular genres across the continent, including by female artists. The Nigerian woman singer St Janet performs lyrics regarded by many as not only obscene and blasphemous, but also flagrantly misogynistic. The multiple implications of women performers taking a more conspicuous place in a wide range of popular genres is a theme which future research could try to map and explore comparatively and historically.

Finally, there is the question of how history is experienced and articulated by popular culture creators themselves. A history of popular culture must include the history *in* popular culture, that is, how popular forms are experienced, and constituted, in relation to the passage of time. Scholarly literature on African popular culture has emphasised its ephemerality and volatility. New forms would catch on, spread like wildfire and then apparently disappear. Genres would mutate, themes would migrate from one genre to another. Even genres that look well established can suddenly collapse: that was certainly my own experience when I worked on Yoruba popular travelling theatre. In the early 1980s, when I started my research project, there were more than 100 professional, commercial travelling companies plying the roads of western Nigeria and beyond. Each had ten or more paid performers, their own repertoire of plays and their own stage lighting, sound system, scenery, costumes and props. Though their plays were improvised and unscripted and new ones were continually being invented, there was a stability in their repertoires. The most popular plays had lasted, with incremental modifications, for upwards of thirty years. This looked like a stable, established tradition if ever there was one. Yet by the late 1980s, fifty years after its inception, the

Yoruba popular theatre was disappearing. The economic crash made maintaining large troupes impossible, the rise of armed robbery made audiences unwilling to go out at night and the rising cost of imported spare parts made it difficult to keep their vehicles on the road. And the advent of video film provided an attractive alternative for both theatre troupes and audiences: the live acting profession moved *en masse* into video drama. In the process, though they retained many features of their improvised performance style, they also changed the shape of their dramas and their mode of textual constitution. Their representational reach expanded, but the intense linguistic creativity that was sustained by interaction with live audiences more or less dried up. And very soon, the Yoruba-language video industry was eclipsed by English-language Nollywood, discussed in Chapter 6.

This sudden mutation and disappearance of a huge, widely popular genre illustrates the fragility of popular culture institutions. Lacking infrastructural support and investment, official sanction, the procedures by which elite cultural forms are vetted, edited, reviewed and eventually canonised – all the mechanisms by which socially valorised art forms are perpetuated – African popular culture lacks not only the inscription that would enable us to retrieve it as a historical object (see Chapter 2), but also the officialising mechanisms that stabilise and consolidate cultural production.

And yet there is a countercurrent running against this narrative of volatility, another history, seen in examples that have appeared throughout this book. This countercurrent is the history of popular memory and memorialisation. As we have seen, people retrieve songs, sayings and anecdotes from many decades ago. Appropriation, remediation and repurposing of cultural materials should not be associated exclusively with the kind of transactions between the local and the global referred to in Chapter 6. Equally important is the interface between the present and the past. Indeed, remediation or recreation ('copying with a difference') is basically how all creative work happens. In the case of fugitive, fluid, apparently ephemeral popular arts, the already constituted forms available to present-day creators are not always documented or easily identifiable, but from time to time examples crop up showing how resilient popular memory can be.

Why do people retain and recreate these stories, songs and sayings long after the event that gave rise to them has passed? One reason may be that they capture and give a name to a significant collective experience. A much-cited example from Ghana is Nana Ampadu and his African Brothers Band, who brought out a song called 'Ebi te yie' ('Some sit well') in 1967, not long after the 1966 military coup that deposed President Nkrumah. The song retells a folk story about a meeting of the animals in the forest, in which the menacing Leopard harasses the little Duiker until the latter asks for an adjournment, because 'Some of us are well seated, some are not so well seated, but others are not well seated at all.' This was understood as a criticism of the increasing gap after independence between the well-off military and commercial elites and the struggling majority. The phrase 'Ebi te yie' became a popular way of naming the experience of a new kind of inequality that previously had no name. It expressed disillusionment with the current regime, a fact not lost on the military authorities. But when they summoned Nana Ampadu for questioning, he stated that it was just a tale he had heard from his father, and he was released (Collins 1976:66–7). The phrase was more powerful and effective as a name for people's experience than a plain descriptive term (such as 'post-independence social inequality') would have been, precisely because it was metaphorical. It required listeners to make an imaginative link between the story and their collective situation, in an act of complicit recognition that bound them together – while at the same time retaining the possibility of denial when questioned by authority. Fifteen years later, the phrase 'Ebi te yie' was still in circulation as a jocular but critical term for inequality (Van der Geest and Asante-Darko 1982).

Particular kernels of expression may be singled out, treasured and passed on by a community because they represent an enduring and deeply significant experience. In nineteenth-century Mozambique, the Portuguese Paiva family acquired vast estates in the lower Zambesi valley, where they established cruelly exploitative and autocratically controlled sugar plantations. The first generation of plantation workers in the 1890s created a song in which the key line, retained in all versions, was a complaint in the form of an obscene insult directed at the then-boss, José Paiva, who was reputed to understand the local language, Sena: 'Paiva – ndampera dinyero ache – nsondo wache' ('Paiva – we've killed his money for him – his penis!'). As the sugar plantations were extended, the labourers taught the song to new recruits, including those whose first language was not Sena. In the 1930s, the newly installed Portuguese government in Mozambique imposed a system of compulsory cotton cultivation, which on the Sena sugar estate had to be carried out by the women and children. Women, drawn into the harsh labour regime, took over the song and elaborated it as a women's genre, sung in a circle, with dancing and improvised drama satirising the officials and overseers. When Leroy Vail and Landeg White collected oral history in the region in the 1970s, people told them, 'This song can't be forgotten'; 'We have to know it, because it's about what people suffered.' It was still being sung by young girls who knew nothing about the Paiva family as people; it even was sung after 1975 to celebrate the overthrow by Frelimo of 'Paiva', now standing for the all-pervasive oppression and exploitation of the past. Thus the song travelled over time and space, moved from a male performance context to a female one and took on many forms, but all versions kept the rhymed epigram. The irreducible kernel of the song was retained, because it was a key to the memory of a wide and long-lasting shared experience of humiliation, pain and defiance. In Vail and White's view, it represented a small space of freedom from the all-pervasive power of the plantation system, a way of 'preserving in an image or slogan or even a curse one small region of the mind which refuses to capitulate completely' (Vail and White 1978:25).

The 'out-there-ness', or detachability, and thus potential for re-contextualisation, which all creative forms share, and which enables them to be transmitted over time and space, also presupposes a collectivity. The text or performance is out there so as *to be heard* by other people, and to be jointly constituted in performance. And when it is passed down through the generations, the collectivity includes the dead:

> The singer of *Paiva* belongs to a community of singers, both in the cane-fields where the lead line demands a response, and at home, with every village developing its own version of the song. But the community is not only of the living ... the link is established with those performances of the past when "our fathers" expressed what "they suffered". What is secured in *Paiva* is not just a private rebellion but a whole tradition of rejection.
>
> (Vail and White 1978:25)

Historical memory in popular culture, then, may be more than the transmission of ideas or information. It may be the extension over time of a collectivity, convened around a shared experience which is encapsulated in a creative form.

Future research could explore further the question of which popular culture forms persist, and how and why, which are abandoned or converted into something different, and what it is that long-lasting genres bring with them from the past.

There is a sense in which history is about failures. For every novel that was published, read and passed from hand to hand, there are dozens that remained in boxes under people's beds, or gathered dust in local publishers' offices, or were published and forgotten. For every rap song that was recorded, played on radio or disseminated over the Internet, there were dozens that remained 'underground'. These creations, below the radar of the histories that are generally written in the mainstream academic sphere, show what was thought to be possible, desirable and interesting by their creators at the time. If they could be accessed, they would demonstrate how ubiquitous was the desire to create and leave a mark. Only by recognising the existence of this desire can we truly understand the works that did end up being popularly recognised and celebrated.

To recapitulate: creative forms are the products of particular historical conjunctures, particular situations, and bear the imprint of the forces and preoccupations that made up the conditions of their emergence. But there is a sense in which they are created so as to escape time. They are made to be detachable from the here-and-now context of their enunciation. They are made to be 'out there', awaiting response, interpretation and recontextualisation which cannot be controlled by the enunciator. But neither do listeners, readers, spectators and cultural producers, all of whom are appropriating and reusing these forms, wholly possess what they appropriate. And this detachment contains potentiality; it hints that things could have been, and perhaps still could be, different. The great Xhosa cattle-killing of 1856 was a disaster for the Xhosa people, hastening their conquest by the whites and reducing to servitude many of those who escaped starvation. And yet, Jennifer Wenzel tells us, narratives of Nongqause, the girl whose prophecies instigated the cattle-killing, continue to have resonance, for literary and cultural texts can be 'sites where unrealised visions of anticolonial projects continue to assert their power' (Wenzel 2009:5). It is not only prophetic utterance that has this capacity to open onto a new configuration of events. Many kinds of texts, in their constitutive detachability from the actual context that precipitated them, can have an afterlife in which they become the focus of new struggles or social initiatives. Thus, texts or images encapsulating memory – whether of past crises, hardships and collective uprisings, or of human predicaments, moral alternatives and incidents treasured for their comic or dramatic potential – are not purely memories of the past, but kernels of collective popular experience which may produce future growth.

Bibliography

Abdulaziz, Mohamed H. 1979 *Muyaka: 19th Century Swahili Popular Poetry*. Nairobi: Kenya Literature Bureau.

Abdullah, Ibrahim 1994 'Rethinking the Freetown crowd: the moral economy of the 1919 strikes and riot in Sierra Leone', *Canadian Journal of African Studies* 28 (2): 197–218.

Abrahams, Peter 1989 [1946] *Mine Boy*. London: Heinemann.

Adamu, Abdalla Uba, Yusuf M. Adamu and Umar Faruk Jibril (eds.) 2004 *Hausa Home Videos: Technology, Economy and Society*. Kano, Nigeria: Center for Hausa Cultural Studies.

Adejunmọbi, Moradewun 2004 *Vernacular Palaver: Imaginations of the Local and Non-native Languages in West Africa*. Clevedon: Multilingual Matters.

Agwuele, Augustine and Toyin Falọla 2009 'Introduction', in *Africans and the Politics of Popular Culture*, ed. Toyin Falọla and Augustine Agwuele. Rochester, NY: University of Rochester Press.

Ahadzie, Sika 2007 'Exploring language patterns, social motivations and discourse strategies: an investigation of contemporary FM broadcast in Ghana'. PhD thesis, University of Birmingham.

Akpan, Ekwere Otu and Violetta I. Ekpo 1988 *The Women's War of 1929: A Popular Uprising in South Eastern Nigeria*. Calabar, Nigeria: The Government Printer.

Akurang-Parry, Kwabena Opare 2000 'Colonial forced labor policies for road-building in southern Ghana and international anti-forced labor pressures, 1900–1940', *African Economic History* 28: 1–25.

Allen, Lara 2003 'Commerce, politics, musical hybridity: vocalising urban black South African identity during the 1950s', *Ethnomusicology* 47 (2): 228–49.

2004 'Kwaito versus crossed-over: music and identity during South Africa's rainbow years, 1994–9', *Social Dynamics* 30 (2): 82–111.

Andersson, Muff 1981 *Music in the Mix: The Story of South African Popular Music*. Johannesburg: Ravan Press.

Andersson, Ruben 2014 *Illegality, Inc.: Clandestine Migration and the Business of Bordering Europe*. Oakland: University of California Press.

Anorue, J. C. n.d. *How to Become Rich and Avoid Poverty*. Awo-Idemili: Providence Printing Press.

Askew, Kelly M. 2000 'Following in the tracks of Beni: the diffusion of the Tanga Taarab tradition', in *Mashindano! Competitive Music Performance in East Africa*, ed. Frank Gunderson and Gregory Barz. Dar es Salaam: Mkuki na Nyota Publishers (21–38).

2002 *Performing the Nation: Swahili Music and Cultural Politics in Tanzania*. Chicago: University of Chicago Press.

Bakhtin, M. M. 1984 *Rabelais and His World*, trans. Helene Iswolsky. Bloomington: Indiana University Press.

1986 *Speech Genres and Other Late Essays*, trans. Vern W. McGee. Austin: University of Texas Press.

Bame, Kwabena N. 1985 *Come to Laugh: African Traditional Theatre in Ghana*. New York: Lilian Barber Press.

Bank, Leslie J. 2011 *Home Spaces, Street Styles: Contesting Power and Identity in a South African City*. New York: Pluto Press; Johannesburg: Wits University Press.

Barber, Karin 1987 'Popular Arts in Africa', *special issue of African Studies Review* 30 (3): 1–78, 105–32.

1997 'Introduction', in *Readings in African Popular Culture*, ed. Karin Barber. Bloomington: Indiana University Press for the International African Institute.

2000 *The Generation of Plays: Yoruba Popular Life in Theatre*. Bloomington: Indiana University Press.

(ed.). 2006 *Africa's Hidden Histories: Everyday Literacy and Making the Self*. Bloomington: Indiana University Press.

2007 *The Anthropology of Texts, Persons and Publics*. Cambridge: Cambridge University Press.

2012 *Print Culture and the First Yoruba Novel: I. B. Thomas's 'Life Story of Me, Ṣẹgilọla' and Other Texts*. Leiden: Brill.

Barber, Karin, John Collins and Alain Ricard 1997 *West African Popular Theatre*. Bloomington: Indiana University Press.

Becker, Heike 2012 'Anthropology and the study of popular culture: a perspective from the southern tip of Africa', *Research in African Literatures* 43 (4): 17–37.

2013 'Nollywood in urban South Africa: Nigerian video films and their audiences in Cape Town and Windhoek', in *Global Nollywood: The Transnational Dimensions of an African Video Film Industry*, ed. Matthias Krings and Onookome Okome. Bloomington: Indiana University Press (179–98).

Birmingham, David 1988 'Carnival at Luanda', *Journal of African History* 29 (1): 93–103.

Björkman, Ingrid 1989 *Mother Sing for Me: People's Theatre in Kenya*. London: Zed Press.

Bosman, William [Willem] 1967 [1705] *A New and Accurate Description of the Coast of Guinea: Divided into The Gold, The Slave, and The Ivory Coasts*. Original edition of 1705 translated from the Dutch by unknown translator. This edition with introduction by John Ralph Willis and notes by J. D. Fage and R. E. Bradbury. London: Frank Cass.

Bouchard, Vincent 2010 'Commentary and orality in African film reception', in *Viewing African Cinema in the Twenty-first Century: Art Films and the Nollywood Video Revolution*, ed. Mahir Şaul and Ralph A. Austen. Athens: Ohio University Press (95–107).

Boyd, Jean 1989 *The Caliph's Sister: Nana Asma'u 1793–1865. Teacher, Poet and Islamic Leader*. London: Frank Cass.

Brown, Carolyn A. 2003 *'We Were All Slaves': African Miners, Culture, and Resistance at the Enugu Government Colliery*. Portsmouth, NH: Heinemann.

Bryce, Jane 2010 'Outside the machine? Donor values and the case of film in Tanzania', in *Viewing African Cinema in the Twenty-first Century: Art Films and the Nollywood Video Revolution*, ed. Mahir Şaul and Ralph A. Austen. Athens: Ohio University Press (160–77).

Burke, Peter 1978 *Popular Culture in Early Modern Europe*. London: Maurice Temple Smith Ltd.

Callaci, Emily 2017. *Street Archives and City Life: Popular Intellectuals in Postcolonial Tanzania*. Durham and London: Duke University Press.

Callinicos, Luli 1981 *Gold and Workers 1886–1924. A People's History of South Africa*, vol. 1. Johannesburg: Ravan Press.

1982 *Working Life 1886–1940: Factories, Townships and Popular Culture on the Rand. A People's History of South Africa*, vol. 2. Johannesburg: Ravan Press.

1985 *A Place in the City: The Rand on the Eve of Apartheid. A People's History of South Africa*, vol. 3. Johannesburg: Ravan Press.

Chartier, Roger 1987 *The Cultural Uses of Print in Early Modern France*, trans. Lydia G. Cochrane. Princeton, NJ: Princeton University Press.

Chernoff, John M. 2003 *Hustling Is Not Stealing: Stories of an African Bar Girl*. Chicago: University of Chicago Press.

Chirambo, Reuben M. 2013 'Traditional and popular music, hegemonic power and censorship in Malawi, 1964–1994', in *Popular Music Censorship in Africa*, ed. Martin Cloonan, Michael Drewett and Derek B. Scott. London: Ashgate (109–26).

Cole, Catherine M. 2001 *Ghana's Concert Party Theatre*. Bloomington: Indiana University Press.

Collins, E. J. [John] 1976 'Ghanaian highlife', *African Arts* 10 (1): 62–8, 100.

Cooper, Frederick 1987 *On the African Waterfront: Urban Disorder and the Transformation of Work in Colonial Mombasa*. New Haven: Yale University Press.

1996 *Decolonisation and African Society*. Cambridge: Cambridge University Press.

Coplan, David B. 1994 *In the Time of Cannibals: The Word Music of South Africa's Basotho Migrants*. Chicago: University of Chicago Press.

2008 *In Township Tonight! South African Black City Music and Theatre*, 2nd ed. Chicago: University of Chicago Press.

Crais, Clifton 2002 *The Politics of Evil: Magic, State Power, and the Political Imagination in South Africa*. Cambridge: Cambridge University Press.

Crisp, Jeff 1984 *The Story of an African Working Class: Ghanaian Miners' Struggles 1870–1980*. London: Zed Books.

De Boeck, Filip and Marie-Françoise Plissart 2004 *Kinshasa: Tales of the Invisible City*. Ghent and Amsterdam: Ludion.

Delius, Peter 1996 *A Lion Among the Cattle: Reconstruction and Resistance in the Northern Transvaal*. Portsmouth, NH: Heinemann; Oxford: James Currey.

Diawara, Mamadou 1989 'Women, servitude and history: the oral historical traditions of women of servile condition in the kingdom of Jaara (Mali) from the fifteenth to the mid-nineteenth century', in *Discourse and Its Disguises: The Interpretation of African Oral Texts*, ed. Karin Barber and P. F. de Moraes Farias. Birmingham: Centre of West African Studies (109–37).

1997 'Mande oral popular culture revisited by the electronic media', in *Readings in African Popular Culture*, ed. Karin Barber. London: James Currey (40–8).

Diawara, Manthia 1992 *African Cinema: Politics and Culture*. Bloomington: Indiana University Press.

Dikobe, Modikwe 1973 *The Marabi Dance*. London: Heinemann.

Diouf, Mamadou 2003 'Engaging postcolonial cultures: African youth and public space', *African Studies Review* 46 (2): 1–12.

Dodson, Don 1973 'The role of the publisher in Onitsha market literature', *Research in African Literatures*, 4 (2): 172–88.

Dolby, Nadine 2006 'Popular culture and public space in Africa: the possibilities of cultural citizenship', *African Studies Review* 49 (3): 31–47.

Durán, Lucy 1995, 'Jelimusow: the superwomen of Malian music', in *Power, Marginality and African Oral Literature*, ed. Liz Gunner and Graham Furniss. Cambridge: Cambridge University Press.

Edmondson, Laura 2007 *Performance and Politics in Tanzania: The Nation on Stage*. Bloomington: Indiana University Press.

Ekwensi, Cyprian 1978 [1961] *Jagua Nana*. London: Heinemann.

Englund, Harri 2011 *Human Rights and African Airwaves: Mediating Equality on the Chichewa Radio*. Bloomington: Indiana University Press.

Enwezor, Okwui, Carlos Basualdo, Ute Meta Bauer, Susanne Ghez, Sarat Maharaj, Mark Nash and Octavio Zaya (eds) 2002 *Under Siege: Four African Cities. Freetown, Johannesburg, Kinshasa, Lagos*. Ostfildern-Ruit, Germany: Hatje Cantz Publishers.

Epstein, A. L. 1958 *Politics in an Urban African Community*. Manchester: Manchester University Press.

1959 'Linguistic innovation and culture on the Copperbelt, Northern Rhodesia', *Southwestern Journal of Anthropology* 15 (3): 235–53; reprinted in Epstein 1992.

1992 *Scenes from African Urban Life*. Edinburgh: Edinburgh University Press.

Erlmann, Veit 1996 *Nightsong: Performance, Power and Practice in South Africa*. Chicago: University of Chicago Press.

Esan, Oluyinka 2008 'Appreciating Nollywood: audiences and Nigerian films', *Particip@tions* 5 (1).

Fabian, Johannes 1978 'Popular culture in Africa: findings and conjectures. To the memory of Placide Tempels (1906–1977)', *Africa* 48 (4): 315–34.

1990 *Power and Performance: Ethnographic Exploration through Proverbial Wisdom and Theatre in Shaba, Zaire*. Madison: University of Wisconsin Press.

1998 *Moments of Freedom: Anthropology and Popular Culture*. Charlottesville: University Press of Virginia.

Fair, Laura 2010 'Songs, stories, action! Audience preferences in Tanzania, 1950s-1980s', in *Viewing African Cinema in the Twenty-first Century: Art Films and the Nollywood Video Revolution*, ed. Mahir Şaul and Ralph A. Austen. Athens: Ohio University Press (108–30).

Fardon, Richard and Graham Furniss (eds.) 2000 *African Broadcast Cultures: Radio in Transition*. Oxford: James Currey.

Ferguson, James 1999 *Expectations of Modernity: Myths and Meanings of Urban Life on the Zambian Copperbelt*. Berkeley, Los Angeles, London: University of California Press.

2006 *Global Shadows: Africa in the Neoliberal World Order*. Durham, NC: Duke University Press.

First, Ruth 1957 'The bus boycott', *Africa South* 1 (4): 55–64.

1983 *Black Gold: The Mozambican Miner, Proletarian and Peasant*. Sussex: Harvester Press.

Frederiksen, Bodil Folke 1994 *Making popular culture from above: leisure in Nairobi 1940–60*. Occasional Paper 145. Calcutta: Centre for Studies in Social Sciences.

Freund, Bill 1981 *Capital and Labour in the Nigerian Tin Mines*. London: Longman.

Fuglesang, Minou 1994 *Veils and Videos: Female Youth Culture on the Kenyan Coast*. Stockholm: Almqvist and Wiksell.

Furniss, Graham 1996 *Poetry, Prose and Popular Culture in Hausa*. Edinburgh: Edinburgh University Press for the International African Institute.

2006 'Innovation and persistence: literary circles, new opportunities and continuing debates in Hausa literary production', in *Africa's Hidden Histories: Everyday Literacy and Making the Self*, ed. Karin Barber. Bloomington: Indiana University Press.

Geenen, Kristien 2009 ' "Sleep occupies no space": the use of public space by street gangs in Kinshasa', *Africa* 79 (3): 347–68.

Gikandi, Simon 2010 'Foreword. In praise of Afro-optimism: towards a poetics of survival', in *Hard Work, Hard Times: Global Volatility and African Subjectivities*, ed. Anne-Maria Makhulu, Beth A. Buggenhagen and Stephen Jackson. Berkeley: University of California Press (xi-xvi).

Goldstein, Joshua and Juliana Rotich 2010 'Digitally networked technology in Kenya's 2007–08 post-election crisis', in *SMS Uprising: Mobile Activism in Africa*, ed. Sokari Ekine. Cape Town: Pambazuka Press (124–37).

Graebner, Werner 1989 'Whose music? The songs of Remmy Ongala and Orchestra Super Matimila', *Popular Music* 8 (2): 243–58.

   2000 'Ngoma ya Ukae: competitive social structure in Tanzanian dance music songs', in *Mashindano! Competitive Music Performance in East Africa*, ed. Frank Gunderson and Gregory Barz. Dar es Salaam: Mkuki na Nyota Publishers (295–318).

Grant, Andrea Mariko 2017 'The making of a "superstar": the politics of playback and live performance in post-genocide Rwanda', *Africa* 87 (1): 155–79.

Green, Margaret M. 1964 [1947] *Ibo Village Affairs*. London: Frank Cass.

Green-Simms, Lindsey 2010 'The return of the Mercedes: from Ousmane Sembene to Kenneth Nnebue', in *Viewing African Cinema in the Twenty-first Century: Art Films and the Nollywood Video Revolution*, ed. Mahir Şaul and Ralph A. Austen. Athens: Ohio University Press (209–24).

Guma, S. M. 1966 *The Form, Content and Technique of Traditional Literature in Southern Sotho*. Pretoria: J. L. van Schaik.

Gunderson, Frank and Gregory Barz (eds.) 2000 *Mashindano! Competitive Music Performance in East Africa*. Dar es Salaam: Mkuki na Nyota Publishers.

Gunner, Liz 1989 'Orality and literacy: dialogue and silence', in *Discourse and Its Disguises: The Interpretation of African Oral Texts*, ed. Karin Barber and P. F. de Moraes Farias. Birmingham: Birmingham University African Studies Series 1.

   2011 'IsiZulu radio drama and the modern subject: restless identities in South Africa in the 1970s', in *Radio in Africa: Publics, Cultures, Communities*, ed. Liz Gunner, Dina Ligaga and Dumisani Moyo. Johannesburg: Wits University Press (163–79).

Gunner, Liz, Dina Ligaga and Dumisani Moyo (eds.) 2011 *Radio in Africa: Publics, Cultures, Communities*. Johannesburg: Wits University Press.

Gutkind, P. C. W. 1974 *Urban Anthropology: Perspectives on 'Third World' Urbanisation and Urbanism*. Assen: Van Gorcum.

Guyer, Jane I. 1996 'Traditions of Invention in Equatorial Africa', *African Studies Review* 39 (3): 1–28.

   2015 'Introduction to the question: is confusion a form?', *Social Dynamics* 41 (1): 1–16.

Guyer, Jane I., LaRay Denzer and Adigun A. B. Agbaje (eds.) 2002 *Money Struggles and City Life: Devaluation in Ibadan and Other Urban Centers in Southern Nigeria, 1986–1996*. Portsmouth, NH: Heinemann.

Haas, Peter Jan and Thomas Gasthuizen 2000 'Ndani ya Bongo: KiSwahili rap keeping it real', in *Mashindano! Competitive Music Performance in East Africa*, ed. Frank Gunderson and Gregory Barz. Dar es Salaam: Mkuki na Nyota Publishers (279–94).

Hall, Stuart 1981 'Notes on deconstructing "The Popular"', in *People's History and Socialist Theory*, ed. Raphael Samuel. London: Routledge and Kegan Paul (227–41).

Hardt, Michael and Antonio Negri 2000 *Empire*. Cambridge, MA: Harvard University Press.

Harris, Jack 1940 'The position of women in a Nigerian society', *Transactions of the New York Academy of Sciences Series II*, 2 (5): 141–8.

Harvey, David 1989 *The Condition of Postmodernity: An Enquiry into the Origin of Cultural Change*. Oxford: Blackwell.

Haynes, Jonathan (ed.) 2000 *Nigerian Video Films*. Athens: Ohio University Press.

Heap, Simon 1990 'The development of motor transport in the Gold Coast, 1900–1939', *Journal of Transport History* 11 (2): 19–37.

Hellmann, Ellen 1948 *Rooiyard: A Sociological Survey of an Urban Native Slum Yard*. Rhodes-Livingstone Papers No. 13. Manchester: Manchester University Press.

Higginson, John 1989 *A Working Class in the Making: Belgian Colonial Labour Policy, Private Enterprise, and the African Mineworker 1907–1951*. Madison: University of Wisconsin Press.

Hiskett, Mervyn 1975 *A History of Hausa Islamic Verse*. London: University of London School of Oriental and African Studies.

Hofmeyr, Isabel 2004 *The Portable Bunyan: A Transnational History of* The Pilgrim's Progress. Johannesburg: Wits University Press.

Hone, Richard B. (ed.) 1877 *Seventeen Years in the Yoruba Country: Memorials of Anna Hinderer*. London: Religious Tract Society.

Honwana, Alcinda and Filip De Boeck (eds.) 2005 *Makers and Breakers: Children and Youth in Postcolonial Africa*. Oxford: James Currey.

Hunwick, John O. 1993 'Not yet *the* Kano Chronicle: king-lists with and without narrative elaboration from nineteenth-century Kano', *Sudanic Africa* IV (95–130).

Ibn Battuta 1994 *The Travels of Ibn Battuta 1325–1354*, vol. IV. Translated and annotated by H. A. R. Gibb and C. F. Beckingham. London: The Hakluyt Society, 2nd series, vol. 178.

Ivaska, Andrew 2011 *Cultured States: Youth, Gender, and Modern Style in 1960s Dar es Salaam*. Durham, NC: Duke University Press.

Jaekel, Francis 1997 *The History of the Nigerian Railway*, 3 vols. Ibadan: Spectrum Books.

James, Deborah 2015 *Money from Nothing: Indebtedness and Aspiration in South Africa*. Stanford, CA: Stanford University Press.

James, Wilmot G. 1992 *Our Precious Metal: African Labour in South Africa's Gold Industry, 1970–1990*. London: James Currey.

Jedlowski, Alessandro 2013 'From Nollywood to Nollyworld: processes of transnationalization in the Nigerian video film industry', in *Global Nollywood: The Transnational Dimensions of an African Video Film Industry*, ed. Matthias Krings and Onookome Okome. Bloomington: Indiana University Press (25–45).

Jewsiewicki, Bogumil 1990 'Collective memory and its images: popular urban painting in Zaire – a source of "present past"', in *Between Memory and History*, ed. Maria Noelle Bourget, Lusette Valensi and Nathan Wachtel. Chur, Switzerland: Harwood Academic Publishers.

1997 'Painting in Zaire: from the invention of the West to the representation of social self', in *Readings in African Popular Culture*, ed. Karin Barber. Oxford: James Currey (99–110).

Johnson, John William 1995 'Power, marginality and Somali oral poetry: case studies in the dynamics of tradition', in *Power, Marginality and African Oral Literature*, ed. Graham Furniss and Liz Gunner. Cambridge: Cambridge University Press (111–21).

Johnson, Samuel 1921 *The History of the Yorubas: From the Earliest Times to the Beginning of the British Protectorate*. Lagos: CMS Bookshops.

Jones, Adam, Robin Law and P. E. H. Hair (eds.) 1992 *Barbot on Guinea: The Writings of Jean Barbot on West Africa, 1678–1712*, vol. 1. London: Hakluyt Society.

Kaarsholm, Preben (ed.) 2006 *Violence, Political Culture and Development in Africa*. Oxford: James Currey.

Kavanagh, Robert 1985 *Theatre and Cultural Struggle in South Africa*. London: Zed Books.

Kea, Ray A. 1982 *Settlements, Trade, and Politics in the Seventeenth-Century Gold Coast*. Baltimore and London: Johns Hopkins University Press.

Kerr, David 2018 'From the margins to the mainstream: making and remaking an alternative music economy in Dar es Salaam', *Journal of African Cultural Studies*. 30 (1): 65–80

Kimble, Judy 1982 'Labour migration in Basutoland c. 1870–1885', in *Industrialisation and Social Change in South Africa: African Class Formation, Culture and Consciousness 1870–1930*, ed. Shula Marks and Richard Rathbone. London: Longman (119–41).

Korieh, Chima J. 2004 'Urban food supply and vulnerability in Nigeria during the Second World War', in *Nigerian Cities*, ed. Toyin Falola and Steven J. Salm. Trenton, NJ: Africa World Press.

Krings, Matthias 2015 *African Appropriations: Cultural Difference, Mimesis and Media*. Bloomington: Indiana University Press.

Krings, Matthias and Onookome Okome (eds.) 2013 *Global Nollywood: The Transnational Dimensions of an African Video Film Industry*. Bloomington: Indiana University Press.

Künzler, Daniel 2011 'South African rap music, counter discourses, identity and commodification beyond the Prophets of Da City', *Journal of Southern African Studies* 37 (1): 27–43.

Lange, Siri 2000 'Muungano and TOT: rivals on the urban cultural scene', in *Mashindano! Competitive Music Performance in East Africa*, ed. Frank Gunderson and Gregory Barz. Dar es Salaam: Mkuki na Nyota Publishers (67–85).

2002 'Managing modernity: gender, state, and nation in the popular drama of Dar es Salaam, Tanzania'. PhD thesis, University of Bergen, Norway.

Larkin, Brian 2004 'Bandiri music, globalization and urban experience in Nigeria', *Social Text* 22 (4): 91–112.

2008 *Signal and Noise: Media, Infrastructure, and Urban Culture in Nigeria*. Durham, NC: Duke University Press.

Larmer, Miles 2007 *Mineworkers in Zambia: Labour and Political Change in Post-colonial Africa*. London and New York: Tauris Academic Studies.

Ligaga, Dina 2012 ' "Virtual Expressions": alternative online spaces and the staging of Kenyan popular cultures', *Research in African Literatures* 43 (4): 1–16.

Lijadu, E. M. 1886 *Kekere Iwe Orin Aribiloṣo* [Little Book of Aribiloṣo's Songs]. Exeter: James Townsend.

Lodge, Tom 1983 *Black Politics in South Africa since 1945*. London and New York: Longman.

Maake, Nhlanhla 2012 ' "I sing of the woes of my travels": the lifela of Lesotho', in *Cambridge History of South African Literature*, ed. David Attwell and Derek Attridge. Cambridge: Cambridge University Press (60–76).

Mack, Beverly B. and Jean Boyd 2000 *One Woman's Jihad: Nana Asma'u, Scholar and Scribe*. Bloomington: Indiana University Press.

Magaziner, Daniel 2016 *The Art of Life in South Africa*. Athens: Ohio University Press.

Malaquais, Dominique 2006 'Douala/Johannesburg/New York: cityscapes imagined', in *Cities in Contemporary Africa*, ed. Martin J. Murray and Garth A. Myers. Basingstoke: Palgrave Macmillan (31–52).

Martin, Phyllis 1995 *Leisure and Society in Colonial Brazzaville*. Cambridge: Cambridge University Press.

Masquelier, Adeline 2013 'Teatime: boredom and the temporalities of young men in Niger', *Africa* 83 (3): 385–402.

Matera, Marc, Misty L. Bastian and Susan Kingsley Kent 2012 *The Women's War of 1929: Gender and Violence in Colonial Nigeria*. Basingstoke: Palgrave Macmillan.

Mayer, Philip, with Iona Mayer 1961 *Townsmen or Tribesmen: Conservatism and the Process of Urbanization in a South African City*. Cape Town: Oxford University Press.

Mbembe, Achille 1997 'The "Thing" and its double in Cameroonian cartoons', in *Readings in African Popular Culture*, ed. Karin Barber. Oxford: James Currey (151–63).

2001 *On the Postcolony*. Berkeley: University of California Press.

Mbembe, Achille and Janet Roitman 2002 'Figures of the subject in times of crisis', in *Under Siege: Four African Cities. Freetown, Johannesburg, Kinshasa, Lagos*, ed. Okwui Enwezor, Carlos Basualdo, Ute Meta Bauer, Susanne Ghez, Sarat Maharaj, Mark Nash, and Octavio Zaya. Kassel: Hatje Cantz Publishers (99–126).

Mbodj-Pouye, Aïssatou 2013 *Le fil de l'écrit: une anthropologie de l'alphabétisation au Mali*. Lyon: ENS Editions.

McLaughlin, Fiona 1997 'Islam and popular music in Senegal: the emergence of a "new tradition"', *Africa* 67 (4): 560–81.

McNeill, Fraser G. 2011 *AIDS, Politics and Music in South Africa*. Cambridge: Cambridge University Press for the International African Institute.

Medvedev, P. N. and M. M. Bakhtin 1978 [1928] *The Formal Method in Literary Scholarship: A Critical Introduction to Sociological Poetics*. Trans. Albert J. Wehrle. Baltimore and London: Johns Hopkins University Press.

Meyer, Birgit and Peter Geschiere (eds.) 1999 *Globalization and Identity: Dialectics of Flow and Closure*. Oxford: Blackwell.

Mhlambi, Innocentia J. 2014 '"Hail to the King": da hip-hop empire and the question of marginalscapes in post-1994 neoliberal South Africa', *English Studies in Africa* 57 (1): 81–91.

Mitchell, J. C. 1956 *The Kalela Dance*. Rhodes-Livingstone Paper No. 27. Manchester: Manchester University Press.

Mitchell, Timothy 2000 'The stage of modernity', in *Questions of Modernity*, ed. Timothy Mitchell. Minneapolis: University of Minnesota Press (1–34).

Mlama, Penina Muhando 1991 *Culture and Development in Africa: The Popular Theatre Approach*. Uppsala: Nordiska Afrikainstitutet.

Mokitimi, M. I. P. 1982 'A Literary Analysis of Lifela tsa Litsamaea-naha Poetry', 2 vols. MA thesis, University of Nairobi.

    1998 *Lifela tsa Litsamaea-naha Poetry: A Literary Analysis*. Pretoria: J. L. van Schaik Publishers.

Moodie, T. Dunbar, with Vivienne Ndatshe 1994 *Going for Gold: Men, Mines and Migration*. Berkeley, Los Angeles and London: University of California Press.

Moorman, Marissa J. 2008 *Intonations: A Social History of Music and Nation in Luanda, Angola, from 1945 to Recent Times*. Athens: Ohio University Press.

Moraes Farias, P. F. de 2015 'Modern transformations of written materials into "traditional" oral wisdom (Mali, West Africa)', in *Métamorphoses de l'oralité entre écrit et image*, ed. Gaetano Ciarcia and Éric Jolly. Paris: Karthala (95–108).

Morris, Rosalind C. 2008 'The miner's ear', *Transition* 98: 96–115.

Moulard-Kouka, Sophie 2005 'Le rap sénégalais: un mode d'expression inédit entre oral et écrit?' in *Interfaces between the Oral and the Written: Versions and Subversions in African Literatures 2*, ed. Alain Ricard and Flora Veit–Wild. *Matatu* 31–2: Amsterdam and New York: Editions Rodopi (233–346).

    2008 '"Sénégal Yewuleen!" Analyse anthropologique du rap à Dakar: liminarité, contestation et culture populaire', 3 vols. PhD thesis, University of Bordeaux 2.

Muller, Carol A. 2004 *South African Music: A Century of Traditions in Transformation*. Oxford: ABC-CLIO.

Murray, Colin 1981 *Families Divided: The Impact of Migrant Labour in Lesotho*. Cambridge: Cambridge University Press.

Murray, Martin J. and Garth A. Myers (eds.) 2006 *Cities in Contemporary Africa*. Basingstoke: Palgrave Macmillan.

Mutongi, Kenda 2006 'Thugs or entrepreneurs? Perceptions of *matatu* operators in Nairobi, 1970 to the present', *Africa* 76 (4): 549–68.

Myers, Garth A. and Martin J. Murray 2006 'Introduction: situating contemporary cities in Africa', in *Cities in Contemporary Africa*, ed. Martin J. Murray and Garth A. Myers. Basingstoke: Palgrave Macmillan (1–25).

Nasson, Bill 1989 ' "She preferred living in a cave with Harry the snake-catcher": towards an oral history of popular leisure and class expression in District Six, Cape Town, c. 1920s–1950s', in *Holding Their Ground: Class, Locality and Culture in 19th and 20th Century South Africa*, ed. Philip Bonner, Isabel Hofmeyr, Deborah James and Tom Lodge. Johannesburg: Witwatersrand University Press and Ravan Press (285–309).

Nesbitt, L. M. 1936 *Gold Fever*. London: Jonathan Cape.

Neveu-Kringelbach, Hélène 2013 *Dance Circles: Movement, Morality and Self-fashioning in Urban Senegal*. New York: Berghahn Books.

Newell, Sasha 2009 'Godrap girls, Draou boys, and the sexual economy of the bluff in Abidjan, Côte d'Ivoire', *Ethnos* 74 (3): 379–402.

Newell, Stephanie 1997 'Making up their own minds: readers, interpretations and difference of view in Ghanaian popular narratives', *Africa* 67 (3): 389–405.

2000 *Ghanaian Popular Fiction: 'Thrilling Discoveries in Conjugal Life' and Other Tales*. Oxford: James Currey.

2002a *Literary Culture in Colonial Ghana: 'How to Play the Game of Life'*. Manchester: Manchester University Press.

(ed.) 2002b *Readings in African Popular Fiction*. Oxford: James Currey.

Newell, Stephanie and Onookome Okome (eds.) 2014 *Popular Culture in Africa: The Episteme of the Everyday*. New York and London: Routledge.

Niven, Sir Rex 1982 *Nigerian Kaleidoscope: Memoirs of a Colonial Servant*. London: C. Nurst and Co.

Nixon, Rob 1994 *Homelands, Harlem and Hollywood: South African Culture and the World Beyond*. London: Routledge.

Ntarangwi, Mwenda 2009 *East African Hip Hop: Youth Culture and Globalization*. Urbana and Chicago: University of Illinois Press.

Nuttall, Sarah 2009 *Entanglement: Literary and Cultural Reflections on Post-apartheid*. Johannesburg: Wits University Press.

Nyamede, Abner 1996 'Martha has no land: the tragedy of identity in *The Marabi Dance*', in *Text, Theory, Space*, ed. Kate Darian-Smith, Liz Gunner and Sarah Nuttall. London: Routledge (191–201).

Nyamnjoh, Francis B. 2005 *Africa's Media, Democracy and the Politics of Belonging*. London: Zed; Pretoria: Unisa Press.

Obadare, Ebenezer 2016 *Humor, Silence, and Civil Society in Nigeria*. Rochester, NY: University of Rochester Press.

Obiechina, E. N. 1972 *Onitsha Market Literature*. London: Heinemann.

Odhiambo, Christopher Joseph 2011 'From diffusion to dialogic spaces: FM radio stations in Kenya', in *Radio in Africa: Publics, Cultures, Communities*, ed. Liz Gunner, Dina Ligaga and Dumisani Moyo. Johannesburg: Wits University Press (36–48).

Ogali, Ogali A. 1977 *Coal City*. Enugu: Fourth Dimension Publishers.

Ola, Yomi 2013 *Satires of Power in Yoruba Visual Culture*. Durham, NC: Carolina Academic Press.

Otiono, Nduka 2011 'Street stories: orality, media, popular culture and the postcolonial condition in Nigeria'. PhD thesis, University of Alberta at Edmonton, Canada.

Oyegoke, Lekan 1994 '"Sade's testimony": a new genre of autobiography in African folklore', *Research in African Literatures* 25 (3): 131–40.

Perullo, Alex 2011 *Live from Dar es Salaam: Popular Music and Tanzania's Music Economy*. Bloomington: Indiana University Press.

Peterson, Bhekizizwe 2002 'Yizo Yizo: reading the swagger in Soweto youth culture', in *Africa's Young Majority*, ed. Barbara Trudell, Kenneth King, Simon McGrath and Paul Nugent. Edinburgh: Centre for African Studies (321–42).

Peterson, Derek R. 2004 *Creative Writing: Translation, Bookkeeping, and the Work of Imagination in Colonial Kenya*. Portsmouth, NH: Heinemann.

Pieterse, Edgar 2010 'Hip-hop cultures and political agency in Brazil and South Africa', *Social Dynamics* 36 (2):428–47.

Powdermaker, Hortense 1962 *Copper Town: Changing Africa*. New York and Evanston, IL: Harper and Row.

Priebe, Richard 1978 'Popular writing in Ghana: a sociology and rhetoric', *Research in African Literatures* 9 (3): 395–432.

Pype, Katrien 2011 'Visual media and political communication: reporting about suffering in Kinshasa', *Journal of Modern African Studies* 49 (4): 625–45.

2012 *The Making of the Pentecostal Melodrama: Religion, Media, and Gender in Kinshasa*. New York/Oxford: Berghahn Books.

2013 'Religion, migration, and media aesthetics: notes on the circulation and reception of Nigerian films in Kinshasa', in *Global Nollywood: The Transnational Dimensions of an African Video Film Industry*, ed. Matthias Krings and Onookome Okome. Bloomington: Indiana University Press (199–222).

Quayson, Ato 2014 *Oxford Street, Accra: City Life and the Itineraries of Transnationalism*. Durham, NC: Duke University Press.

Ranger, T. O. [Terence] 1975 *Dance and Society in Eastern Africa 1890–1970: The Beni Ngoma*. London: Heinemann.

Reuster-Jahn, Uta 2016 'The growing use of the internet for the publication of Swahili fiction in Tanzania', paper presented at Colloque ELLAF, INALCO, Paris, 29 September to 1 October.

Robinson, Charles Henry 2010 [1896] *Specimens of Hausa Literature*. Cambridge: Cambridge University Press.

Salter, Thomas 2008 'Rumba from Congo to Cape Town'. PhD thesis, University of Edinburgh.

Samuel, Raphael (ed.) 1981 *People's History and Socialist Theory*. London: Routledge and Kegan Paul.

Şaul, Mahir and Ralph A. Austen (eds.) 2010 *Viewing African Cinema in the Twenty-first Century: Art Films and the Nollywood Video Revolution*. Athens: Ohio University Press.

Scheld, Suzanne 2007 'Clothing, the city and globalization in Dakar, Senegal', *City and Society* 19 (2): 232–53.

Schulz, Dorothea E. 2012 *Muslims and New Media in West Africa: Pathways to God.* Bloomington, Indiana: Indiana University Press.

Schumann, Anne 2012 'A generation of orphans: the socio-economic crisis in Côte d'Ivoire as seen through popular music', *Africa* 82 (4): 535–55.

Shipley, Jesse Weaver 2009 'Aesthetic of the entrepreneur: Afro-cosmopolitan rap and moral circulation in Accra, Ghana', *Anthropological Quarterly* 82 (3): 631–68.

2013 *Living the Hiplife: Celebrity and Entrepreneurship in Ghanaian Popular Music.* Durham, NC: Duke University Press.

Simone, AbdouMaliq 2002 'The visible and invisible: remaking cities in Africa', in *Under Siege: Four African Cities. Freetown, Johannesburg, Kinshasa, Lagos*, ed. Okwui Enwezor, Carlos Basualdo, Ute Meta Bauer, Susanne Ghez, Sarat Maharaj, Mark Nash, and Octavio Zaya. Kassel: Hatje Cantz Publishers (23–43).

2004 *For the City Yet to Come: Changing African Life in Four Cities.* Durham, NC: Duke University Press.

Smith, Pierre 1975 *Le récit populaire au Rwanda.* Paris: Armand Colin.

Solberg, Rolf 1999 *Alternative Theatre in South Africa: Talks with Prime Movers Since the 1970s.* Scottsville: University of Natal Press.

Sole, Kelwyn and Eddie Koch 1990 'The Marabi Dance: a working class novel?' in *Rendering Things Visible: Essays on South African Literary Culture*, ed. M. Trump. Johannesburg: Ravan (205–24).

Soyinka, Wọle 1984 *Six Plays* (Plays I). London: Methuen.

Spitzer, Leo 1974 *The Creoles of Sierra Leone: Responses to Colonialism, 1870–1945.* Madison: University of Wisconsin Press.

Szombati-Fabian, Ilona and Johannes Fabian 1976 'Art, history, and society: popular painting in Shaba, Zaire', *Studies in the Anthropology of Visual Communication* 3 (1): 1–21.

Tettey, Wisdom J. 2011 'Talk radio and politics in Ghana: exploring civic and (un)civil discourse in the public sphere', in *Radio in Africa: Publics, Cultures, Communities*, ed. Liz Gunner, Dina Ligaga and Dumisani Moyo. Johannesburg: Wits University Press (19–35).

Thometz, Kurt 2001 *Life Turns Man Up and Down: High Life, Useful Advice, and Mad English: African Market Literature.* New York: Pantheon Books.

Thompson, E. P. 1963 *The Making of the English Working Class.* London: Victor Gollancz.

Thompson, Katrina Daly 2008 'Keeping it real: reality and representation in Maasai hip-hop', *Journal of African Cultural Studies* 20 (1): 33–44.

Topp Fargion, Janet 1993 'The role of women in taarab in Zanzibar: an historical examination of a process of Africanization', *The World of Music* 35 (2): 109–25.

2000 '"Hot Kabisa!" The mpasho phenomenon and *Taarab* in Zanzibar', in *Mashindano! Competitive Music Performance in East Africa*, ed. Frank Gunderson and Gregory Barz. Dar es Salaam: Mkuki na Nyota Publishers (39–53).

Turino, Thomas 2000 *Nationalists, Cosmopolitans, and Popular Music in Zimbabwe.* Chicago: University of Chicago Press.

Ugor, Paul 2016 *Nollywood: Popular Culture and Narratives of Youth Struggles in Nigeria*. Durham, NC: Carolina Academic Press.

Ukadike, Nwachukwu Frank 1994 *Black African Cinema*. Berkeley: University of California Press.

Urban, Greg 2001 *Metaculture: How Culture Moves through the World*. Minneapolis: University of Minnesota Press.

Vail, Leroy and Landeg White 1978 'Plantation protest: the history of a Mozambican song', *Journal of Southern African Studies* 5 (1): 1–25.

Van der Geest, Sjaak 2004 'Orphans in highlife: an anthropological interpretation', *History in Africa* 31: 425–40.

Van der Geest, Sjaak and Nimrod K. Asante-Darko 1982 'The political meaning of highlife songs in Ghana', *African Studies Review* 25 (1): 27–35.

Van der Laan, H. Laurens 1981 'Modern inland transport and the European trading firms in colonial West Africa', *Cahiers d'Études Africaines* 21 (cahier 84): 547–75.

Van Onselen, Charles 1976 *Chibaro: African Mine Labour in Southern Rhodesia, 1900–1933*. London: Pluto Press.

Vansina, Jan 2004 *Antecedents to Modern Rwanda: The Nyiginya Kingdom*. Oxford: James Currey; Kampala: Fountain Publishers.

Wa Mũngai, Mbũgua 2013 *Nairobi's Matatu Men: portrait of a subculture*. Goethe-Institut Kenya, Native Intelligence and the Jomo Kenyatta Foundation: Contact Zones NRB Text.

Waterman, Christopher A. 1990 *Jùjú: A Social History and Ethnography of an African Popular Music*. Chicago: University of Chicago Press.

2002 'Big Man, Black President, Masked One: models of the celebrity self in Yoruba popular music in Nigeria', in *Playing with Identities in Contemporary Music in Africa*, ed. M. Palmberg and A. Kirkegaard. Uppsala: Nordiska Afrikainstitutet (19–34).

Weiss, Brad 2009 *Street Dreams and Hip Hop Barbershops: Global Fantasy in Urban Tanzania*. Bloomington: Indiana University Press.

Wells, Robin E. 1994 *An Introduction to the Music of the Basotho*. Morija, Lesotho: Morija Museum and Archives.

Wenzel, Jennifer 2009 *Bulletproof: Afterlives of Anticolonial Prophecy in South Africa and Beyond*. Chicago: University of Chicago Press.

White, Bob W. 2008 *Rumba Rules: The Politics of Dance Music in Mobutu's Zaire*. Durham, NC: Duke University Press.

(ed.) 2012 *Music and Globalization: Critical Encounters*. Bloomington: Indiana University Press.

Wilson, Francis 1972 *Labour in the South African Gold Mines 1911–1969*. Cambridge: Cambridge University Press.

Wilson, Monica and Archie Mafeje 1963 *Langa: A Study of Social Groups in an African Township*. London: Oxford University Press.

Yékú, James 2016 'Akpos don come again: Nigerian cyberpop hero as trickster', *Journal of African Cultural Studies* 28 (3): 245–61.

Zeleza, Paul Tiyambe 2003 'Introduction. The creation and consumption of leisure: theoretical and methodological considerations', in *Leisure in Urban Africa*, ed. Paul Tiyambe Zeleza and Cassandra Rachel Veney. Trenton, NJ: Africa World Press (vii–xli).

Index

Indian films, 147
Islamic literacy, 26–28
juju music, 5, 99
mines, 45, 46, 72
music, 11, 174
nineteenth-century wars, 33
northern, 76
romantic novels, 174
schools, 90
theatre, 8, 98, 131
video film, 146
western, 34, 174
Nixon, Rob, 70, 71, 132
Nkrumah, Kwame, 89, 120, 176
Nollywood, 147–52, 160, 173, 175
   distribution within Africa, 151–52
   Face of Africa (video film), 143F16, 149, 150
   Glamour Girls (video film), 149–50
   Living in Bondage (video film), 149
Nongqawuse, 102, 103
Northern Rhodesia, 6, 46, 52, 72, 103, 167, See also Zambia; Copperbelt
Ntarangwi, Mwenda, 154, 158–59
Nupe, 37
Nuttall, Sarah, 156
Nyame, E.K., 82
Nyamnjoh, Francis, 134, 141, 145
Nyasaland, 6, 167, See also Malawi
Nyerere, President Julius, 102, 121, 123, 124

Obadare, Ebenezer, 162
Obiechina, E. N., 90, 91–92, 93
Odhiambo, Christopher, 139, 140
Ogali, Ogali A., 92, 93, 94
Okome, Onookome, 151, 152
Ongala, Remmy, 168–69
Onitsha, Nigeria, 89–90
   market literature, 5, 89–97, 98, 99, 151, 171
orality
   continued vitality of, 41
   interface with literacy, 40, 170
   oral genres, 9, 13, 14, 17, 28, 32, 101
   oral genres and media, 131, 142
   oral genres as historical sources, 28–33
   oral genres in rap, 153
   oral performance, 27, 172

oral traditions, 7, 27–29, 37, 121, 132, 148, 167, See also Aribiloso; Mali: oral genres; Mali: Sunjata epic; Muyaka bin Haji; Rwanda: oral genres; Xhosa: praise poetry; Yoruba: poetry; Zulu: praise poetry
oral transmission, 21
Orphan Do Not Glance (concert party play), 87–88
Otiono, Nduka, 162
Ouedraogo, Idrissa, 148
Ousmane, Sembène, 148
Oyegoke, Lekan, 15
Oyo, Nigeria, 34

Paiva family, Mozambique, 176–77
Pan-African Congress (PAC), 109
Pedi, 44, 51
Perullo, Alex, 122
Peterson, Derek, 79
photographs, 131
Pieterse, Edgar, 155, 156
Pongweni, Alec, 117–19
popular
   culture, as field of study, 4–12, 130
   definitions of, 4, 7–12, 32, 36, 41–42
Powdermaker, Hortense, 4, 5
Pype, Katrien, 140, 146, 151

Qabula, A. T., 41
Quaresma, 162–63
Quayson, Ato, 160–62

radio. See media: radio
railways, 57, 73, 74–77, 81, 89–90, 99, 105
   employees, 81, 103, 106–07
Ranger, Terence, 5–6, 52, 53, 54, 109, 115–17
rap/hip hop, 11, 15, 146, 152–59, 178, See also Cape Town; Dakar; Dar es Salaam; Luganda; South Africa; Swahili; Tanzania; Wolof; X-Plastaz; Zulu
   Scenti no!!, 161–62
Reuster-Jahn, Uta, 144
Rhodes, Cecil, 114
Rhodes-Livingstone Institute, 4–5, 14
roads, 99
   in colonial period, 73, 75–77, 81, 90, 98
   in concert party plays, 87